Reflections of

Asian Diaspora

Asian Diaspora Christianity Series—3

"Migration and mission are of utmost importance to the biblical faith. It may be right to say that without migration, perhaps, the biblical faith—the Jewish as well as the Christian faith—would not have come into existence. Migration and the diasporic life of the people of God are foundational for the expansion and establishment of the Christian faith and also for the final formation of one new human in Christ in the world without dividing walls of separation—the ultimate goal of God's mission in the world. I congratulate Dr. Sam George for taking up this project."

Simon Samuel
Professor of New Testament and Christian Origins,
New Theological College, Dehradun, India

Reflections of Asian Diaspora

Mapping Theologies and Ministries

Edited by Sam George

FORTRESS PRESS
MINNEAPOLIS

REFLECTIONS OF ASIAN DIASPORA
Mapping Theologies and Ministries

Cover image: Grungy Wall texture by jessicahyde and Background of passport stamps by ugurhan
Cover design: Kristin Miller

Print ISBN: 978-1-5064-8748-9
eBook ISBN: 978-1-5064-8749-6

Dedicated to
Professor Daniel Jeyaraj
Scholar, Teacher, and Mentor

Contents

Acknowledgments

A book of this kind is truly a labor of love and the fruit of global friendship cultivated over more than a decade. Sustained interactions over emails, phone calls, Zoom meetings, and the like to collaborate on this edited volume have only strengthened those bonds. I had the good fortune of visiting some of their countries, eating with them, staying with their families, learning from them, preaching at their churches, teaching their seminary classes, and simply hanging out with them. So first of all, kudos to an exceptional bunch of scholars and friends who have contributed to this volume. Thank you for sharing your insights on your community, what God is doing in your part of the country through your community, and your passion for the mission to and through people on the move.

This is the third and final volume of the Asian Diaspora Christianity series but not the last word on the subject. The three dozen of us who contributed to these books and several others who guided, reviewed, participated in, and endorsed this writing project greatly benefited from our many interactions and exchanges of our wanderings. I hope and pray that these essays will be catalytic to generate further reflection and writing on this distinctive continental diasporic vantage point, for I firmly believe that in the making of World Christianity, Asian diasporas will play a critical role in the transformation and advance of the Christian faith in the twenty-first century and will stand to both richly benefit from and have much to contribute to the dispersion of Asians worldwide.

I am grateful for my association with the Lausanne Movement, which permits me to travel widely and to serve the global church. However, the unanticipated pandemic lockdown forced me to stay put and providentially created space and time to write and edit this series. Lausanne has provided connections with exceptional global leaders and many opportunities to learn and see what God is doing in different parts of the world. Being on the front lines across the globe in the last five years has offered an incredibly rich perspective and comprehension of the critical nature of diaspora peoples in reshaping and advancing the Christian faith in the early decades of the twenty-first century.

I express my sincere gratitude to the endorsers of the third volume of this book series on Asian diaspora Christianity: Dr. Wonsuk Ma of Oral Roberts University, Tulsa (United States); Dr. Finny Philip, New Testament professor and principal of Filadelfia Bible College (Udaipur, India); Dr. David Ro, Regional Director for East Asia of the Lausanne Movement; and Dr. Simon Samuel of New Theological College, Dehradun (India). I appreciate the kind words, valuable feedback, and many encouragements you have given over the last many years. Your passion to teach, burden for the lost, and passion for the cause of Christ around the world are contagious. I thank God for the exceptional leaders of the Global Diaspora Institute at the Wheaton College Billy Graham Center, like Ed Stetzer, Andrew Y. Lee, Joel Wright, Yoman Mann, and Zaki L. Zaki. I am grateful for my co-catalyst for diasporas of the Lausanne Movement—Bulus Galadima—and the executive team of the Global Diaspora

Network, especially to T. V. Thomas, Barnabas Moon, Art Medina, Paul Sydnor, Mauricio Sanchez, and Elizabeth Mburu, all of whom embody an unmatched passion for serving diaspora peoples globally.

I am much obliged to Jesudas Athyal of Fortress Press for his invaluable guidance in developing this entire series. I am grateful to Fortress Press for their partnership in producing and marketing this book series and their interest in writings on global Christianity. A special word of appreciation to Elvis Ramirez for his editorial assistance and diligent work on these manuscripts. Thanks to all who worked behind the scenes on the copyediting, book layout, and cover design.

I dedicate this book to my teacher and mentor Professor Daniel Jeyaraj, whom I first met in the late 1990s at Princeton Theological Seminary and later when he was teaching at Andover Newton Theological School in Boston. He currently serves as the director of the Andrew F. Walls Centre for African and Asian Christianity at Liverpool Hope University, besides serving as the professor of World Christianity and university pastor. He was my doctoral advisor and continues to be a great encourager in all my missionary and scholarly endeavors. Having lived, studied, and taught in several countries, he embodies the struggles of diasporic wanderings firsthand. Because he is a leading Indian historian and scholar of World Christianity, I turn to him for guidance from time to time. His love of learning and unmatched humility and simplicity are worth emulating by all Christ followers. He had the unique privilege to work closely with Professor Andrew F. Walls until the latter's passing away in August 2021 and embodies Walls's eponymous center's vision for the study of World Christianity.

Not least of all, I express my sincere gratitude to my wife, Mary M. George, who, with much wisdom, patience, and prayers, has supported all my ministry undertakings, including this book series. Also, I have much appreciation for our boys, Daniel and Joshua, who now stand taller than both of us. I thank God for the many meals and time we got to spend together as a family during the global pandemic lockdown that drew us closer to one another and gave us the experience of divine protection and providence.

Sam George
Advent 2021

Series Introduction

Asian Diaspora Christianity

Sam George

Migration, diaspora, and displacement have become defining issues of our time. They appear daily on the front pages of newspapers, in breaking news reports on television, on Twitter feeds, and in academic discourses and political debates. Though human migration is as ancient as our history, the scale, volume, urge, speed, and direction of human displacements have reached unprecedented levels in recent decades. It is perceived to be at the crux of many of the dramatic transformations happening in our societies, economies, and nations. Since the prevailing frameworks of cultural, legal, financial, political, and religious orders are found inadequate to deal with contemporary migration, serious deliberations are occurring about this new reality in many circles and disciplinary domains. At the same time, innovative technologies, mass communication, and affordable transportation are creating new conflicts and crises owing to increased human mobility and connectivity.

The movement of people is of the utmost consequence to Christianity, as migrants and diaspora communities have shaped and reshaped the contours of its growth and expansion throughout history. At its core, Christianity is a faith that must move from place to place because it is a quintessential missionary and translatable faith. It is not bound to any particular land, geography, culture, or people. Since the beginning, it has continually diffused across cultural and geographical borders, and many different people in different places have been chief representatives of the Christian faith. Christianity cannot be held captive to a geographic location or domesticated by any people because its nature is to break free of the prisons that we enshrine it in.

Being the largest continent, Asia comprises forty-eight nations and has the most diverse population in the world, with nearly 4.7 billion people as of 2021 (about 60 percent of the world population), which is expected to swell to 5.3 billion by 2050. Among the top ten most populous countries of the world, five are in Asia (China, India, Indonesia, Pakistan, and Bangladesh), and Asia will continue to scatter multitudes globally year after year. Asia remains the largest source and destination of international migrants, with over 40 percent (110 million in 2019) of the world's international migrants and more than half of them (66 million) residing in other countries of Asia. There have been substantial surges into and out of Asia in the last decade, and much of the out-migration from the continent has been to Europe and North America (nearly 45 million).[1]

Asians are a widely dispersed populace and can be found in every nook and corner of the globe. This has been in the making over long periods in history, yet the Asian diaspora only makes up a minuscule part of the large population of the continent. Asia is a site marked by multivalent histories, peoples, cultures, economies, and religions, and

Asians' dispersion worldwide—resulting from globalization, neoliberalism, ethnic conflicts, wars, and political and ecological crises—has created tectonic transformations in our understanding of ecclesiology, missiology, and theology. The existential ontology of diasporic living necessitates new ways of perceiving and interpreting reality concerning oneself, others, the cosmos, and ultimately, God. In this volume, when we refer to Asia, we mean the whole continent, from its eastern edge in the Pacific Ocean to the Mediterranean states at the borders of Europe and Africa, not merely to the popular subregions of Asia that tend to dominate many writings. Yet due to limitations of space and scholarship, this book does not include all the immigrant groups of the continent or their divergent expressions of the faith.

This series brings together scholars of Asian backgrounds and a few others (who have served in Asian contexts or among Asians for decades) who are situated in diverse locations all over the world to draw insights from Christian ministry from a diasporic insider perspective. These volumes articulate the voices of Asian migrants and their progeny to weave a kaleidoscopic intercultural theological tapestry. These manifold expressions of displacement, encounters, struggles, and complexities compel us to reimagine faith from a distinctive vantage point to develop theological reflections and explore the missiological implications of Asian wanderings.

Migration and Mission: The Movement of People Transforming Christianity

Migration is fundamentally a disruptive phenomenon. The globalized diasporas seek social and economic upward mobility to break out of the bondage to geography and assimilate into other cultures while experiencing rejection and marginalization in their host societies. They seek emancipation by migrating to nearby cities and faraway nations to live in relative anonymity, free from obligation bound up in a locality, and defying sociocultural and religious restraints while also comparing and exploring new ideas and worldviews. Some explore business ventures and partnerships abroad, while others invest in the land of their forefathers and send remittances to dear ones back in their native lands. Some pursue studies, jobs, and marital alliances overseas to escape coercion into antiquated traditions and the limited options available to their ancestors. A record number of people are forced to flee their homelands to seek refuge abroad. Many are victimized by native strangers in foreign lands who are threatened by their arrival and legislations that are quick to discriminate against and exploit the newcomers. These journeys involve unexpected turns and misfortunes that no one can foresee or know how to navigate, even as the migrants grieve over many inevitable losses that come alongside their gains.

Just as the Jewish diaspora shaped the trajectory of Christianity in the first century, today's diasporas are shaping the frontiers of the faith and have become global missionary forces in an era of missions from everywhere to everywhere. This series explores the contours of Asian diaspora (the largest contemporary diaspora group in the world) and

Christian mission to, by, among, through, and beyond these dispersed communities from a global perspective. These writings have benefited from the recent proliferation of diaspora missiology and theology and hope to contribute further to migration/diaspora mission conversations using the lens of World Christianity. This series covers diaspora communities of Chinese, Indian, Korean, Japanese, Filipino, Vietnamese, Hmong, Sri Lankan, Pakistani, Indonesian, Nepalese, Iranian, Lebanese, and Israeli people while spanning intersecting angles of Buddhist, Hindu, Islamic, and Jewish religious contexts. These essays come from different continents of the world, with divergent sociocultural, geopolitical, and economic realities, and distill insights from multiple disciplinary domains, such as anthropology, sociology, history, economics, psychology, literature, and politics, in addition to the Bible, theology, and missiology. They are written by missionaries, pastors, professors, entrepreneurs, scientists, counselors, lay leaders, and doctoral students.

Taking diaspora as its primary lens and focusing on the continent of Asia, this project invited a select group of Christian scholars of Asian origin to reflect on and address issues related to their respective communities from the distinctive vantage points of their geographical and historical locations. They come from wide-ranging backgrounds, institutions, and theological positions, though most come under the canopy of the Reformed, Protestant, Evangelical, and Pentecostal traditions, with diverse experiences and advanced scholarship in varied fields. They encompass the ongoing and contested processes involving identity, belonging, meaning, affiliation, and allegiance while being embedded within varied social, cultural, and political webs of relations that are sustained concurrently.

Asian Christianity: Now Global

Christianity began in Asia and has now become the most global and diverse religion in the world.[2] At the turn of the third millennium, Christianity is returning to Asia and Asians around the world in some noteworthy manner. Many scholars have argued about the rise of Christianity in the Global South, which includes Asia, and how some Asian countries are playing an increasingly vital role in missionary undertakings and concomitant mission activities worldwide. Economic rise, the substantial growth of Christianity in some parts of Asia, religious persecution, and a host of other factors have resulted in the large-scale dispersion of Asian people globally. They have taken their distinctive spirituality, practices, hermeneutics, and institutions along with them to all parts of the world and have the potential to renew and revitalize Christianity in the coming centuries. On any Sunday morning, Christian worship services are conducted in Asian languages like Mandarin, Korean, Tagalog, and Malayalam in every major time zone, and families keep track of the news where their relatives are dispersed. The churches in Asia receive remittances in all major currencies of the world, and Asian pastors, evangelists, and leaders make frequent visits to their scattered sheep and followers everywhere. As a result, churches in Asia are catching a more global vision of Christianity and their role in the mission of Jesus Christ worldwide.

Because Christians are a minority faith group in much of Asia, they necessarily make immediate connections with Christians elsewhere. Coming from pluralistic societies with multireligious orientations, the Asian diasporas are transforming the religious landscape globally. The Christian faith breaks the bondages to geographical locations, present in many traditional Asian religions and cultures, and brings an openness to people that allows them to explore lands far beyond their places of birth. The educational prospects, language skills, economic progress, and positive outlook of Asians have scattered millions within and outside of their countries and continent, and many have embraced the Christian faith in the places of their sojourning and settlements. Asian Christianity is not monolithic in any fashion, and its dispersion is making Asian ecclesial bodies more global and producing a great diversity within the larger body of Christ worldwide.

One central thesis of this series is that the large-scale dispersion of Asians to far-flung corners of the globe over the past century or more is transforming Christianity itself—just as migration has always done with other peoples of the world. Subsequent to the Protestant Reformation in Europe in the sixteenth century, many Europeans relocated across the continent and around the world. This event came to be called the Great European Migration, and an estimated sixty million people relocated over three centuries until the middle of the twentieth century. An unexpected consequence of this widespread out-migration from Europe was that it made Christianity look European all over the world. Upon migrating abroad, Europeans established their distinctive religious orders and engaged in mission practices wherever they went, making Christianity take on their cultural garb. Likewise, the growth of Christianity in Asia and large-scale migration out of Asia are exporting Asian Christianity globally, and diasporic connections and resources are helping Asian Christians become a more global and missionary force.

Christians are at the forefront of migratory tendencies, as they are more likely to be mobile than others and better connected with Christians elsewhere. Some say, "If you are a Christian, you will travel, and if you travel, you will become a Christian." Their bent toward education, their motivation to work hard and succeed, and their expectations of a more hopeful future take them across borders and oceans. The Christian faith and practices have been translated, and Asian migrants and their offspring are actively engaged in adapting and renewing Christianity within their host cultures and nations. It is migration that necessitates the translation of the gospel into other contexts, and migrants act as natural translators by straddling multiple realities all the time. As missionaries, with intercultural sensibilities and acquired linguistic competencies, engaged in translating the gospel into diverse languages and cultures, today's migrants—whether their migration be volitional or involuntary—serve as mission agents and perform a missionary function. They translate the truths of the gospel into their new host cultures. The experiences of marginality and powerlessness that migrants face force them to harmonize their state of in-between-ness, in-both and in-beyond, making them adept at interpreting the world of their ancestors to the new world of their neighbors and vice versa using theological terms—infusing new meaning while reinterpreting prevailing cultural norms and predicaments.

The diasporic culture is about being here (hostland) and there (homeland) simultaneously. People do not fully belong to either place yet feel incomplete without both, and their diasporic existence calls for continual interaction between and dynamic attachment to both worlds.[3] Their culture and religion provide a strong link between homeland and hostland. The cultural flows between both places as people grieve the loss of the old world while also re-creating it in the new world and integrating into the host society. As James Clifford puts it, "Diaspora cultures mediate, in a lived tension, the experiences of separation and entanglement, of living there and remembering/desiring another place."[4] The remittances act as currencies of care and are used to negotiate and consolidate the soft power of the diasporas. The dispersed people become two-way conduits for the expansion of religious traditions while at the same time for the flow of new ideas and practices imbibed from their new environments, which together result in remarkable religious changes. The transformational power of diasporic people lies in their heightened awareness of both the perils and the rewards of multiple belonging and in their exemplary grappling with the paradoxes of identity and belonging. In short, the diaspora communities remain transformative forces to both sending and receiving places because of their transnational orientation and mission. No wonder uprooted and transplanted people make exceptional missionaries, even without knowing it.

As they pitch their tents in the far corners of the globe, many uprooted Asians are becoming Christians in their new homelands. They are exposed to and come closer to the claims of Jesus in foreign lands, whereas Asian Christians are reinvigorated in their faith in overseas locations. They are drawn to the life and teachings of Jesus Christ, which can cleanse their souls after their polluting voyages. In the process of liberating themselves from the bondages of the past, migrating to new places brings them face-to-face with new ideas, and they tend to compare and contrast inherited beliefs and worldviews of their native lands against those in their adopted homelands. They seek deliverance from cultural trappings and religious encumbrances while pursuing deeper spiritual realities. They are quick to abandon some identity markers, while others are reinforced, and subsequent generations assimilate into the host cultures and become estranged from their ancestral homelands. They find a new freedom in Christianity, which is more suited for the peripatetic ambiguities and resourceful in navigating contemporary meanderings. They have established distinctively Asian churches by worshipping in their own languages and cultures while also interfacing with local Christians and others from different regions of the world. Many people of Asian diasporas are joining local evangelical and charismatic churches in their host nations and now play increasingly visible roles in the leadership of many churches and institutions globally.

Global Christianity: Asian Version

The phenomenal growth of Christianity in the Global South is dramatically transforming the face of Christianity worldwide.[5] Although the percentage of Christians worldwide has remained constant since 1900, where those Christians live has moved southward and eastward. In 1900, only 18 percent of Christians lived in the Global South, but by 2020, that figure surged to 67 percent, which translates to 667 million Christians in Africa, 612 million in Latin America, and 407 million in Asia and Oceania (see the appendix in volume 1: *Journeys of Asian Diaspora*). Andrew F. Walls had the foresight to note the shifting of the center of gravity of Christianity from its Euro-American center to Africa, Asia, and Latin America.[6] The continental shift of the locus of Christianity coincided with the surge in global migration and new missionary movements. Lamin Sanneh claims that the teachings of Jesus and the apostles are not confined to a place—"territoriality [had] ceased to be a requirement of faith"—and when it takes root in a new place, the faith itself takes on something from there.[7]

Though Christianity began in West Asia in the first century, it soon moved east to Asia, south to Africa, and northwest to Europe, and in the process, the "new" places became home to Christianity. Throughout its history, the chief representatives of Christianity have altered from time to time to new places and peoples. As a result of the startling surge of Christianity in Africa, Asia, and Latin America and the massive migration from those regions to its former heartlands in the Global North, the portrait of Christianity is being remade with traits of people, cultures, and theologies from the Global South.

Contemporary examples abound. The current head of the Catholic Church is Pope Francis, who was born and raised in Argentina and is the first pope from the Southern Hemisphere. As a result, Latin American ethos and influence are clearly evident in the Vatican now. Likewise, among the Protestants, many current presidents of the World Council of Churches come from Asia, Africa, and Latin America. Several leaders of the Anglican Church are from Nigeria, and there are more Anglicans in sub-Saharan Africa than in the United Kingdom, Canada, the United States, and Australia put together. The same is true of European denominations like Presbyterians, Lutherans, Methodists, and others. The largest churches in major European cities are now led by Africans, and the common perception of Christianity is undergoing a dramatic makeover. The organization that I serve, the Lausanne Movement—which was started by Billy Graham and John Stott, two major voices in the latter half of the twentieth century from the United States and the United Kingdom, respectively—is now being headed by a Korean American who was a missionary in Japan. Global South Christians are rising to the highest ranks of many ecclesial bodies and global Christian organizations. Another case in my context is that the new leader of the National Association of Evangelicals, an influential body of Christians in the United States, is again a Korean American. Many Asians are among the senior leaders of churches and ministries in North America, in Europe, and elsewhere around the world.

This growing trend of the role Asians are playing is evident in other spheres as well, such as missionary sending, missionary funding, mission resources, scholarship, theologies, and so on. Peter C. Phan makes a case for the emerging Asian face of Christianity by presenting theologies rooted in the Asian American experience with christological portrayals of Jesus with a Chinese face and as an eldest son, an ancestor, and a poor monk using liberation and enculturation lenses.[8] Likewise, others have noted the changing face of Christianity in recent years, arguing that "cultural variety and plurality . . . were inscribed into the original character of Christianity."[9] Missiologists have been quick to note the seismic changes on the global Christian landscape, and several chapters in this series cite the impact of migration and changing demographics on world missions.[10] Others have explored Asian migration from biblical and theological perspectives by using migrations of the Bible and comparing contemporary immigrant generations to the Jewish exile.[11] Non-Western churches are surging ahead in missions with sizable numbers from China, India, South Korea, and the Philippines who are involved worldwide, including the Western nations. It could be argued that missions themselves are decentering Christianity from its former heartlands and expanding its spread and adherence in other places. Pentecostalism has been a decisive factor in the transformation of World Christianity, as it took root in remarkable ways in the Global South.[12] The Asian diaspora peoples are reviving Christianity in their places of settlement as it wanes there, and they also provide strategic linkages to churches in their ancestral homelands to engage globally and partner with their Western counterparts, leveraging one another's resources and strengths to reach everyone everywhere. Along with other dispersed Christians of the world, Asian diasporas are helping the global church transition into a new era of missions.

Series Outline

This series comprises three volumes: (1) *Journeys of Asian Diaspora: Mapping Originations and Destinations*, (2) *Interconnections of Asian Diaspora: Mapping the Linkages and Discontinuities*, and (3) *Reflections of Asian Diaspora: Mapping Theologies and Ministries*. The first volume traces select major Asian diaspora communities from discrete locations in the world, while the second volume sketches the wide array of connections and disconnections arising out of migratory displacements of Asians through various disciplinary lenses. The final volume showcases an assortment of theological and missiological deliberations on migration, diaspora displacement, and movement from biblical and evangelical perspectives of Asian diasporas and demonstrates select cases of ministry by and among Asian diasporas worldwide.

This series is pan-Asian in scope and attempts to cover all major regions of Asia, ranging from its eastern end in the Pacific Ocean to its western edge in the Mediterranean Sea, comprising diverse socioreligious contexts, migratory histories, and ecclesial traditions. It is not, however, comprehensive in any manner or intended to have the final say on this matter. It strives to argue that the widespread dispersion of Asians over the past few centuries and more so in recent decades has firmly established a distinctively Asian form of Christianity all over the world. Asian Christians have flourished abroad and have added diversity to Christian expressions in their host nations. Their presence and faith practices are bringing fresh vitality and renewal to Christianity and changing its face in many parts of the world. Altogether, this series paints a compelling portrait of Global Christianity with a distinctive Asian face and flavor.

The first volume, subtitled "Mapping Originations and Destinations," focuses on the journeys of Asian diaspora Christians and comprises twelve chapters that provide diasporic narratives of select Asians from wide-ranging geographical locations, such as Chinese in the United Kingdom, Japanese in Brazil and the United States, Koreans in Central and Latin America, Vietnamese and Hmong worldwide, Indonesians in Australia, Nepalese in the United States, Iranians in Europe, Lebanese around the world, Christians in the Persian Gulf, and ministry among dispersed people of Israel. All authors provide insider perspectives on their respective communities from disparate diasporic settings. The appendix at the end provides select charts and infographics related to Asian diaspora communities collated from various reports of the United Nations, the World Bank, and other agencies, particularly the *World Migration Report 2020*.

The second volume in the series, subtitled "Mapping the Linkages and Discontinuities," contains another twelve chapters that survey various connections of Asian diaspora Christians from different parts of the world. This volume explores a wide range of themes, such as religious faith in diasporas with a particular focus on Buddhism and Hinduism, family life in transnational contexts, women and migration, cultural assimilation and hybridization, hyphenated identities, the future of ministry for foreign-born and foreign-raised Asians, diaspora writings in English, the globalizing of Indian denominations, bridging the digital divide as a mission strategy, mental health, and the leadership styles of Asian diasporas. These essays are written by scholars and practitioners situated in places as broad as Thailand, India, the Philippines, the United Kingdom, the United States, South Korea, Laos, Singapore, China, and Lebanon. The contributors employ divergent disciplinary lenses such as missiology, religion, anthropology, migration, literature, sociology, psychology, economics, and technology management. By drawing insights from diverse disciplinary fields, the volume showcases the vital need for interdisciplinary work in diasporic studies and missions.

The third volume in the series, subtitled "Mapping Theologies and Ministries," contains another dozen chapters that attempt to trace divergent ministries and theologies developed in the context of diasporic Asians worldwide. In it, a Korean Australian sketches a biblical trajectory for a theology of migration, and an Indian Bible scholar explores exilic theology for immigrants in terms of the absence and presence of God. Then, a Filipino American develops a theology of nations and citizenship in the context of transnationalism, and I develop a new theology of mission for the age of migration using the concept of *motus Dei* (the move of God). Later, a Korean American critiques the use of the term *diaspora* using Asian American theology, and a Filipino Canadian compares the concepts of reverse missions and diaspora missions. Afterward, a Korean American missionary based in Japan assesses the state of global engagement of Korean missionaries and the challenges they are facing. Subsequently, a Chinese American pastor contemplates the future of English ministries in Asian churches in the United States, and a Korean missionary in East Africa investigates mobilization and cross-cultural dynamics in rural sub-Saharan contexts. The next two chapters are written by non-Asians, one British and another Australian, who have lived in Malaysia and China, respectively, for many years and explore the discipleship of Asian migrants and ministry among international students studying in China. Finally, a British Pakistani closes with a diasporic doxology that narrates the story of the use of the contextualized Punjabi Psalter in Indo-Pakistani congregations in North America. After perusing these diverse renderings of Asian diaspora Christians worldwide, one may conclude that Asian diaspora Christians are indeed globalizing Asian Christianity and Asianizing global Christianity.

Like Asia itself, Asian Christianity and its global manifestations are extremely complex, and it is preposterous to claim this series is a definitive account of it. Instead, at the risk of being accused of distortion and colossal generalization, the authors of these volumes present a few broad brushstrokes on the multifaceted canvas of Asian Christianity from the distinctive vantage points of their global locations without asserting them as comprehensive or conclusive on this matter. This Asian migratory rendering of World Christianity defies a simple explanation or any particular cultural formulation, as is evident in the ensuing chapters by the voluminous themes and perspectives covered herein. They are featured here as illustrative cases with suggestive themes and contextual realities that together must constitute a much larger whole, hoping that this will generate further interest and spark nuanced deliberations on the nature of Christianity and the role diasporas play in reshaping World Christianity in the twenty-first century.

Notes

1 See the appendix of *Journeys of Asian Diaspora: Mapping Originations and Destinations*, ed. Sam George, vol. 1 (Minneapolis: Fortress, 2021), 223–33. All numbers are based on International Organization for Migration (IOM), *World Migration Report 2020* (Geneva: IOM, 2019). See the latest reports at IOM (website), accessed September 1, 2021, https://www.iom.int/wmr/.

2 See Todd Johnson and Gina Zurlo, eds., *World Christian Encyclopedia*, 3rd ed. (Edinburgh: Edinburgh University Press, 2020).

3 Robin Cohen, *Global Diasporas: An Introduction* (Seattle: University of Washington Press, 1997). Also see Patrick Johnstone, *The Future of the Global Church: History, Trends and Possibilities* (Downers Grove, IL: InterVarsity, 2011).

4 James Clifford, "Diasporas," *Cultural Anthropology* 9, no. 3 (1994): 311.

5 This is a popular geopolitical category defined by the United Nations. The Global South includes Asia, Africa, and Latin America, while the Global North includes Europe, North America, and Oceania. See Philip Jenkins, *The Next Christendom: The Coming of Global Christianity* (New York: Oxford University Press, 2002); Mark Noll, *The New Shape of World Christianity* (Downers Grove, IL: InterVarsity Academic, 2009); and others.

6 Andrew F. Walls, *The Cross-Cultural Process in Christian History: Studies in the Transmission and Appropriation of Faith* (Maryknoll, NY: Orbis, 2007), 64.

7 Lamin Sanneh, *Disciples of All Nations: Pillars of World Christianity* (New York: Oxford University Press, 2008), 7.

8 Peter C. Phan, *Christianity with an Asian Face: Asian American Theology in the Making* (Maryknoll, NY: Orbis, 2003).

9 Lamin Sanneh and Joel Carpenter, eds., *The Changing Face of Christianity: Africa, the West, and the World* (New York: Oxford University Press, 2005), 214. See also Philip Jenkins, *The New Faces of Christianity: Believing in the Bible in the Global South* (New York: Oxford University Press, 2006).

10 Michael Pocock, Gailyn Van Rheenen, and Douglas McConnell, *The Changing Face of World Missions* (Grand Rapids, MI: Baker Academic, 2005).

11 See, for example, Fabio Baggio and Agnes M. Brazal, eds., *Faith on the Move: Toward a Theology of Migration in Asia* (Honolulu: University of Hawaii Press, 2009); John J. Ahn, *Exile and Forced Migration* (Berlin: Walter de Gruyter, 2011).

12 See Allan Anderson, *To the Ends of the Earth: Pentecostalism and the Transformation of World Christianity* (Oxford: Oxford University Press, 2013); Amos Yong, *The Missiological Spirit: Christian Mission Theology in the Third Millennium Global Context* (Eugene, OR: Cascade, 2014).

Bibliography

Ahn, John J. *Exile and Forced Migration.* Berlin: Walter de Gruyter, 2011.

Anderson, Allan. *To the Ends of the Earth: Pentecostalism and the Transformation of World Christianity.* Oxford: Oxford University Press, 2013.

Baggio, Fabio, and Agnes M. Brazal, eds. *Faith on the Move: Toward a Theology of Migration in Asia.* Honolulu: University of Hawaii Press, 2009.

Clifford, James. "Diasporas." *Cultural Anthropology* 9, no. 3 (1994): 302–338.

Cohen, Robin. *Global Diasporas: An Introduction.* Seattle: University of Washington Press, 1997.

George, Sam, ed. *Journeys of Asian Diaspora: Mapping Originations and Destinations.* Vol. 1. Minneapolis: Fortress, 2021.

International Organization for Migration (IOM). *World Migration Report 2020.* Geneva: IOM, 2019.

Jenkins, Philip. *The Next Christendom: The Coming of Global Christianity.* New York: Oxford University Press, 2002.

Johnson, Todd, and Gina Zurlo, eds. *World Christian Encyclopedia.* 3rd ed. Edinburgh: Edinburgh University Press, 2020.

Johnstone, Patrick. *The Future of the Global Church: History, Trends and Possibilities.* Downers Grove, IL: InterVarsity, 2011.

Noll, Mark. *The New Shape of World Christianity.* Downers Grove, IL: InterVarsity Academic, 2009.

Phan, Peter C. *Christianity with an Asian Face: Asian American Theology in the Making.* Maryknoll, NY: Orbis, 2003.

Pocock, Michael, Gailyn Van Rheenen, and Douglas McConnell. *The Changing Face of World Missions.* Grand Rapids, MI: Baker Academic, 2005.

Sanneh, Lamin. *Disciples of All Nations: Pillars of World Christianity.* New York: Oxford University Press, 2008.

Sanneh, Lamin, and Joel Carpenter, eds. *The Changing Face of Christianity: Africa, the West, and the World.* New York: Oxford University Press, 2005.

Walls, Andrew F. *The Cross-Cultural Process in Christian History: Studies in the Transmission and Appropriation of Faith.* Maryknoll, NY: Orbis, 2007.

Yong, Amos. *The Missiological Spirit: Christian Mission Theology in the Third Millennium Global Context.* Eugene, OR: Cascade, 2014.

Introduction

Sam George

A *National Geographic* cover story titled "A World on the Move" in August 2019 made an audacious claim: "We are all migrants. . . . We are a migratory species. . . . All of us are descended from migrants."[1] If we dare to trace our ancestries back a few decades—or centuries in certain cases—we will soon realize that none of us are native to the places where we currently make our homes. Human beings are a wandering kind because we move in search of home and hearth, for survival and livelihood, to work and play, for love and belonging, and for safety and security. When where we are becomes intolerable and unlivable, we escape to other places. In the face of danger, we relocate to safer locales and are more cognizant of perceived greener pastures far beyond our current domiciles. Some choose to move, while others are compelled to. For some, it turns out favorably, while others languish for the rest of their lives, and many others disappear entirely from the face of the earth.

This volume explores diasporic reflections of widely dispersed Asians from different parts of the world in the form of their theologies and contemplations on select ministries. In the first volume, we scanned the globe to locate the "journeys" of Asian diaspora Christians who have settled in every continent by mapping their divergent origins, routes, and destinations. In the first volume, the chapters were geographically and historically wide ranging, with varied points of beginnings and endings, and in the second volume, we focused on disciplinary breadth by inviting scholars from diverse domains to locate "interconnections" of global Asian Christians to provide insights from their fields of expertise into the wanderings of Asian Christians. These two volumes bring us to the present one, where we dig deeper to glean "reflections" of Asian Christian scholars about their global movements. We investigate diasporic narratives of Scripture for theological insights on our lived reality in foreign lands and the missiological implications of the growing trend of Asian dispersion out of and within Asia.

Migration as a Theologizing and Missionizing Experience

Over forty years ago, the American historian Timothy L. Smith claimed that migration is "a theologizing experience," which had stirred some deliberations.[2] According to him, when migration involves traumatic events of uprooting, separation, disorientation, and settlement, it forces migrants to probe deeper into existential issues concerning the meaning of life and their displacement using spiritual terms. There is an amplification of the psychic basis for theological consideration and ethnoreligious commitment owing to dislocation, settling in distant places, the process of othering, and loss, pain, and rejection suffered in foreign nations. The alienation and disruptions resulting from migratory displacements intensify the ontological quest for a life purpose, for which faith and a faith community remain inestimable resources.[3]

Immigrants become more religious after relocating to a new place and turn to their inherited as well as new surrounding religious beliefs and practices to answer the deeper spiritual angst they are sensing on account of displacements.[4] This is clearly evident from the new vigor and significance of religious rituals for immigrants, the prevalence of ethnoreligious organizations, and the vital role belief systems play in navigating diasporic nomadism. Other immigrants are disillusioned with religious and sociocultural customs of the old world, their irrelevance in the new world, and tend to explore tenable alternatives, all of which result in their eventual disavowal of inherited traditions and embrace of the dominant faith of the host nation or whatever else is most beneficial to them.

Christian migrants are revived in their faith and quick to re-create childhood faith practices in the new world, which renews and globalizes Christianity in their host nations, while simultaneously appropriating faith practices from their new contexts—from both host nations and other Christian immigrants from other parts of the world—and exerting significant influence on their families and communities back in their ancestral homelands. They shed the baggage of the past and add fresh vibrancy to Christianity in their host nations, both of which force them to reimagine the nature of the Christian gospel and its mission to all people. The migrant faith communities exhibit tremendous creative energy and an innovative spirit for theological contemplation on lived theology from the perspective of World Christianity as these new streams join the mainstream of earlier eras of migrants from different parts of the world. This is particularly true of the North American context. Christianity is not native to this continent; it was brought here by immigrants from many different shores of the world. Every wave of immigration has enriched the North American church in inimitable ways and helped it become more global and diverse while also reengaging with the world with a revived spirit, a renewed vision, and expanded connections for missionary undertakings.

Migration is not only a theologizing experience but also a missionizing experience because the immigrants carry out the missionary function without even fully realizing it. The mission historian Jehu J. Hanciles has traced the critical role common Christian migrants have played in the making of contemporary Christianity and claims that "every Christian migrant is a potential missionary."[5] Christians get unhinged from locality and its geographical bondage, besides becoming more aware of and connected with Christians from other parts of the world. They are a disproportionate share of the international migrant populace and are more likely to migrate than others. Many who are not Christian embrace the Christian faith after moving to new locales, whatever the motives and destinations. After relocating, Christians are invigorated spiritually and turn into natural evangelists. They start Bible studies, host fellowship groups, practice hospitality, plant new churches, and support ministries—in adopted as well as ancestral homelands. They read Scripture with a new pair of eyes, interpret its many diasporic narratives in novel ways, are empathetic toward the hurting, develop insight into migratory struggles, and become generous with resources to assist other migrants in addition to family and friends back home. Their faith provides much-needed buoyancy in life, which helps them overcome socioeconomic challenges, and most end up thriving despite many odds stacked up against them in the host countries.

Migrants are an enterprising lot and have spawned new religious ventures unlike any that exist on either end of their migratory journeys while borrowing heavily from both ends of their Spirit-led faith adventures. They are quick to circumvent religious institutional orders to pioneer and expand ethnic denominations to their diasporic settlements for the sake of communal solidarity, civic participation, fiscal benefits, and political recognition in foreign lands. Migratory displacement proffers a strong impulse toward rejuvenation, innovations, and expansionist propensities. Over decades and generations, migrants and their progeny assimilate through cultural osmosis, whether of their deliberate choosing for its apparent benefits or as an unintended consequence of prolonged accommodations. The diasporic liminality possesses a creative bent and essential reserve needed to fuel fresh reimagination. When departure occurs in operose conditions and return does not seem plausible anytime in the near future, the immigrants become determined to exploit every given opportunity. Leaving their home countries—whether by choice, by need, or by force—transforms migrants to have an exceptional work ethic, motivation, and an uncanny ability to overcome all obstacles in their adopted countries. They find ingenious means to resolve issues and are exceptionally resourceful because of their entrepreneurial spirit and ability to take risks. Since they have to succeed and prove to many in their homelands the wisdom of their decision to migrate, most thrive and even help fellow immigrants thrive in their host nations.

Just to illustrate, I reiterate a few examples of the missionizing tendencies of diasporic Asian Christians. In volume 1 of this series, Alexander Chow narrates the account of how Chinese restaurant workers laid the foundation of British Chinese Christianity,[6] while Daniel Nam Y. Choe recounts the role faith and church played in the account of agrarian Koreans turning into garment makers in Latin America.[7] Godfrey Harold tells the story of Indian indentured laborers in South Africa and how the cane cutters have become church planters.[8] Likewise, Vietnamese and Nepali refugees have become pastors and missionaries to care for their own dispersed communities in many nations, whereas Iranian converts from Islamic backgrounds are bringing new enthusiasm to Christians in Europe.[9] Filipino sailors conduct church services on ocean liners in the high seas, while Indian software techies create virtual and hybrid ministry platforms to reach people in numerous nations. Many international traders and investment bankers of Asian Christian origin hold discipleship classes in their corporate boardrooms. Migrant international students from Buddhist, Hindu, and Muslim backgrounds are drawn to Jesus Christ by the witness of fellow students along with campus ministry leaders abroad. God is moving among people who are on the move, and these Asian migrants have proven to be exceptional missionaries.

In all of these cases, most of the Asian emigrants are bypassing the existing ecclesiastical structures and economic models by inventing novel ways of doing ministry. Most of these pioneers are not formally sent by or affiliated with any church or Christian organization, nor do they have any theological education but are simply obedient to the work of the Spirit, and most serve as bivocational ministers instead of seeking ecclesial ordination and professional association. They defy prevailing modes of mission funding and ministry operations while carrying out the missionary mandate by becoming conduits for gospel diffusion to new places and people. Just as missionaries of the past may perhaps be considered migrants for traversing national and cultural boundaries for the sake of mission work, now migrants could be construed to perform a missionary function, although they may have migrated abroad for other reasons.

Book Outline

This third volume of the Asian Diaspora Christianity series begins with a biblical theology of diaspora developed by the Korean Australian theologian Miyon Chung, in which she traces the language of dispersion in the Bible and argues that dispersion itself is missional. Later, the Indian Old Testament scholar Prince Kumar Tamilarasan explores the exilic theology from the book of Ezekiel to present the interplay between the divine absence and the divine presence for the deportees and argues that God does not have any spatial or temporal limitations and has many implications for today's displaced peoples of the world.

The next three chapters come from systematic theological perspectives. The third chapter is written by the Filipino theologian Tereso C. Casiño, who traces the notion of nations in the Bible and its connection to the current understanding of world missions. He investigates the implication of identity and belonging for diaspora missiology by developing a theological understanding of nation, citizenship, and transnationalism. Afterward, I briefly examine the Christian doctrines of creation, the Trinity, humanity, the fall, the incarnation, salvation, and eschatology in motile terms to argue that the God of the Bible is a living and moving being, which makes Christianity an exceptional transportable and translatable faith. Next, the Korean American theologian Daniel D. Lee argues the need for deep contextual awareness that includes Asian American origins by delineating particularities of personal, ethnic, racial, and postcolonial histories to do the work of theology and discern our vocational calling to bear witness to Christ in the world.

The subsequent three chapters come from global missiological perspectives. First, the Filipino Canadian pastor Narry F. Santos contrasts reverse mission and diaspora mission while presenting a case study of a church in Manila planting a new multiethnic and multigenerational church in Toronto. Later, the Korean American missiologist Chandler H. Im, who is based in Japan, evaluates the latest data on South Korean Protestant missionaries worldwide and identifies five areas of concern facing them in regard to their global missionary engagement. Then the Chinese American Andrew Y. Lee—who has pastored the largest Chinese churches in the Chinatowns of New York and Chicago—explores the future of English ministry developed for American-born and American-raised generations of Chinese and Asian immigrants to the United States.

The following three chapters look at the issue of leadership training in diasporic contexts using divergent strategies and in distinctive contexts, beginning with the Korean missionary Paul Sungro Lee, who has been actively involved in the cross-cultural training of missionaries in East Africa for over two decades. He presents the challenges of designing a non-Western training manual in different languages for the contextual realities of the Global South, which has been field-tested in several countries in Asia, Africa, Oceania, and South America. This is a good example of a Global

South–South partnership—totally eclipsing mission training offered by the Global North. The next chapter is written by the British mission trainer David Mark Ball, who is based in Thailand and employs the church-based model of theological education by extension (TEE) to disciple diaspora leaders, thus transcending the national boundaries conventionally associated with the TEE movement. The next chapter is written by Phil Jones, an Australian international student ministry leader based in East Asia who analyzes the Asian student diasporas from both sending and receiving contexts inside as well as outside of Asia. He identifies several challenges and exciting opportunities in ministries to Asian international students in Asia as well as around the world.

Finally, the book closes with a diasporic doxology, a narrative of the contextualized worship of the Punjabi psalms in South Asia that deals with the missiological implications of the translation of biblical poetry using local musical customs by American missionaries in the late nineteenth century and its role in the migration of people in the early twenty-first century from the region to the same American city where the missionaries had come from. Yousaf Sadiq emphasizes the essential role these translated psalms play in the development of diasporic spirituality among South Asian Punjabi churches worldwide.

What is significant about the essays in this series on Asian diaspora Christianity is that nearly all are by Asians in diasporic contexts globally with distinct voices and points of view. Their unique methodological approaches and theological stances—depending on their domain of expertise and for most of whom English often is not their first language—add to the complexity of the discourse on the intersectionality of Asian studies, migration/diaspora literature, and Christian mission. Most of them do not know one another or are not conversant with the others' ministry or writings. Several others could have contributed substantial essays to this series but were unable to do so because of the disruptions caused by Covid-19 or the demands of family, academic, or ministerial commitments. What remains remarkable about this series is how it all came together when we all were grounded and were forced to reconnect virtually to produce these writings and how one book enlarged into a three-volume series to cover the great diversity of Asia and Asian diasporas.

Mapping a Moving World and Migrating Mission

Since this final volume does not have any formal conclusion at the end, nor did the previous two volumes, allow me to make some closing remarks here. These three volumes were planned to be explorative and open ended by design. Each chapter and the multifarious themes covered therein illustrate some particularities but also reveal complexities associated with the study of the faith of contemporary diasporas and reveal some generalities about the mission of God in the world without being definitive or final. Though migration is as old as human history, large-scale and long-distance human migration is only beginning to unfold in a significant manner, and it is too soon to pontificate about it or draw any conclusive inferences. Yet migration remains one of the most profound and defining issues of our time that will hold a far-reaching sway on the reconfiguration of Christianity in the coming decades.

I have used a common thread to tie the entire series together and have used it in the subtitle of each book. The word is *mapping* and is used intentionally in its present continuous tense. This series on Asian diaspora Christianity is an emerging story, and much more is going to be mapped and written in the coming years and decades. Many more characters, sets, and plots must be drawn up in order to enrich this chronicle. A lot more will be deliberated, discussed, and debated about it, including materials in other languages and perspectives. These three dozen voices and forty essays are only elemental to get a feel for the lay of the land, but I hope they steer readers in a direction that broadens and deepens their understanding of the story of Christianity in the twenty-first century.

This series intends to map out some points on the contours of the current dispersion of Asian Christians worldwide and its missional implication and role in the transformation of global Christianity itself. It has only located a few sites in the trajectory of contemporary Christianity, and I invite other scholars along this exploration to plot additional points, expressions, and loci of this fast-emerging reality. These are a few broad brushstrokes to portray the complex dimensions of how diasporas transform and advance Christianity. I welcome Asian and other practitioners and scholars to review, modify, and expand this cartographical attempt to discern the catalytic role diasporas play in reimagining the missionary nature of the Christian faith. Along with numerous other ethnic, linguistic, regional, national, and continental diasporas, this Asian diasporic account aims to render a fuller and richer portrait of Christianity that is consistent with the eschatological vision of "a great multitude that no one could count, from every nation, from all tribes and peoples and languages, standing before the throne and before the Lamb" (Rev 7:9).

Maps and missions are intricately tied together in history. The father of the modern mission movement, William Carey, penned his famous mission treatise and included many maps of the nations, populations, and religious preferences of peoples of the world before setting out to British India.[10] Later missionaries like David Livingstone drew up maps of Africa for the British public, and Hudson Taylor used maps of China to mobilize more workers to join him. Since European colonial times, mission societies have relied on official maps, census reports, and other data in addition to traveling on colonial ships to their mission fields, which proves the nexus between colonialism and the mission enterprise. The imperial ambitions and conquering of the seas changed the vision of the world for the masses. The late fifteenth-century maiden voyages of Christopher Columbus and Vasco da Gama were "the most important events in the human history" not because they provided wealth for Europe but because they made people vastly more mobile than they had ever been before.[11] Maps were central in reshaping our conception of the nations and the peoples of the world, which eventually led to the development of faster modes of transportation, increased human interactions, and migration around the world.

Maps have proven to be strategic implements used by churches and missionary agencies to mobilize personnel and funds, to deploy missionaries to select areas, to avoid duplication and redundancy, and to develop synergy. The notions of frontiers, boundaries, margins, and crossings are widely prevalent in mission literature, all of which are drawn from the field of cartography. In recent decades, mission strategies such as those involving unreached people groups charted people anthropologically and geographically, while the 10/40 Window prioritized mission efforts within certain latitudes and longitudes till the end of the last millennium. Prayer mobilization tools like *Operation World* and Christian census reference guides like *World Christian Encyclopedia* rely heavily on geographical profiling and have proven to be strategic resources for missions.[12] Territorial metaphors and geographical expressions are widespread in mission writings, and these pieces of literature contain many colonial, militaristic, and business jargons. Though practical and helpful in relating to diverse audiences, they can lead to a managerial mission mentality and fail to recognize that the mission of God is so much more.

However, in this age of migration, people cannot be defined by geography anymore, since they are mobile, possess multiple identities, and are simultaneously associated with several localities. The reality of transnational linkages and multiple belonging—having many passports or living in multiple places regularly—makes things complicated in networked societies. The ethnolinguistic or cultural distinctives are less discrete than before, as more people are globalized or use technological tools to interact with people from other parts of the world. The increased global flow of information, music, video, and money is disrupting traditional societal and economic orders in many parts of the world. Large-scale diasporic intermingling and hybridity due to mixed marriage and global living make it problematic to define people by parameters that we used in the past.

All of this beckons us to engage in cartographical tasks afresh, wearing new pairs of glasses to look at the world through the lens of migration while reading Scripture using the spectacles of diaspora and seeing God as a moving being who is at work in the world in new ways. It requires us to understand who is moving from where (origination) and to where (destination). It demands us to comprehend the transnational belonging (linkages) and alienation (discontinuities) arising out of diasporic displacements. It asks a new set of questions about divinity (theology) and divine activity in the world (ministries). Our theologies and mission engagements have to be completely reinvented in the context of global diasporas. It is forcing us to develop a bifocal sensibility and reimagine our ministries for the new world. A helpful comparison in this regard is learning to "shoot a moving target." In archery, the strategies to shoot a fixed target and a moving target are poles apart, and archers are trained to shoot not where a target is currently but where it will be after shooting the arrow. This requires us to anticipate where a target will go, be creative and quick, have mastery over our equipment, account for climatic conditions, and prepare for high failure rates.

The study of Global Christianity is redrawing the map of the theology and mission of the church around the world. The unreached peoples of the world are no longer bound to any geographical borders but have moved to live next door to us everywhere. Missions are no longer from the West to the Rest but from everywhere to everyone everywhere. Christianity is a de facto missionary religion par excellence not because of a few random verses at the end of a Gospel. Its tenets and practices are not static or confined to any geographic region but are dynamic, are translatable, and move unceasingly. It is a translatable faith, since no one language is considered exclusive to Christianity. It is never confined to a place, culture, or people, as different regions and peoples have been chief representatives of the Christian faith. It possesses an innate power to diffuse across cultures and geographies. It is a mobile faith, and its mobility brings about fresh reconceptualization, which causes cross-cultural diffusion, and Jesus incarnates into all cultures of the world. Migration, whether voluntary or forced, has played an enormous and determinative role in the expansion and transformation of Christianity throughout its history.

This series need not be relegated as something for Asians or merely as a mission strategy to reach dispersed Asians or some category of an exotic theology of Asians. Rather, the entire enterprise of Christian theology and missiology needs to be reconfigured on account of the end of Christendom and the emergence of World Christianity, especially in the wake of surging global migration, diaspora networks, a new global consciousness, and missionary movements arising from everywhere. This series is an attempt to do just that—a process of remapping the world of Asian diaspora Christianity—and is best depicted in its descriptive title: Globalizing of Asian Christianity and Asianizing of Global Christianity.

Notes

1 Mohsin Hamid, "We Are All Migrants," *National Geographic*, August 2019, https://www.nationalgeographic.com/magazine/issue/august -2019.

2 Timothy L. Smith, "Religion and Ethnicity in America," *American Historical Review* 83, no. 5 (1978): 1175; Jehu J. Hanciles, *Beyond Christendom: Globalization, African Migration, and the Transformation of the West* (Maryknoll, NY: Orbis, 2008), 4, 297; John Corrie,

"Migration as a Theologizing Experience: The Promise of Interculturality for Transformative Mission," *Mission Studies* 31 (2014): 9–21; Eunil David Cho, "Re-understanding Migration as a Theologizing Experience," *Practical Matters*, no. 11 (October 2018), http:// practicalmattersjournal.org/2018/10/15/re-understanding-migration -as-a-theologizing-experience/.

3 See Philip Connor, "Religion as Resource: Religion and Immigrant Economic Incorporation," *Social Science Research* 40, no. 5 (2011): 1350–61; Pyong G. Min and Jung Ha Kim, *Religion in Asian America: Building Faith Communities* (Walnut Creek, CA: AltaMira, 2002); Michael Foley and Dean R. Hoge, *Religion and the New Immigrants: How Faith Communities Form Our Newest Citizens* (New York: Oxford University Press, 2007).

4 See Prema Kurien, *Ethnic Church Meets Megachurch: Indian American Christianity in Motion* (Philadelphia: Temple University Press, 2017); R. Stephen Warner and Judith G. Wittner, *Gatherings in Diaspora: Religious Communities and the New Immigration* (Philadelphia: Temple University Press, 1998).

5 Hanciles, *Beyond Christendom*, 378. Also see Jehu J. Hanciles, *Migration and the Making of Global Christianity* (Grand Rapids, MI: Eerdmans, 2021).

6 Alexander Chow, "From Takeaways to British Chinese: Christianity among Overseas Chinese in the United Kingdom," in *Journeys of Asian Diaspora: Mapping Originations and Destinations*, ed. Sam George (Minneapolis: Fortress, 2021), 1:9–24.

7 Daniel Nam Y. Choe, "Korean Christians in Central and Latin America," in George, *Journeys of Asian Diaspora*, 1:61–82.

8 Godfrey Harold, "From Cane Cutters to Church Planters: The Story of the Indian Church in South Africa," in *Diaspora Christianities: Global Scattering and Gathering of South Asian Christians*, ed. Sam George (Minneapolis: Fortress, 2018), 57–68.

9 See Sam George and Miriam Adeney, eds., *Refugee Diaspora: Missions amid the Greatest Humanitarian Crisis of Our Times* (Littleton, CO: William Carey, 2018).

10 William Carey, *An Enquiry into the Obligation of Christians to Use Means for the Conversion of the Heathens* (Leicester, UK: Ann Ireland, 1792), https://www.wmcarey.edu/carey/enquiry/anenquiry.pdf.

11 Anthony Pagden, *Peoples and Empires: A Short History of European Migration, Exploration and Conquests from Greece to the Present* (New York: Modern Library, 2003), 56; Adam Smith, *An Inquiry into the Nature and Causes of the Wealth of Nations*, ed. R. H. Campbell and A. S. Skinner (Oxford: Clarendon, 1976), 560.

12 Jason Mandryk, *Operation World*, 7th ed. (Downers Grove, IL: InterVarsity, 2016); Todd Johnson and Gina Zurlo, eds., *World Christian Encyclopedia*, 3rd ed. (Edinburgh: Edinburgh University Press, 2020).

Bibliography

Carey, William. *An Enquiry into the Obligation of Christians to Use Means for the Conversion of the Heathens.* Leicester, UK: Ann Ireland, 1792. https://www.wmcarey.edu/carey/enquiry/anenquiry.pdf.

Cho, Eunil David. "Re-understanding Migration as a Theologizing Experience." *Practical Matters*, no. 11 (October 2018). http://practicalmattersjournal.org/2018/10/15/re-understanding-migration-as-a-theologizing-experience/.

Choe, Daniel Nam Y. "Korean Christians in Central and Latin America." In George, *Journeys of Asian Diaspora*, 61–82.

Connor, Philip. "Religion as Resource: Religion and Immigrant Economic Incorporation." *Social Science Research* 40, no. 5 (2011): 1350–1361.

Corrie, John. "Migration as a Theologizing Experience: The Promise of Interculturality for Transformative Mission." *Mission Studies* 31 (2014): 9–21.

Foley, Michael, and Dean R. Hoge. *Religion and the New Immigrants: How Faith Communities Form Our Newest Citizens.* New York: Oxford University Press, 2007.

George, Sam, ed. *Diaspora Christianities: Global Scattering and Gathering of South Asian Christians.* Minneapolis: Fortress, 2018.

———. *Journeys of Asian Diaspora: Mapping Originations and Destinations.* Vol. 1. Minneapolis: Fortress, 2021.

George, Sam, and Miriam Adeney, eds. *Refugee Diaspora: Missions amid the Greatest Humanitarian Crisis of Our Times.* Littleton, CO: William Carey, 2018.

Hamid, Mohsin. "We Are All Migrants." *National Geographic*, August 2019. https://www.nationalgeographic.com/magazine/issue/august-2019.

Hanciles, Jehu J. *Beyond Christendom: Globalization, African Migration, and the Transformation of the West.* Maryknoll, NY: Orbis, 2008.

———. *Migration and the Making of Global Christianity.* Grand Rapids, MI: Eerdmans, 2021.

Harold, Godfrey. "From Cane Cutters to Church Planters: The Story of the Indian Church in South Africa." In George, *Diaspora Christianities*, 57–68.

Johnson, Todd, and Gina Zurlo, eds. *World Christian Encyclopedia.* 3rd ed. Edinburgh: Edinburgh University Press, 2020.

Kurien, Prema. *Ethnic Church Meets Megachurch: Indian American Christianity in Motion.* Philadelphia: Temple University Press, 2017.

Mandryk, Jason. *Operation World.* 7th ed. Downers Grove, IL: InterVarsity, 2010.

Min, Pyong G., and Jung Ha Kim. *Religion in Asian America: Building Faith Communities.* Walnut Creek, CA: AltaMira, 2002.

Pagden, Anthony. *Peoples and Empires: A Short History of European Migration, Exploration and Conquests from Greece to the Present.* New York: Modern Library, 2003.

Smith, Adam. *An Inquiry into the Nature and Causes of the Wealth of Nations.* Edited by R. H. Campbell and A. S. Skinner. Oxford: Clarendon, 1976.

Smith, Timothy L. "Religion and Ethnicity in America." *American Historical Review* 83, no. 5 (1978): 1155–1185.

Warner, R. Stephen, and Judith G. Wittner. *Gatherings in Diaspora: Religious Communities and the New Immigration.* Philadelphia: Temple University Press, 1998.

A Biblical Trajectory for a Theology of Diaspora

Miyon Chung

As a result of globalization, people are moving about at unprecedented rates all over the world. Christianity has truly become a world religion and has gained new momentum for mission through dispersed peoples. So what does mass migration mean for the nature and purpose of the church of Jesus Christ? Christianity was primarily associated with the West in the past few centuries, and local churches were composed of people with similar racial, ethnic, cultural-linguistic backgrounds, and they were largely clustered in certain regions of the world. The unreached people groups were located outside of Christendom, where missionaries were sent. Thus, Christian missionaries were migrants who traveled and engaged in foreign languages and cultures to share the gospel.

Today, however, we are witnessing the reality of God's grace permeating across the world as God's people migrate. The gospel advances as people move, and the term *diaspora* is being applied, though not without dispute, to migrants who settle in foreign places for both religious and other purposes.

Therefore, we require a timely, biblically sound, and theologically cohesive reflection on Christian identity and vocation that renders strategic modifications of the traditional notions and methods of mission. This essay traces the trajectory of diaspora in the Bible to unpack what it has to do with the church and mission. The thesis is that dispersion in the Bible is not simply a result of punishment but a transformed way in and through which God demonstrates his saving grace, and for this reason, the condition and experience of diaspora are basic to the church's identity, vocation, and mission.

The Language of Dispersion in the Bible

Diaspora is a Greek word that means "dispersion" or "scattering."[1] Appearing most frequently in the LXX and extrabiblical Jewish literature, it was originally and technically used to refer to the Jewish deportations and exile that Nebuchadnezzar had enforced in the late sixth century BCE and the Jewish dispersion among the gentiles away from Palestine. The term also includes the deportations by the Assyrians and "to a lesser extent later conquerors" such as Pompey. In the New Testament, *diaspora* designates the Jewish dispersion throughout the Roman Empire to Egypt, Asia Minor, Greece, and Italy.[2] This section delineates the historical and theological trajectory of the term in the Bible to develop a theological reflection relevant and constructive for the meaning and purpose of contemporary diasporas.

Lexically, multiple Hebrew words correspond to the Greek term *diaspora*. The most often used are the various forms of *pwṣ*, *ndḥ*, and *zrḥ*, which describe the displacement, banishment, scattering, or dispersion of people.[3] In

Genesis 11:8 (the Tower of Babel), the inhabitants of the land are scattered (*pwṣ*) as a result of God's punishment for their sin. Similarly, most instances of the scattering of people in the Old Testament are portrayed as undesirable and threatening experiences. Here are climactic expressions of God's warning against disobedience that will lead to Israel's scattering among the nations:

> And you I will scatter [*zrh*] among the nations, and I will unsheathe the sword against you; your land shall be a desolation, and your cities a waste. (Lev 26:33)

> The Lord will scatter [*pwṣ*] you among all peoples, from one end of the earth to the other; and there you shall serve other gods, of wood and stone, which neither you nor your ancestors have known. (Deut 28:64)

Likewise, Solomon's Temple Dedication Prayer in 1 Kings 8:46 also uses *pwṣ* to speak of the prospect of being scattered as a punishment for sin. In the Prophets, Jeremiah 9:16 declares that God "will scatter [*pwṣ*] them among nations" to places unknown to "their ancestors" because of their recalcitrant rebellion against him. Approximately half of the Old Testament's scattering expressions occur in Jeremiah and Ezekiel.

One would expect, therefore, the LXX and the extrabiblical Jewish literature to use *diaspora* to translate the aforementioned Hebrew terms. In other words, *diaspora* should have been used to translate the Hebrew forms of *pwṣ*, *ndḥ*, and *zrh*. On the contrary, *diaspora* was employed to translate the Hebrew terms for exile—*golah* and *galut*, two nominal forms of the lexical *glh*.[4] The word *exile* deals with the experience of forced migration or displacement, and the condition of being scattered (i.e., dispersion) and that of "exile" are intimately related to each other in biblical narratives. But the Hebrew terms for exile (variants of *glh*) occur predominantly in Jeremiah and Ezekiel to refer to the Jewish deportations to Babylon in 597, 587, and 582 BCE. Also, the Jewish dispersion during biblical times was extensive and complex, and the term *glh* was embedded with pregnant expressions related to the historical and theological causes of the Jewish deportations. In the course of history, however, the concrete and immediate sense of the term was not carried into its Greek translation, and its use broadened.

The above observation is substantive because the actual Greek word for "banishment as punishment" is *phuge*, not *diaspora*, as used in Matthew 24:20.[5] More significantly, the New Testament applies *diaspora* not just to the dispersed Jews or even the dispersed Jewish Christians of the first century but also to the dispersed gentile Christians (John 12:20; Jas 1:1; 1 Pet 1:1; and in verb forms in Acts 8:1, 4; 11:19). Consequently, the following questions that are important for this essay emerge: (1) Why do the LXX and the extrabiblical Jewish literature use *diaspora* to speak of both the Jewish exile and the Jewish dispersion outside Palestine? and (2) Why does the New Testament apply *diaspora* to refer to the Jewish and Christian dispersions?

Grace through and in Dispersion

As observed earlier, the Old Testament narratives of dispersion are primarily conveyed in the context of divine judgment and punishment for sin and consequently executed coercively. Surprisingly, they are commingled with God's grace that operates in and out of the context of punishment. In the Old Testament, dispersion is ultimately disclosed as grace even though it is occasioned by God's punishment for and wrath against sin. For dispersion reorients the sinful people to turn to God in repentance and faith to receive God's restoring and renewing grace.

A foundational example is given in Genesis 11. The Tower of Babel is one of the zenith expressions of human hubris and self-idolization. A cursory reading of the story concludes that God punishes the people by diversifying their language and scattering them. A careful reader, however, will discover that these are actually the gracious means by which God restrains and terminates the people's effort to establish security by centralizing (the megacity) and absolutizing (the tower) civilization. The language diversification and the ensuing scattering in Genesis 11, therefore, are not ultimately punitive in direction; rather, they function as "the gift of new beginnings, liberation from a blind alley."[6] The graciousness of God demonstrated in Genesis 11 reaches its fulfillment at Pentecost: "When the day of Pentecost had come, they were all together in one place. And suddenly from heaven there came a sound like the rush of a violent wind, and it filled the entire house where they were sitting. Divided tongues, as of fire, appeared among them, and a tongue rested on each of them. All of them were filled with the Holy Spirit and began to speak in other languages, as the Spirit gave them ability" (Acts 2:1–4). Here the Holy Spirit heals the experience of dispersion by language division in Genesis 11 through the gift of speaking in tongues. Miraculously, the diaspora Jews and some proselytes from a vast geographical region are able to hear the Galilean disciples of Jesus speaking about

"God's deeds of power" in their "own languages": "Parthians, Medes, Elamites, and residents of Mesopotamia, Judea and Cappadocia, Pontus and Asia, Phrygia and Pamphylia, Egypt and the parts of Libya belonging to Cyrene, and visitors from Rome, both Jews and proselytes, Cretans and Arabs—in our own languages we hear them speaking about God's deeds of power" (Acts 2:9–11). Soon after, the gift of tongues is extended to gentiles who are brought into the family of God (such as Cornelius and some of the Corinthian Christians), thus disclosing Pentecost as the eschatological sign that overturns the scattering and confusion in Genesis 11 by unity and clarity of salvation through Jesus Christ and the power of the Holy Spirit.

Moreover, the grace that inheres in the scattering in Genesis 11 is likewise traceable in the trajectory of the ensuing scattering narratives in the Old Testament. A stunning illustration emerges in Jeremiah's letter to the exiles in chapter 29.[7] It functions like a trope that is quintessentially important for unfolding the thesis of this essay. A few preliminary observations that affirm the above proposition and simultaneously move the discussion forward are as follows. First of all, Jeremiah 29:4 (and also Jer 29:14) attributes God as the agent of the scattering and exile to Babylon. Counterproductive to the reason for the dispersion, however, God's message to the Jewish exiles is to flourish in the new place rather than to mourn and decline: "Build houses and live in them; plant gardens and eat what they produce. Take wives and have sons and daughters; take wives for your sons, and give your daughters in marriage, that they may bear sons and daughters; multiply there, and do not decrease" (Jer 29:5–6). The message from God is clear. The exiled Israelites are not to falter into a hiatus from living until they return "home" but to begin establishing a robust community in the distant land ruled by their subjugators. As unremittingly disparaging as they were in their incipience, the traumatic memory of the forced dispersion and the humiliating condition of exile are not to shape the people's lives, for the exile is the transforming initiative for thriving in the land to which God has brought them.

Second, in Jeremiah 29:14, God's speech brings the scattering and exile events close together and amplifies the future gathering as an act of restoration and enrichment: "I will let you find me, says the Lord, and I will restore your fortunes and gather you from all the nations and all the places where I have driven you [*ndh*], says the Lord, and I will bring you back to the place from which I sent you into exile [*glh*]." It can be deduced from this text that the scattering and exile are unified into a single theme. This semantic suggestion is important for the Greek term *diaspora*, for it is used to translate the Hebrew terms for exile—*golah* and *galut*—not scattering.

Third, in later passages in Jeremiah and Ezekiel, where a concentration of references to the scattering and exile occurs, the term "exile" (*glh*) is rarely used in the context of a threat, humiliation, or retribution. Increasingly, they express God's concern for the scattered Israelites and the promise of gathering, renewal, and restoration. In other words, whereas the Hebrew term for scattering is used negatively, the variants of *glh* are used in reference to the future blessings planned for Israel. For instance, Ezekiel 36 declares God's profound concern for his holy name, which has become profaned among the nations due to Israel's defilement and demise. For his name's sake, therefore, God promises to renew Israel thoroughly and declares an eschatological promise that is to be fulfilled in the New Testament: "I will sprinkle clean water upon you. . . . A new heart I will give you, and a new spirit I will put within you" (Ezek 36:25–26).

Fourth, in texts such as Isaiah 60, although dating Isaiah pericopes can be an issue, the incipient cause of the exilic life (forced deportation and dispersion) recedes to the background, and the exiles become reclassified as the remnants of Israel who will rebuild a new community of God. God's promise of restoration, renewal, and gathering back to the homeland is to be accomplished not by those who had remained in Judah but by the remnants of the exiled Judeans who were carried off to Babylon. The textual and historical movements discussed above, therefore, elucidate and qualify why the LXX, for instance, uses *diaspora* to translate the Hebrew term for exile (*glh*); by the time the text was written in 2 BCE, the descendants of the original Jewish exiles were well established in foreign lands. Although the Greek term *diaspora* was associated with experiences of compulsory migration, it privileged the semantics of "emigration and colonization."[8] We can infer that the intentional use of *diaspora* highlights that later Jewish communities were not necessarily characterized by an urgent desire to return to the homeland.

Undoubtedly, the memory of the forced deportation from Judea remained an essential constitutive element of the diaspora Jews' identity. They continued to maintain their Jewish national identity and regularly made pilgrimage to Jerusalem. But the memory of the plight of the exile ceased to function as a central existential condition that determined their lives. Returning home was no longer an urgent imperative for them. The extrabiblical literature such as 1 Maccabees 15:22–24 confirms the dispersion was maintained and spread throughout the Roman world. The Jewish community in Alexandria, Egypt, for instance, was "undoubtedly large and influential."[9] By the first century CE, as Roman citizenship became more accessible, many Jews were able to procure it in exchange for favors (like the apostle Paul's ancestors [Acts 22:25–28]). In this way, though "seemingly counterintuitive, the Greek use of 'diaspora' frames both the threat and the promise of life-under-God," for dispersion is not the absence of grace but a paradoxical and profound partaking of it.[10]

Lastly, important corroborating evidence is also found in the New Testament. Matthew 1:11, 12, and 17 use *metoikesia* to refer to the Babylonian exile. To address the Jewish dispersion in totality, however, other books of the New Testament follow the LXX's usage of *diaspora* (John 7:35; Jas 1:1). Linguistically, a separation is created between the original Babylonian exile and consequent dispersions. More importantly, the New Testament makes a critical linguistic and theological initiative by applying *diaspora* to the scattered Jewish Christians—like Peter addressing his readers as "the exiles of the Dispersion in Pontus, Galatia, Cappadocia, Asia, and Bithynia" (1 Pet 1:1).

What is the significance of this appellation? The dispersion Peter speaks of in the text had no causative connection to divine punishment, for they scattered due to persecution. Moreover, various verb forms of *diaspora* are used in Acts (8:1, 4; 11:19) to record how the Hellenistic Jewish Christians spread the gospel to Judea, Samaria, Phoenicia, Cyprus, and Antioch through the mode of dispersion. The implication is clear. The term *diaspora* in the New Testament is not associated with punishment. Rather, the scattering was a result of the persecution against the unwavering demonstrations of their loyalty and commitment to Jesus Christ.

It, furthermore, was used as the principal mode through which the gospel spread among the gentiles. Thus, *diaspora* in the New Testament illustrates the culmination of the grace embedded in the experiences of the dispersion and exile.

Diaspora as an Identity and a Calling

Inasmuch as dispersion is grace, it is the heart of God's people's calling. Early in Genesis, displacement and dispersion are already revealed as the providentially structured modes of life that are formative of the identity and lifestyle of God's elect. Genesis 15 is a striking illustration against the illusion of making settlement or rootedness the ultimate mode of achieving contentedness in life. God comes to Abram in a vision on a starry night to remind him of the extravagant promises that were made earlier (Gen 12:1–3)—those of the land (home) and countless descendants (heirs). But the promises here include a distressful, starkly dark calling for Abraham's posterity to live as enslaved aliens for four hundred years.

Consequently, tension is created between the promises of the land and a rooted life and the prolonged, detouring dislocation. The tension seems to compromise the prospect of fully enjoying the gift. Hence what kind of "home" will it be to return to? What kind of identity formation will this experience produce? When Abraham's heirs finally enter Canaan, the land will have numerous Indigenous occupants, and the situation will force the Israelites to yet again face the paradoxical situation of being strangers and aliens in their newly conquered promised land: "For so many generations living enslaved in a foreign land, the 'return' to Canaan will amount to a new exile, for there will be nothing familiar in the land to which they will come. Genesis 15:13–16 writes alien status into the very origin of the identity of the people of Abraham. And appeal to the land will not solve the identity crisis, for this land is teeming with others: Kenites, Kenizzites, Kadmonites, Hittites, Perizzites, Rephaim, Amorites, Canaanites, Girgashites, and Jebusites (Genesis 15:19–20)."[11]

The formation of Israel's identity was far more nuanced than can superficially be surmised. For it was not derived from the land, rootedness, or the Canaanite conquest. Instead, it was to be grounded in the memory of the dispersion and God's abiding presence with the people. As shown above, the looming threat of dispersion was there if the people of Israel were to sin against God. Henceforth, the diaspora was far more significant for Israel's identity even before the Babylonian captivity.

Israel's diasporic identity is preeminently demonstrated in the celebrative cultic prescriptions in Deuteronomy 26: the Feast of First Fruits and offering of tithes. This text will be discussed in the subsequent section, and at this junction, we will only look at the command that the entire congregation of Israel was required to recite from generation to generation (Deut 26:5): "A wandering Aramean was my ancestor; he went down into Egypt and lived there as an alien, few in number, and there he became a great nation, mighty and populous." While celebrating the annual harvest by offering the first fruits of the land to God and generously sharing their tithes with the Levites, the Israelites were commanded to recall collectively the diaspora root of their identity. In addition, through the grafting of the select Canaanites via Moses, Rahab, and Ruth (to name a few) into the twelve tribes and ultimately into the lineage of Jesus Christ (Matt 1:1–17), the diaspora experience was fixed as the normative constituent of Israel's and therefore Christian's identity. The text generates profound implications:

1. Insofar as Israel's identity was ingrained in Abraham's diasporic calling, Israel's calling was thoroughly constituted by multicultural contexts. For one cannot live as a foreigner or graft foreigners into the lineage without interacting with the host culture or the cultures that others bring to the homeland, and multicultural engagement was normative to Israel's constitution.

2. Although seemingly counterintuitive, Israel's annual reenactment of its diasporic heritage in the context of a celebration makes the status and condition of diaspora normative, not merely transitory or superfluous.

3. By implication, the distinction that Abraham's descendants were to enjoy was not going to be derived from the land, its bountiful produce, or assimilation into their neighbor's established culture. For Israel's identity and security were to be grounded in the presence of God alone. Living out of this complex, tension-filled resident alien status, they were constantly directed to desire God and God only (Exod 20:4–5; 34:14; Deut 6:15). After all, is this not what Moses pleads for in the face of God's incumbent and imminent wrath at Mount Sinai? In interceding for his people, he cries out, "If your presence will not go, do not carry us up from here. For how shall it be known that I have found favor in your sight, I and

your people, unless you go with us? In this way, we shall be distinct, I and your people, from every people on the face of the earth" (Exod 33:15–16).

4. Hence Israel's diasporic identity and vocation could be reinterpreted as a paradigmatically unique and decisively optimum context in which to live *coram Deo*.

Furthermore, precisely because diaspora is grace, "it functions as a metaphor for God's renewing life of faith anywhere."[12] It is the mode of dispersion, not settlement, that is to be the vocation of God's people. This imperative is articulated climactically in Jeremiah's message to the Jews in Babylon (Jer 29:5–6). John Yoder retrieves the following groundbreaking insight from the text regarding diaspora: "To be scattered is not a hiatus, after which normalcy will resume. From Jeremiah's time on, rather, according to the message of the play, dispersion shall be the calling of the Jewish faith community."[13] The Jeremian model of life instructs the Jews in Babylon to settle into the *galut* ("exile"), for it is not a temporary "hiatus" until the reinstallation of Israel's royal line and reconstruction of the temple in Jerusalem. The dispersion is not a situation to escape by returning home; rather, it is the people's calling, which is revealed to be eschatological in the New Testament.

The divine imperative of the dispersion is presented as being radically and emphatically predestined and eschatological (Acts 17:26–28; 1 Pet 1:1–2). That God fulfilled his salvific promise through Jesus Christ and extended the application of his saving grace to all people through the Holy Spirit in the event of Pentecost affords us with two prime implications: (1) diaspora is the unconditional vocation of all Christians, and (2) it is to be the universally implemented strategy for mission. As such, the occasion for Christian dispersion is completely detached from the imposition of punishment for sin. The tension imbued in the dual quality of the diasporic life simultaneously as punishment and grace is no longer operative. Instead, the scattering of Christians was singularly caused by the persecution against their faithfulness to Jesus Christ, and it was transformed into the chief method for spreading the gospel. In this way, diaspora became inseparable from the unconditional vocation of all Christians to spread the gospel.

Peter's first epistle is enormously significant for understanding diaspora as a foundational eschatological identity and universal vocation of Christians.[14] Although it was written to the scattered Jewish Christians, it inclusively addresses the gentile Christians in 1:14, 18; 2:9–10, 25; 3:6; and 4:3–4. Peter opens his letter with words that strongly deconstruct any identity intimately tied to the land and rootedness: "Peter, an apostle of Jesus Christ, To the exiles of the Dispersion in Pontus, Galatia, Cappadocia, Asia, and Bithynia, who have been chosen and destined by God the Father and sanctified by the Spirit to be obedient to Jesus Christ and to be sprinkled with his blood: May grace and peace be yours in abundance" (1 Pet 1:1–2).

These verses completely dissociate any notion of negativity from the states of exile and dispersion. The subsequent chapter reveals that the Christians are exiles because their home to return to is not of the world but in heaven. Peter reaches back to God's primal declaration of Israel's priesthood and nationhood in the wilderness before the people were to reach Canaan (1 Pet 2:9–10) and applies what was uniquely Israel's identity to all scattered Christians. After all, Peter was forced to realize that the scope of God's salvific work covered the gentiles unconditionally upon the conversion of Cornelius and his household (Acts 10:1–11:19).

Peter's text, henceforth, directly affirms that Christians are grafted into the historic identity and calling of Israel. Insofar as they are grafted into Abraham's lineage, they are aliens/strangers, pilgrims/sojourners living outside of their ultimate home in the heavenly city (1 Pet 2:11). Christians, therefore, must understand that their identity and calling are inescapably diasporic. This means that dispersion, not establishment, is normative for a Christian vocation and mode of life.

Diaspora as a Social Ethic

Israel's social-ethical responsibilities toward the marginalized given in the form of God's command are paradigmatically unprecedented and strikingly fresh even for twenty-first-century readers. Thousands of years before drafting the international laws regarding human rights for migrants and resident aliens, the biblical Israelites were already commanded to do justice toward the aliens in their land. This command was not given as a tangential or superfluous addendum. Obeying the command to love the strangers in the land was issued and inseparably bound up with (1) Israel's central commandment to love, serve, and worship God and (2) Israel's distinctive heritage/identity built on the Abrahamic lineage and circumcision. The implication is clear: Israel's unique status among all other peoples on the face of the earth was intrinsically and indispensably related to Israel's social-ethical responsibilities toward the marginalized.

First of all, before reaching the promised land, God spoke to Moses on Mount Sinai and gave Israel the book of the covenant, which included the Ten Commandments (Exod 20:1–17) and the detailed instructions to be performed in keeping them (Exod 21:22–31:18). The people of Israel were commanded to not "wrong" or "oppress" the foreigners in their land (Exod 22:21). This is reiterated wherever Israel's unique social-ethical responsibility is articulated. But what about God's directive to purge the Canaanites from the land (Deut 20:16–18)? To heighten the tension between the two commands, the "foreigners" in the land in which Israel was to settle clearly included the original settlers in Canaan. Although there is no simple way of flattening the tension between the two seemingly contradicting commands, priority must be given to the charge to love the "foreigners" because it was intricately interwoven into the laws as a standing, normative command. This responsibility appears not only in the Mosaic law but also throughout historical, Wisdom, and Prophetic writings—even in the last Old Testament book (Zech 7:10).

Second, Deuteronomy 10:12–22 is a par excellence text. The significance of this text is amplified by its resemblance to the Shema (Deut 6:4–9; 11:13–21; Num 15:37–41) and the connection of the commandments to Israel's distinctive quality—circumcision. Israel was to observe God's command to love the foreigners as an expression of having had their hearts "circumcise[d]" (Deut 10:16) when they entered the promised land:

So now, O Israel, what does the Lord your God require of you? Only to fear the Lord your God, to walk in all his ways, to love him, to serve the Lord your God with all your heart and with all your soul, and to keep the commandments of the Lord your God and his decrees that I am commanding you today, for your own well-being. . . . Who executes justice for the orphan and the widow, and who loves the strangers, providing them food and clothing. You shall also love the stranger, for you were strangers in the land of Egypt. . . . Your ancestors went down to Egypt seventy persons; and now the Lord your God has made you as numerous as the stars in heaven. (Deut 10:12–13, 18–19, 22)

The principal ethical imports of the text are as follows: the command to love the strangers was simply and intrinsically obligatory because it was incumbent upon God's impartiality and justice. Israel's calling was to love the strangers in the land to be occupied, not to subjugate or to merely tolerate. It was not an optional or exceptional practice:

1. Implicit in the command is that mistreating the strangers in the land was an offense against God. For God's electing and saving grace shown upon Israel did not limit the bestowment of God's grace to Israel only.
2. Loving the cohabiting strangers or foreigners—along with other marginalized people, such as orphans and widows—in the land was inescapably linked to Israel's identity and well-being. This connection is fully reinforced in Deuteronomy 11:26–32.
3. Israel's special status before God and therefore its distinguishing quality from all other tribes was to be expressed by loving the marginalized in society.
4. Because the command to love the stranger was given when Israel was still journeying in the wilderness, the

force of the command is intensified on existential and prescriptive grounds.

Third, we must revisit Deuteronomy 26, which lays out the laws regarding the celebration of first fruits and offering of tithes:

"When the Egyptians treated us harshly and afflicted us, by imposing hard labor on us, we cried to the Lord, the God of our ancestors; the Lord heard our voice and saw our affliction, our toil, and our oppression. The Lord brought us out of Egypt . . . into . . . a land flowing with milk and honey. So now I bring the first of the fruit of the ground that you, O Lord, have given me." . . . Then you, together with the Levites and the aliens who reside among you, shall celebrate with all the bounty that the Lord your God has given to you and to your house. When you have finished paying all the tithe of your produce in the third year (which is the year of the tithe), giving it to the Levites, the aliens, the orphans, and the widows, so that they may eat their fill within your towns, then you shall say before the Lord your God: "I have removed the sacred portion from the house, and I have given it to the Levites, the resident aliens, the orphans, and the widows, in accordance with your entire commandment that you commanded me." (Deut 26:6–13)

This is a sober reminder of Israel's heritage formed out of Abraham's diasporic life as a wandering Aramean. The text compels the people of Israel to remember the misery of having lived as resident aliens in a foreign land. Hence before they were to live as resident aliens in a newly conquered land, they were told to live out a radical social ethic as they anticipated celebrating in freedom the prosperous life in the promised land. The context for performing generosity to the marginalized in society, therefore, is to spring not from a sense of superiority but from the memory of Israel's own plight and God's transforming grace.

By instituting the offering of first fruits together with tithing, the people of Israel are instructed to act generously in response to God's faithfulness and generosity shown toward them. By binding Israel's well-being with its advocacy for the strangers in the land, God redeems their presence as part of its destiny. In this way, Israel's social-ethical obligations toward the marginalized are elevated to the status of demonstrating God's general grace to the inhabitants of the promised land, thereby anticipating the future fulfillment of extending God's special grace to all people on earth. This idea is thoroughly disturbing for those whose aim in life is to cultivate the prerogatives of the establishment but a refreshing initiative and a powerfully redeeming invitation for the church that is willing to externalize the implications of it as God's diaspora community on earth.

Diaspora as a Mission

The diasporic identity, calling, and social ethic lead to the gospel-centered missional mandate for all Christians. In this essay's final section, therefore, we will delineate how the theological trajectory of diaspora finally consummates in the church's mission. First, we need to return to Jeremiah 29 to retrieve how Israel's exilic experience was structured to stretch the scope and depth of God's command to love the "others" in the land. God's directive was for the people of Israel not only to settle into the diasporic life but also to radicalize their diasporic social ethic regarding the "foreigners." The subversiveness of the command was extraordinarily consistent with God's own character but unfathomably challenging for, even offensive to, Israel. The exiled Israelites were called to love the worst kind of enemy, the one who destroyed their nation and God's temple: "But seek the welfare of the city where I have sent you into exile, and pray to the Lord on its behalf, for in its welfare you will find your welfare" (Jer 29:7).

The text makes it explicit that God's grace for Israel was not an exclusive gift, nor was it given simply to relativize or mitigate the dreadful exilic experience. On the contrary, the diaspora experience was issued as the heart of God's mission to lead Israel to embrace its mission, which was to intercede on behalf of the enemy so that it also could partake in God's grace. Herein the dispersion is shown as the transforming initiative to forgive and make peace with Israel's subjugators and to build a good life along with them. This time, the circumstance was completely reversed, for the people of Israel were once again the resident aliens. But the Mosaic command to love the "others" in the land was reissued as an intensified command.

Second, Jeremiah 29:7 is recontextualized by Paul's exhortation to the diaspora church in Rome. Paul instructs the people of the church to pray for their "governing authorities" or "rulers" (Rom 13:1–7). In interpreting this text, we must first recognize that it was written to the scattered and persecuted Christians. Consequently, Paul's exhortation is directly in line with Jeremiah 29:7, and the immediate application of the exhortation was for the Roman Christians to pray for their persecutors. Herein lies the radicality of the biblical social ethic: God's people as sojourners on earth pray not necessarily to maintain the power of their own nations but for the sake of the general prosperity of those in which they reside.

Third, Jeremiah 29:7 makes diaspora the normative condition of and command for Christians of all times, for its fulfillment is eschatologically accomplished by Jesus Christ through the Holy Spirit.[15] Diaspora is not simply a method for mission; rather, it is the preeminent calling and mission. In Matthew's genealogy of Jesus, the names included reinforce the diasporic identity and vocation discussed above. In the incarnation of Jesus, the Jewish diasporic identity and vocation are reshaped as God's decisive salvific plans to be fulfilled through the mission of Jesus Christ in the power of the Spirit. Also, Peter reminds us that the church is to do mission as the diaspora community on earth (1 Pet 2:9–11).

Fourth, Peter illumines that the imperative to the church's journey as a diaspora community is suffering. According to him, the preeminent theme of suffering as the intrinsic mode of the church's life is equally operative for its mission (1 Pet 4:12–19). The entwining of God's people's diasporic identity, vocation, and mission with their correlative condition of suffering is epitomized in the Letter to the Hebrews: "Others were tortured, refusing to accept release, in order to obtain a better resurrection. Others suffered mocking and flogging, and even chains and imprisonment. They were stoned to death, they were sawn in two, they were killed by the sword; they went about in skins of sheep and goats, destitute, persecuted, tormented—of whom the world was not worthy. They wandered in deserts and mountains, and in caves and holes in the ground" (Heb 11:35b–38).

Therefore, accepting diaspora as a mission leads us to conclude that the culmination of mission lies not in the establishment of a powerful wealthy nation but in obeying the directive to "run with perseverance the race that is set before us" in the company of "so great a cloud of witnesses" (Heb 12:1). By implication, mission cannot be done out of an imperialistic construct, for the church consists of people of another kingdom who are "noncitizens" on earth. This salient but subversive way of carrying out the church's mission has come to full force, as Christianity has become a world religion and mission is being done by "people on the move," not only by the traditional missional method.[16]

Fifth, diaspora as a mission elucidates that mission is not only a cross-cultural mandate but also a multicultural one. The diaspora reality cannot dismiss multicultural engagement. Paul's life and theology are two of the best illustrations of "diaspora as a mission." As a diaspora Jew, he was born and educated in a multicultural, multilingual Jewish background (Phil 3:4b–6; 2 Cor 11:22; Acts 21:37–40). Upon his conversion, Paul's diasporic identity and qualities became vital determinants of his theology and mission.[17] Paul, together with Barnabas, was chosen to proclaim the gospel to the gentiles (Acts 13:2–3), and during the Jerusalem Council, his testimony from the gentile mission was used as a theological and missional norm to reject the imposition of circumcision on the gentile Christians (Acts 15; Gal 2). For Paul, the single determinant of being Christian had nothing to do with race, gender, circumcision, or social status (Gal 3:28; Rom 10:12; Col 1:11). The Christian life was fundamentally distinguished by the empowering presence of the Holy Spirit through Jesus Christ.[18]

Paul recapitulates the aforementioned Old Testament social ethic as it is existentially embodied in his own diasporic, multicultural life experience under the grace of freedom:

> For though I am free with respect to all, I have made myself a slave to all, so that I might win more of them. To the Jews I became as a Jew, in order to win Jews. To those under the law I became as one under the law (though I myself am not under the law) so that I might win those under the law. To those outside the law I became as one outside the law (though I am not free from God's law but am under Christ's law) so that I might win those outside the law. To the weak I became weak, so that I might win the weak. I have become all things to all people, that I might by all means save some. I do it all for the sake of the gospel, so that I may share in its blessings. (1 Cor 9:19–23)

Conclusion

In light of contemporary migratory trends globally, the church can have a fresh prospect to practice the New Testament's ecclesial and missional model. Today, mission fields have come to front doors everywhere, and we cannot afford to think of mission as an exclusive calling for a select group of people to live in a distant land. We must abandon the mistaken notion that only a few select Christians are scattered for mission work, for the entire church is the diaspora community of God on a missional journey to the heavenly abode.

Similarly, the New Testament explicitly states that persecution and suffering are inescapable parts of life for all disciples of Jesus Christ, not sporadic misfortunes that befall some or even glorious destinies for the chosen few. Herein lies what makes the Christian view of mission unique—not that dispersion/diaspora is for mission but that dispersion is itself missional. And as such, the church must be redirected in its understanding of power relations. Its status is not that of powerful earthly rulers but that of the marginalized, noncitizens, and aliens in the land whose commitment is to render the peacemaking grace of God in Jesus Christ through the power of the Holy Spirit. In this way, the church can freely and redemptively engage with people on the move in whatever form wherever they are. In diasporic contexts, the church must proclaim the gospel and administer freely and creatively God's justice and compassion to the displaced migrants who have come to reside in foreign lands.

Notes

1 Karl Ludwig Schmidt, "Διασπορά," in *Theological Dictionary of the New Testament*, ed. Gerhard Kittel, trans. and ed. Geoffrey W. Bromiley, vol. 2 (Grand Rapids, MI: Eerdmans, 1964), 141.

2 See G. A. Ban Alstine, "Dispersion," in *The International Standard Bible Encyclopedia*, ed. Geoffrey W. Bromiley, vol. 1, rev. ed. (Grand Rapids, MI: Eerdmans, 1979), 962–68.

3 David J. Reimer, "Exile, Diaspora, and OT Theology," *Scottish Bulletin of Evangelical Theology* 28, no. 1 (Spring 2010): 10–13.

4 Schmidt, "Διασπορά," 99. See also J. Ahn, "Exile," in *Dictionary of the Old Testament Prophets*, ed. Mark J. Bod and J. Gordon McConville (Nottingham: InterVarsity, 2012), 196–204.

5 Louis H. Feldman, "Concept of Exile in Josephus," in *Exile: Old Testament, Jewish, and Christian Conceptions*, ed. James M. Scott, Supplements to the Journal for the Study of Judaism 56 (Leiden: E. J. Brill, 1997), 145.

6 John Howard Yoder, *For the Nations: Essays Public and Evangelical* (Grand Rapids, MI: Eerdmans, 1997), 63.

7 See Yoder, 51–78; Reimer, "Exile, Diaspora," 10–16.

8 For a comprehensive treatment of the topic, see Feldman, "Concept," 145–72.

9 Alstine, "Dispersion," 962–68. See also Ted Rubesh, "Diaspora Distinctives: The Jewish Diaspora Experience in the Old Testament," *Torch Trinity Journal* 13, no. 2 (2010): 114–36. Rubesh shows that "it was not 'insiders,' but 'outsiders,' like Ezra and Nehemiah, who brought renewal and recommitment to those who had resettled in the Promised Land" (135).

10 Reimer, "Exile, Diaspora," 15.

11 Carolyn J. Sharp, "The Trope of 'Exile' and the Displacement of Old Testament Theology," *Perspectives in Religious Studies* 31, no. 2 (Summer 2004): 166.

12 Yoder, *For the Nations*, 57.

13 Yoder, 52.

14 Narry F. Santos, "Diaspora in the New Testament and Its Impact on Christian Mission," *Torch Trinity Journal* 13, no. 1 (2010): 3–6.

15 Yoder, *For the Nations*, 66–70; Arne Rasmusson, "The Politics of Diaspora: The Post-Christendom Theologies of Karl Barth and John Howard Yoder," in *God, Truth, and Witness: Engaging Stanley Hauerwas*, ed. L. Gregory Jones, Reinhard Hutter, and C. Rosalee Velloso Ewell (Grand Rapids, MI: Eerdmans, 2005), 107–11.

16 Enoch Wan and Sadiri Joy Tira, "Diaspora Missiology and Missions in the Context of the Twenty-First Century," in *The Human Tidal Wave*, ed. Sadiri Joy Tira (Manila: LifeChange, 2013), 151.

17 Steven S. H. Chang, "Paul and Multicultural Education: What Can We Learn?," *Korea Society for Christian Education and Information and Technology* 23, no. 4 (2013): 41.

18 Gordon Fee, *Paul, the Spirit, and the People of God* (Peabody, MA: Hendrickson, 1995), 88.

Bibliography

Ahn, J. "Exile." In *Dictionary of the Old Testament Prophets*, edited by Mark J. Bod and J. Gordon McConville, 196–204. Nottingham: InterVarsity, 2012.

Alstine, G. A. Ban. "Dispersion." In *The International Standard Bible Encyclopedia*, edited by Geoffrey W. Bromiley, 962–968. Vol. 1. Rev. ed. Grand Rapids, MI: Eerdmans, 1979.

Chang, Steven S. H. "Paul and Multicultural Education: What Can We Learn?" *Korea Society for Christian Education and Information and Technology* 23, no. 4 (2013): 41–65.

Fee, Gordon. *Paul, the Spirit, and the People of God.* Peabody, MA: Hendrickson, 1995.

Feldman, Louis H. "Concept of Exile in Josephus." In *Exile: Old Testament, Jewish, and Christian Conceptions*, edited by James M. Scott, 145–172. Supplements to the Journal for the Study of Judaism 56. Leiden: E. J. Brill, 1997.

Rasmusson, Arne. "The Politics of Diaspora: The Post-Christendom Theologies of Karl Barth and John Howard Yoder." In *God, Truth, and Witness: Engaging Stanley Hauerwas*, edited by L. Gregory Jones, Reinhard Hutter, and C. Rosalee Velloso Ewell, 88–111. Grand Rapids, MI: Eerdmans, 2005.

Reimer, David J. "Exile, Diaspora, and OT Theology." *Scottish Bulletin of Evangelical Theology* 28, no. 1 (Spring 2010): 10–13.

Rubesh, Ted. "Diaspora Distinctives: The Jewish Diaspora Experience in the Old Testament." *Torch Trinity Journal* 13, no. 2 (2010): 114–136.

Santos, Narry. "Diaspora in the New Testament and Its Impact on Christian Mission." *Torch Trinity Journal* 13, no. 1 (2010): 3–18.

Schmidt, Karl Ludwig. "Διασπορά." In *Theological Dictionary of the New Testament*, edited by Gerhard Kittel, translated and edited by Geoffrey W. Bromiley, 140. Vol. 2. Grand Rapids, MI: Eerdmans, 1964.

Sharp, Carolyn J. "The Trope of 'Exile' and the Displacement of Old Testament Theology." *Perspectives in Religious Studies* 31, no. 2 (Summer 2004): 153–169.

Wan, Enoch, and Sadiri Joy Tira. "Diaspora Missiology and Missions in the Context of the Twenty-First Century." In *The Human Tidal Wave*, edited by Sadiri Joy Tira, 175–190. Manila: LifeChange, 2013.

Yoder, John Howard. *For the Nations: Essays Public and Evangelical.* Grand Rapids, MI: Eerdmans, 1997.

2

The Displaced and Divine Self-Exile

The Interplay between the Absence and Presence of God

Prince Kumar Tamilarasan

Introduction
===

The final days of the nation of Judah were fraught with large-scale destruction, the devastation of the Jerusalem temple, and the exile of the nation. In the book of Ezekiel, in the wake of Judah's ruination and exile, some people allege that "the way of the Lord is not just" (Ezek 33:17, 20; see also 18:25, 29). Others claim that "the Lord does not see" their plight and that he has "forsaken the land" altogether (Ezek 8:12; 9:9). Ezekiel himself, who is caught among voices like these, seeks to understand and explain the exilic crisis. Ezekiel is best suited for such a task because he receives his call and serves God in exile. His focus is on "the reality of disaster," and in his book, the desolation of Judah and the "experience of exile [are] a central reality."[1] Hence Ezekiel's voice for the displaced in today's world is quintessential.

The History and Impact
of the Babylonian Invasion

The Babylonian Empire, in its heyday, invaded Judah and, in line with its policy toward conquered nations, deported its citizens. There were at least three prominent deportations in the history of Judah under Babylon. Ezekiel's reference to the surrender of Jehoiachin, the king of Judah, to Babylon marks the beginning of the first deportation (Ezek 17:12–13), which is dated to 597 BCE.[2] The parallel account in the book of Kings records that Nebuchadnezzar, the king of Babylon, installed Zedekiah as a puppet king over Judah in place of Jehoiachin (2 Kgs 24:12–17). Further, he took Jehoiachin and his court officials as captives and even carried away temple treasures (2 Kgs 24:12–16). Ezekiel, too, was "taken with the first deported groups" before the eventual fall of Jerusalem and its ruination.[3]

The nation, having lost all its elites and only with the impoverished left behind (2 Kgs 24:14), was ruled by Zedekiah as Babylon's vassal for eleven years (2 Kgs 24:18). However, when Zedekiah himself revolted against Babylon (2 Kgs 24:20), Ezekiel declared his imminent doom (Ezek 17:15–20) and predicted the further destruction and deportation of the people of Judah (Ezek 17:21). It was fulfilled in 586 BCE and is known as the second deportation.[4] While trying to escape, Zedekiah was caught and brought before the king of Babylon. His sons were executed before his eyes, and that was the last thing he would ever see, as his eyes were then gouged out. He was bound in chains and taken as a prisoner to Babylon (2 Kgs 25:5–7; Ezek 19:5–9). More gloomily, any semblance of Judah's hope was irrecoverably crushed when its temple was razed to the ground (2 Kgs 25:8–20).

The loss of hope was profoundly reflected in the non-Davidic replacement for Zedekiah: Gedaliah, who was appointed as the governor of Judah. Thus, the monarchy in Israel came to a crashing halt, and Judah lost its independent statehood to become a province of Babylon. The political power center shifted from Jerusalem to Mizpah, as Gedaliah governed from there (2 Kgs 25:22–26). Hence Mizpah replaced Jerusalem as the seat of power, and Gedaliah's governorship substituted the Davidic dynasty.[5] However, his tenure was short lived, as he was assassinated (2 Kgs 25:25).[6] The third deportation occurred in 582 BCE as Babylon avenged Judah for the murder of Gedaliah (see Jer 52:30).[7] Thus, Judah ended in blood and a bleak future.

Owing to repeated deportations, Oded Lipschits observes, Judah's population gradually dwindled.[8] The voluntary flight of people as refugees and the lack of a standing army to protect the region led to many "seminomadic groups" infiltrating Judah.[9] Corresponding demographic changes severely "affected the boundaries of Judah," and it "shrank" drastically. People of "Arabian-Edomite orientation" settled in the land and established a province known at the beginning of the Hellenistic period as Idumea.[10]

The exile itself was a "terrible experience of forcible displacement" and meant social uprooting and humiliation. Exiles "lost not only their homeland but also their real property and their generally influential position."[11] They were settled in the previous war-ravaged territories of Babylon to repopulate and redevelop them.[12] The elites of Judah ended up in agricultural labor, and that was an "unbearable social degradation."[13] Ezekiel records that the exiles became an object of mockery (Ezek 5:14–15; 7:17–18; 22:4–5; 23:32). Thus, their sense of shame accrued from intense "emotional" exasperation and "social" embarrassment.[14]

The exiles, observes Rainer Albertz, were distraught politically, psychologically, and religiously:[15] politically because the monarchy had come to naught; psychologically because their "homesickness," "helplessness," and concern for their family members left behind in Jerusalem were only aggravated; and religiously because their temple was no more and they lived in the territory of the foreign gods.[16]

The Divine Self-Exile

The book of Ezekiel is structured to show the movement of the glory of the Lord. The initial chapters depict God's glory abandoning and leaving the Jerusalem temple (Ezek 1:1–11:25), while the last section of the book paints a picture of God returning to his temple in all his glory (Ezek 40:1–48:35).[17] God's presence in Babylon in the beginning (Ezek 1:1) implicitly indicates his absence in Jerusalem. This idea becomes increasingly explicit as the theme of divine abandonment develops and culminates in chapters 8–11.

First, in chapter 8, Ezekiel is given a temple tour. He sees abominations committed by Israel inside the temple precinct as he passes through its different stations under the direction of God. The gravity of the people's sin is summarized in the oft repeated indictment "You will see still greater abominations" (Ezek 8:6, 13, 15). In consequence,

God declares that he is outraged by their actions and promises to "act in wrath" (Ezek 8:17–18; 9:10 ESV). Second, in chapter 9, Ezekiel watches the spectacle of God's judgment over Jerusalem, and it is laid waste to at God's command (Ezek 9:7). Third, Ezekiel witnesses God's gradual exit from the holiest place of the temple to the east gate of the temple complex (Ezek 10:4). Fourth, following a brief pause at the east gate (Ezek 10:19), the glory of the Lord departs "from the midst of the city" to the mountain on the "east side" (Ezek 11:23 ESV). Subsequently, the glory of the Lord departs in the direction of Babylon, where the exiles are.[18] Thus, the divine abandonment is reinforced by a picture of the divine glory leaving the temple mount in Jerusalem.

The Divine Self-Exile
in the Ancient Near East

According to Daniel I. Block, in the religions of the ancient Near East (ANE), the idea of deities abandoning the cities of their residence is a common motif recurrent in a variety of literary genres. In a Babylonian account, it is said that the reigning god Marduk abandons his city of residence because of the immorality and ritual violations of humans. The outcome of Marduk's rage is the devastation of Babylon, the devastation of its temples, and the inhabitants' exile and slavery.[19] However, in such similar situations, local gods may represent the "victims of conquest" and "intercede on behalf of their subjects and their shrines" before a superior god.[20] When the high god refuses to relent, the divinities disown their temples "reluctantly and with great lamentation."[21] At times, instead of protecting their temples, "the gods take the side of the invader and unleash all the forces of destruction upon their respective cities."[22]

Politically, the invading nations capitalized well on this belief system. Morton Cogan observes that the conquering nations usually seized the statues of the local deities and transferred them to their countries.[23] In his study of the Assyrian exploitations of foreign nations, he notes, "The captured gods were held hostage until the defeated ruler begged for their return, a public sign of his submission to Assyria."[24] Thorkild Jacobsen argues that confrontation among nations also meant confrontation among the gods of the nations.[25] Hence gods were "drawn into political conflicts," and often their temples were ransacked and statues ravaged.[26] If undamaged idols were carried off to the conquering nation, then their return and the restoration of their temples were at the sheer mercy of the conquering king.[27]

The Meaning of the Divine Self-Exile in Ezekiel

The devastation and exile of Judah engendered doubts about God's power to protect in the face of an invading army and its gods. As mentioned earlier, in the ANE, people perceived their defeat as the local divinities' defeat by a superior deity. It was a widely held belief in Babylon too. The idea of pillaging a conquered nation's temple and carrying away seized religious statues to place them in the temple of Marduk in the city of Babylon was rooted in the state policy of Nebuchadnezzar. It was a powerful declaration of the defeat of a conquered nation's gods.[28] In such a context, it was natural for people in exile to believe their God was weak and unable to protect them from foreign occupation. William A. Tooman says that Ezekiel, by "anticipating" such an "unspoken charge," alleges that God was "neither incapable nor inattentive; rather, he ordained and enacted the destruction himself."[29]

According to Elizabeth Keck, the ideas of the dispossession of the land and dislocation imply that the exiles should "relinquish any claim they might have had to Yahweh as their God." They are no longer in "Yahweh's land with Yahweh's people, but the land of another god and another people."[30] While the Judahites speak as though the Lord is with them and claim that the land is given to them for "possession" and that the exiles "have gone far from the Lord" (Ezek 11:15), God says that in the future, he will give the land to the exiles (Ezek 11:17) and that they are not driven far from him, since he has moved to dwell among them (Ezek 11:16). Thus, in his self-exile, God has, in fact, become a sanctuary for the exiles in the very land in which they are dislocated. He declares, "I have been a sanctuary to them for a while in the countries where they have gone" (Ezek 11:16 ESV).

As a result, even during the exile, God's enduring intimate relationship with Israel is captured in the oft repeated phrase "my people."[31] He also affirms the permanence of his covenant repeatedly by declaring, "I will be your God, and you will be my people."[32] So the exile is not a sign of an annulment of his covenant. Instead, it is an enforcement of the covenant as a punishment for its violation (Lev 26; Deut 28; Ezek 16). It is inviolable and renewable even in and through the exile (Ezek 16:60–63; 37:26–28). Hence those who are in the vicinity of the sanctuary in Jerusalem are "far off" from God, while those who are exiled are in the little sanctuary.[33] This presence of God is affirmed as a reality to the first deportees in Babylon "even before" the final fall and destruction of the Jerusalem temple.[34] God's abandonment of Judah, in turn, spells the end of its history and yet guarantees the "future" for the exiles.[35]

According to Pieter de Vries, the notion behind the metaphor "little sanctuary" could be understood either "temporally" as God's provisional presence with the deportees until the end of the exile or "quantitatively" in the sense of his condensed presence.[36] He identifies the little sanctuary with the departure of the glory of the Lord from Jerusalem and its presence in Babylon with the exiles.[37] Terry R. Clark sees in the vision reports of Ezekiel the "explicit symbols" of the presence of God as a little sanctuary for the exiles.[38] De Vries, too, explains that "the oracles of hope" that Ezekiel receives mediate the presence of God in the exile to the deportees.[39] Furthermore, the little sanctuary could be understood "in terms of the prophet himself," who saw the glory of the Lord in the "exile."[40] Hence not only his message but also the prophet himself mediates the presence of God as a mark of the little sanctuary.

However one may try to understand the metaphor of the little sanctuary during the exile, the point is clear that God is closer to the deportees and that he regards the exiles as his people. Nonetheless, some exiles perceive that their status as deportees in a distant alien land is nothing but death from God, as they have lost access to him. Such a perception of the deportees is captured in their disclosure in Ezekiel 37:11: "Our bones are dried up, and our hope is lost; we are cut off completely." Saul M. Olyan notes that the idea of being "cut off" not only suggests that some exiles see themselves as being dead but also could mean that, "like the dead," the exiled people "are no longer the beneficiaries of Yhwh's covenant loyalty, that they cannot hope in his faithfulness, that they are forgotten by Yhwh, that they are unable to worship him, and that they will never return to their land."[41] However, in contrast to this "traditional perception of exile as a distance and separation from God," Ezekiel contends that God is with the exiles "outside the land of Israel."[42] Not only is God with them, but he promises their return and full restoration (Ezek 11:17), giving them changed hearts and new spirits (Ezek 11:19) so that they can live a life of obedience (Ezek 11:20). Unlike in the past, through the exile, the external observation of rituals will be replaced by an internal change of heart effected by "a new spirit." "This is an act of grace on his [God's] part. The exile is thus both an act of judgment and an act of grace," observes Kim M. Hawtrey.[43] It is also a "message of hope for the exiles."[44] Hence the message and the presence of God as a little sanctuary are, in essence, a "consoling reality" for the exiles.[45]

Although the presence of God during the exile is a comfort, the exile itself is in no sense a pleasant experience. It is full of pain, trauma, and shame.[46] Thus, Ezekiel gives hope that God will bring an end to their shame when he restores them (Ezek 34:29; 36:6, 7, 15, 30). Eric Ortlund argues that in the restoration of Judah, all the foreign nations that mocked it will be ashamed.[47] When the covenant is reinstated, the exiles will no longer grumble about their shame (Ezek 16:63). Instead, they will be ashamed of their past (Ezek 6:9; 16:61; 20:43). Hence Jacqueline E. Lapsley argues that God will indeed remove the "public dimension of shame" through their "private, inner experience of shame."[48] Margaret S. Odell observes that as opposed to the usual notion of shame as the "basis for accusation of the other," Israel will experience shame in the sense of "self-examination."[49] Thus, the very "recognition" of the deserved judgment by the exiles, which is "more humiliating than the destruction itself," will become the "basis of a renewed relationship with YHWH (6.8–10; 16.62–63; 20.43–44)."[50] This is indeed the good that comes from the sufferings of the exile—a deeper relationship with the one true God and the rejection of other gods.

Historically, it is well established that in and through the exile, Israel got rid of syncretism. Rainer Albertz notes that in the history of Israel, the experience of the exile shaped the unique religious and social identity of Israel. Religious reforms gave rise to an unadulterated form of devotion to the God of the Bible that was unparalleled in its history—that too in the absence of the Jerusalem temple.[51] Hence he claims, "Without the experience of the exile, Israel would never have made the discovery of monotheism in the strict sense; without it, Israel would never have transcended the limits of its national religion; without it, the idea of a worldwide mission would never have emerged within Israel."[52] Thus, if the exile was the reason for Israel's unadulterated devotion to one God, then it was accomplished through the divine self-exile. What centuries of those in the Israelite monarchy failed to achieve, in less than a century of the exilic life, God in exile with the exiles accomplished.

The Meaning of Divine Abandonment in Ezekiel vis-à-vis ANE Religions

Ezekiel silhouettes the concept of divine abandonment against the religious belief systems of the ANE but with a marked difference. In Ezekiel, God is infuriated and subsequently abandons his people, land, and temple just like the ANE gods. Nonetheless, he leaves them not because he is impulsive or powerless but because of the sins of his people. The cause of the exile was not because "Babylon or its gods were mightier" than Israel's God, "but rather its cause was the sin of the people of Israel."[53] Hence God's "departure is not the consequence but the *cause* of the destruction of the Temple."[54] Later, when God returns to his new temple just like the gods of the ANE, he does so not because he earnestly desires or needs a temple or territory but because he wishes to dwell among his people (Ezek 43:9).[55] Unlike the ANE religious texts where the change of the gods' hearts to return to their temple is highlighted, in Ezekiel, Yahweh promises to change the hearts of the exiles for them to "walk in his ways."[56]

The king of Babylon did not destroy or deport any idol of Yahweh to assert his political hegemony. There was indeed no statue for Yahweh to despoil or deport: "No human monarch took Yahweh as spoil; Yahweh exiled himself."[57] Nevertheless, God's voluntary self-exile became a sanctuary for the exiles so as to redirect their destiny even outside of his holy city, Jerusalem. While the kings in the ANE repaired and returned the idols of the conquered nations and renovated or rebuilt their temples to express benevolence, John F. Kutsko observes that no human "monarch" attempted to return or restore Yahweh. Instead, it is Yahweh who "restores his people" from the exile.[58] Although an idol in the ANE is understood to have housed the spirit of a god, idols in Ezekiel are held as objects that convey the absence of God.[59] The God of Israel is "present in his absence" even without an idol or temple, whereas for the ANE gods, "the physical existence of idols prove that these gods are absent in their presence."[60] Hence in a pagan idolatrous country, God visits his people, making himself present. He is sovereign over the conquering as well as the conquered nation.

Conclusion

The exilic theology of Ezekiel declares God was never bound to any particular place; he could be with the exiles. Thus, today's displaced communities can look up to a God who actively intervenes in the political affairs of the nations without any spatial or temporal limitations. While Ezekiel's deportees were in a state of crisis in a foreign land, it was partly their own doing. They sinned and deserved punishment. Although contemporary exiles need not share the guilt of offending God for their present crises, they can identify with the sufferings of the exiles in Ezekiel. In such an identity, there is abundant hope. Ezekiel's God, though he punishes his people for their sins, chooses to protect them in a foreign land. How much more would this God desire to protect those who are innocent of the causes of their crises and are merely puppets in the hands of their political masters? Consequently, the interplay between the divine absence and the divine presence powerfully conveys the message that God is ever present with the dispossessed, disentitled, dislocated, and disenfranchised of the world and may simultaneously be absent to those who are unjust and despise him.

While the exile itself was an unpleasant experience, there was a redemptive value to it. It enabled people to become more receptive to the divine teachings. Hence like Ezekiel and his message, Christians should mediate the presence of God to the distressed exiles and displaced people across the globe.

Notes

1 Peter R. Ackroyd, *Exile and Restoration: A Study of Hebrew Thought of the Sixth Century B.C.*, Old Testament Library (Philadelphia: Westminster, 1968), 104.

2 Rainer Albertz, *Israel in Exile: The History and Literature of the Sixth Century B.C.E.*, trans. David Green, Studies in Biblical Literature 3 (Atlanta, GA: Society of Biblical Literature, 2003), 9–10.

3 Daniel L. Smith-Christopher, *A Biblical Theology of Exile*, Overtures to Biblical Theology (Minneapolis: Fortress, 2002), 75.

4 Albertz, *Israel in Exile*, 9–10.

5 Oded Lipschits, *The Fall and Rise of Jerusalem: Judah under Babylonian Rule* (Winona Lake, IN: Eisenbrauns, 2005), 366.

6 See Lipschits, 118.

7 Albertz, *Israel in Exile*, 95.

8 Lipschits, *Fall and Rise*, 367.

9 Lipschits, 69.

10 Lipschits, 134.

11 Albertz, *Israel in Exile*, 98.

12 See Lipschits, *Fall and Rise*, 68.

13 Albertz, *Israel in Exile*, 101.

14 Jacqueline E. Lapsley, *Can These Bones Live? The Problem of the Moral Self in the Book of Ezekiel*, Beihefte Zur Zeitschrift Für Die Alttestamentliche Wissenschaft 301 (Berlin: Walter de Gruyter, 2000), 131.

15 Albertz, *Israel in Exile*, 102.

16 Albertz, 102–5.

17 David Noel Freedman, "XXVII. The Book of Ezekiel," *Interpretation: A Journal of Bible and Theology* 8, no. 4 (October 1, 1954): 456.

18 Note the glory of the Lord returns to the new temple from the east "by the gate facing east" just like it departed from the east gate toward the east (Ezek 43:1–5).

19 See also Peter Machinist, "Literature as Politics: The Tukulti-Ninurta Epic and the Bible," *Catholic Biblical Quarterly* 38, no. 4 (October 1976): 462.

20 Daniel I. Block, *By the River Chebar: Historical, Literary, and Theological Studies in the Book of Ezekiel* (Cambridge: James Clarke, 2014), 89.

21 Block, 80.

22 Daniel I. Block, *The Gods of the Nations: A Study in Ancient Near Eastern Theology* (Eugene, OR: Wipf & Stock, 2013), 123.

23 See Morton Cogan, *Imperialism and Religion: Assyria, Judah, and Israel in the Eighth and Seventh Centuries B.C.E.,* Monograph Series—Society of Biblical Literature 19 (Missoula, MT: Society of Biblical Literature, 1974), 22–40.

24 Cogan, 42.

25 Thorkild Jacobsen, *The Treasures of Darkness: A History of Mesopotamian Religion* (New Haven, CT: Yale University Press, 1976).

26 John F. Kutsko, *Between Heaven and Earth: Divine Presence and Absence in the Book of Ezekiel,* Biblical and Judaic Studies 7 (Winona Lake, IN: Eisenbrauns, 2000), 113.

27 Kutsko, 113–18.

28 Smith-Christopher, *Biblical Theology of Exile,* 60.

29 William A. Tooman, "Ezekiel's Radical Challenge to Inviolability," *Zeitschrift Für Die Alttestamentliche Wissenschaft* 121, no. 4 (December 2009): 512.

30 Elizabeth Keck, "The Glory of Yahweh in Ezekiel and the Pre-tabernacle Wilderness," *Journal for the Study of the Old Testament* 37, no. 2 (December 2012): 214.

31 Ezek 11:20; 13:9, 18, 21, 23; 14:8, 11; 21:12; 25:14; 33:31; 34:30; 36:8, 12, 28; 37:12, 23, 27; 38:14, 16; 39:7; 44:23; 45:8; 46:18.

32 Ezek 11:20; 14:11; 34:24, 30–31; 36:28; 37:23.

33 Tooman, "Ezekiel's Radical Challenge," 507.

34 Tooman, 507.

35 Thomas Renz, *The Rhetorical Function of the Book of Ezekiel* (Boston: Brill Academic, 2002), 69.

36 See Pieter de Vries, "The Presence of YHWH in Exile according to the Book of Ezekiel, with Special Reference to the Meaning of the Expression מִקְדָּשׁ מְעַט in Ezekiel 11:16," *Old Testament Essays* 31, no. 1 (2018): 271.

37 Pieter de Vries, *The Kābôd of YHWH in the Old Testament: With Particular Reference to the Book of Ezekiel*, Studia Semitica Neerlandica 65 (Leiden: Brill, 2016), 283.

38 Terry R. Clark, *I Will Be King over You! The Rhetoric of Divine Kingship in the Book of Ezekiel*, Gorgias Dissertations 59 (Piscataway, NJ: Gorgias, 2014), 123.

39 Vries, "Presence of YHWH," 264.

40 Vries, *Kābôd of YHWH*, 283.

41 Saul M. Olyan, "'We Are Utterly Cut Off': Some Possible Nuances of נגזרנו לנו in Ezek 37:11," *Catholic Biblical Quarterly* 65, no. 1 (January 2003): 51.

42 See Dalit Rom-Shiloni, "Facing Destruction and Exile: Inner-Biblical Exegesis in Jeremiah and Ezekiel," *Zeitschrift Für Die Alttestamentliche Wissenschaft* 117, no. 2 (2005): 201.

43 Kim M. Hawtrey, "The Exile as a Crisis for Cultic Religion: Lamentations and Ezekiel," *Reformed Theological Review* 52, no. 2 (May 1993): 83.

44 Clark, *I Will Be King*, 123.

45 Vries, "Presence of YHWH," 277.

46 For trauma studies in Ezekiel, see Refael Furman, "Trauma and Post-trauma in the Book of Ezekiel," *Old Testament Essays* 33, no. 1 (May 13, 2020): 32–59; and Brad E. Kelle, "Dealing with the Trauma of Defeat: The Rhetoric of the Devastation and Rejuvenation of Nature in Ezekiel," *Journal of Biblical Literature* 128, no. 3 (2009): 469–90.

47 Eric Ortlund, "Shame in Restoration in Ezekiel," *Scandinavian Evangelical E-journal for New Testament Studies* 2, no. 1 (January 2011): 3–5.

48 Lapsley, *Can These Bones Live?*, 145.

49 Margaret S. Odell, "The Inversion of Shame and Forgiveness in Ezekiel 16.59–63," *Journal for the Study of the Old Testament* 17, no. 56 (December 1992): 112.

50 Ellen F. Davis, *Swallowing the Scroll: Textuality and the Dynamics of Discourse in Ezekiel's Prophecy*, Bible and Literature Series 21 (Sheffield, UK: Almond, 1989), 57.

51 See Albertz, *Israel in Exile*, 106–9.

52 Albertz, 435–36.

53 Vries, "Presence of YHWH," 266.

54 Vries, *Kābôd of YHWH*, 285.

55 In the ANE, the deities returned because they needed a home. See Block, *By the River Chebar*, 76–87.

56 Block, 96.

57 Kutsko, *Between Heaven and Earth*, 147.

58 Kutsko, 147.

59 Ezekiel nowhere calls the statues gods. Ezekiel "refuses to acknowledge even a verbal identity of other objects of worship as gods." Unlike other parts of the Old Testament (e.g., Lev 19:4), he avoids using the "generic term" *God* to refer to pagan gods or idols. Kutsko, 35.

60 Kutsko, 148.

Bibliography

Ackroyd, Peter R. *Exile and Restoration: A Study of Hebrew Thought of the Sixth Century B.C.* Old Testament Library. Philadelphia: Westminster, 1968.

Albertz, Rainer. *Israel in Exile: The History and Literature of the Sixth Century B.C.E.* Translated by David Green. Studies in Biblical Literature 3. Atlanta, GA: Society of Biblical Literature, 2003.

Block, Daniel I. *By the River Chebar: Historical, Literary, and Theological Studies in the Book of Ezekiel.* Cambridge: James Clarke, 2014.

———. *The Gods of the Nations: A Study in Ancient Near Eastern Theology.* Eugene, OR: Wipf & Stock, 2013.

Clark, Terry R. *I Will Be King over You! The Rhetoric of Divine Kingship in the Book of Ezekiel.* Gorgias Dissertations 59. Piscataway, NJ: Gorgias, 2014.

Cogan, Morton. *Imperialism and Religion: Assyria, Judah, and Israel in the Eighth and Seventh Centuries B.C.E.* Monograph Series—Society of Biblical Literature 19. Missoula, MT: Society of Biblical Literature, 1974.

Davis, Ellen F. *Swallowing the Scroll: Textuality and the Dynamics of Discourse in Ezekiel's Prophecy.* Bible and Literature Series 21. Sheffield, UK: Almond, 1989.

Freedman, David Noel. "XXVII. The Book of Ezekiel." *Interpretation: A Journal of Bible and Theology* 8, no. 4 (October 1, 1954): 446–471.

Furman, Refael. "Trauma and Post-trauma in the Book of Ezekiel." *Old Testament Essays* 33, no. 1 (May 13, 2020): 32–59.

Hawtrey, Kim M. "The Exile as a Crisis for Cultic Religion: Lamentations and Ezekiel." *Reformed Theological Review* 52, no. 2 (May 1993): 74–83.

Jacobsen, Thorkild. *The Treasures of Darkness: A History of Mesopotamian Religion.* New Haven, CT: Yale University Press, 1976.

Keck, Elizabeth. "The Glory of Yahweh in Ezekiel and the Pre-tabernacle Wilderness." *Journal for the Study of the Old Testament* 37, no. 2 (December 2012): 201–218.

Kelle, Brad E. "Dealing with the Trauma of Defeat: The Rhetoric of the Devastation and Rejuvenation of Nature in Ezekiel." *Journal of Biblical Literature* 128, no. 3 (2009): 469–490.

Kutsko, John F. *Between Heaven and Earth: Divine Presence and Absence in the Book of Ezekiel*. Biblical and Judaic Studies 7. Winona Lake, IN: Eisenbrauns, 2000.

Lapsley, Jacqueline E. *Can These Bones Live? The Problem of the Moral Self in the Book of Ezekiel*. Beihefte Zur Zeitschrift Für Die Alttestamentliche Wissenschaft 301. Berlin: Walter de Gruyter, 2000.

Lipschits, Oded. *The Fall and Rise of Jerusalem: Judah under Babylonian Rule*. Winona Lake, IN: Eisenbrauns, 2005.

Machinist, Peter. "Literature as Politics: The Tukulti-Ninurta Epic and the Bible." *Catholic Biblical Quarterly* 38, no. 4 (October 1976): 455–482.

Odell, Margaret S. "The Inversion of Shame and Forgiveness in Ezekiel 16.59–63." *Journal for the Study of the Old Testament* 17, no. 56 (December 1992): 101–112.

Olyan, Saul M. "'We Are Utterly Cut Off': Some Possible Nuances of נגזרנו לנו in Ezek 37:11." *Catholic Biblical Quarterly* 65, no. 1 (January 2003): 43–51.

Ortlund, Eric. "Shame in Restoration in Ezekiel." *Scandinavian Evangelical E-journal for New Testament Studies* 2, no. 1 (January 2011): 1–17.

Renz, Thomas. *The Rhetorical Function of the Book of Ezekiel*. Boston: Brill Academic, 2002.

Rom-Shiloni, Dalit. "Facing Destruction and Exile: Inner-Biblical Exegesis in Jeremiah and Ezekiel." *Zeitschrift Für Die Alttestamentliche Wissenschaft* 117, no. 2 (2005): 189–205.

Smith-Christopher, Daniel L. *A Biblical Theology of Exile*. Overtures to Biblical Theology. Minneapolis: Fortress, 2002.

Tooman, William A. "Ezekiel's Radical Challenge to Inviolability."
Zeitschrift Für Die Alttestamentliche Wissenschaft 121, no. 4
(December 2009): 498–514.

Vries, Pieter de. *The Kābôd of YHWH in the Old Testament: With
Particular Reference to the Book of Ezekiel.* Studia Semitica
Neerlandica 65. Leiden: Brill, 2016.

———. "The Presence of YHWH in Exile according to the Book of
Ezekiel, with Special Reference to the Meaning of the Expression
מִקְדָּשׁ מְעַט in Ezekiel 11:16." *Old Testament Essays* 31, no. 1 (2018):
264–279.

3

Changing Identity and Disrupted Belongingness

A Theology of Nations, Citizenship, and Transnationalism

Tereso C. Casiño

Human dispersions and migration flows can threaten people's identities and disrupt their sense of belonging. Leaving one's homeland for another nation could destabilize most migrants. Even one who moves within a country could rupture familial links and heritage relationships. No matter how dearly one holds on to their traditional identity, the pressure a person faces in the process of migration and geographic mobility can be heavy. Transitions, both geographical and spatial, could pose a serious threat to one's identity and psychosocial stability. Diaspora missiology offers insights to navigate through these issues related to the intersecting concepts of nations, citizenship, and transnationalism.[1]

Nations and Diasporas

The relation between the concept of nations and the global reality of human dispersion is both unmistakable and indissoluble. Even if one bypasses scholarly depth for the sake of public accessibility, the link among nations for the diasporic people is indispensable. When individuals resettle in places away from their homelands, parts of their nations move with them, as they carry their cultures, religious systems and practices, symbols and metaphors, histories, and varying ideologies. World history is marked by the formation of nations because of human migration. In a sense, nations move when people move.

In the Bible, references to nations span from Genesis to Revelation. The motif of nations is crucial to the development of a biblical theology of mission where mobility and the dispersion of individuals and people groups play strategic roles. Caution should be taken when making a direct application of the ancient word *nations* to twenty-first-century settings, as its rendering and usage may have technical and fundamental differences. In the Old Testament, four major terms stand out as synonymous references to nations. These appear to apply to particular nations, including Israel: "(1) *ammim* (kinship as the basis of the group), (2) *goyim* (stresses political and social rather than kinship bonds), (3) *le'ummim* (used in parallel with *goyim* to refer to a city that could produce a contingent of soldiers to fight wars), and (4) *ummot* or *ummim* (tribes or people)."[2] The key to understanding all these lies in the "tension between the concepts of nationalism and universalism"—between a vision for the salvation of the nations and Israel's identity and task as a light to them. The Old Testament understanding has a missiological currency, especially to refer to people who live in a shared space for a common cause, have similar ideals in life, and bear God's image, which was tainted and now requires redemption. Some scholars single out *goyim* as crucial to any discussion of the redemptive plan and work of God among the nations. When used in its plural form, *goyim* refers to nations other than Israel (the singular is *goy*, "nation").[3] Through it, one can see how nations become representations of all peoples, both righteous and unrighteous. Except for Israel as a "chosen nation," the dividing line between a righteous nation and an ungodly one is straightforward in the Old Testament. *Goyim* has implications for understanding diasporas as missional opportunities.

Israel, of course, is a *goy*, but it was chosen to be a "holy nation" and a "kingdom of priests" (Exod 19:6 NIV). Set apart for a missionary purpose, this "chosen nation" will live among the other *goyim* rather than away from them. Duane L. Christensen explains, "The nations are the matrix of Israel's life, the raison d'être of her very existence."[4] In the Old Testament, God forms a *qahal* to participate in his redemptive work among the nations. Occurring over seventy times in the Septuagint, *qahal* means "to summon," which is "frequently used for the 'assembly' or 'congregation' of the people of Israel."[5] The Greek equivalent of *qahal* is *ekklesia*, which has a secular Greek background, although it is used in four ways—the universal church, the local church, the assembly of believers, and the house church. Whatever the usage and size of the church, David Watson notes, *ekklesia* "always speaks of the coming together of God's people in answer to his call, in order to meet with God in the company of each other and to meet each other in the presence of God."[6] L. A. Hoedaker asserts, however, "The appearance of the church does not stamp the way of Israel as an obsolete or dead-end road."[7]

By the first century, *ethne* in Jewish Greek evolved into a technical term referring to non-Jewish individuals. This rendered the Hebrew *goyim* to mean "gentiles."[8] It is crucial to understand the significance of nations in salvation history, as Christ's mandate to his followers is to "make disciples of all nations" (Matt 28:19–20). The correlation between making disciples and *panta ta ethne* (all nations) is not coincidental. Christ here is not simply giving the Great Commission, as traditionally known in most Western churches; rather, this is a declaration of the Central Commission that defines the core identity and entire missionary thrust of the church from the first century onward.[9] Every fiber of the disciples' very being stems from this mandate. *Panta ta ethne* bears a strong missional currency. The adjective *panta* is accusative, neuter, and plural, and if it is attached to the noun *ethne* (accusative, neuter, plural), it stresses inclusivity, thereby embracing all peoples of the earth regardless of their varying ethnicities, nationalities, or cultures. A failure to interpret *panta ta ethne* through the lens of *missio Dei* could lead to disastrous results, as in the case of the first wave of the Reformation.[10] The global mission was weak as the Reformation expanded across Europe, partly due to an exegetical blunder regarding the church's missionary task.[11] Martin Luther, for example, argued that the church's missionary task was completed in the first century.[12] This move dampened the enthusiasm of the Reformation, especially among Luther's followers.[13] But not everything was lost. As early as 1555, an attempt was made to do what is known as "missionary colonization"—namely, the Calvin-Coligny expedition to Brazil. John C. Thiessen explains, "It was to be a place of refuge for persecuted Protestants and at the same time serve as a center from which to reach the Indians."

Among Lutherans, the first serious effort came only in 1664 courtesy of Baron Justinian von Welz, who "issued a clarion call to the church to assume missionary responsibilities."[14] Scholarly debates on *panta ta ethne* have been classified traditionally, sociologically, and missiologically.[15]

Traditional interpretations of *panta ta ethne* vary: from Jews only, gentiles only, or both Jews and gentiles as objects of God's redemptive work.[16] Some identify *ethne* as exclusively meaning "Jews" or "Israel," referring to Jesus's specific instruction to go to the "lost house of Israel" (Matt 10:6), which highlights the intersection between *goyim* and *ta ethne*.[17] Others identify *ethne* as referring to gentiles only and argue that they are the focal point of God's redemptive work because they are not participants in the covenant that God established with ancient Israel.[18] As "excluded people" who live outside the realm of the covenantal relationship, they are the only ones Jesus envisions to receive God's favor of salvation. Others embrace an integrationist rendering of *panta ta ethne* that unpacks the inclusivity of mission. Richard R. De Ridder writes, "When used in the sense of the Gentiles, [*panta ta ethne*] is often used with no sense of plurality of the nations; that is, it is used non-sociologically. It designates, then, all the individuals who do not belong to the chosen people. The significance of this designation is that the community of the Gentiles (together with the Jews) has taken over the place of Israel as the locus of the redemptive work of God."[19] In this sense, Jews, like their gentile neighbors, are integral to the composition of all nations.[20] The debates, of course, continue.

Sociological interpretations of *panta ta ethne* emerged by way of Donald A. McGavran's church growth movement in the late 1960s. Gleaning heavily from his experiences in

India, he developed "people group" thinking, which had huge ramifications in mission circles and still does even to this day. The Catholic missionary priest Vincent J. Donovan also developed a people group approach to mission work with the Maasai tribe in Kenya. He explains, "*Ethne* would refer more to ethnic, cultural groups, the natural building blocks of the human race."[21] While the people group notion fails to consider the pluralistic social strata of contemporary society, it succeeds in promoting *panta ta ethne* as referring to the families of mankind—that is, tongues, tribes, castes, lineages, or "peoples of the earth."[22] Some claim that "all nations may not mean every individual, but people from among all nations,"[23] while others argue that "geographical ends of the earth have disappeared in a time of jet travel and a worldwide Church, but there are social, cultural, ideological, and spiritual 'far ends' of human society in profusion."[24]

The meaning of *panta ta ethne* as applied to human migration emerged at the dawn of the twenty-first century with the advent of diaspora missiology. Although the scattering of people is as old as human history, a coherent interpretation of migration through the lens of *missio Dei*—both as a missionary practice and as a theological reflection—is a new development. The proponents view diaspora missiology as an emerging biblical and strategic field of missiology, not to supplant general missiology but to augment it.[25] The types of diasporas vary: victim diasporas, labor diasporas, imperial diasporas, trade diasporas, homeland diasporas, and cultural diasporas.[26] People move for various reasons—some permanently and others temporarily—either by forces like famine, war, or persecution or by choice to improve living conditions or to pursue a dream.[27] Most struggle with uprooting, culture shock, grief, and the pressure to integrate.

Those with legal status have opportunities to obtain residency and eventually citizenship, but those without the necessary documents drift into obscurity.

Panta ta ethne also includes those living in conflict zones, unreached peoples, and closed nations. People who live in conflict zones always face dangers, and some opt to stay, while many decide to go elsewhere for safety either as refugees or as asylum seekers. There are also people living in unreached communities, where the gospel has never been heard. Christian witness is weak in those areas, and some are considered "closed nations," where the host cultures are resistant to the gospel or become openly hostile to it and in the process hamper the missionary presence and task of the body of Christ. Christians who live in these locations go through many difficulties, and most barely *survive*. Yet they stay because of their family heritage and love for their homelands. Seok-Hwan Kim reasons that Christians have no freedom to exclude some nations when Jesus said "all nations," and disciples have to go not only to places that welcome and praise them but also to places where they are not wanted.[28] Thus, a narrow reading of *panta ta ethne* violates the original, inclusive missionary intent of the Central Commission. God's redemptive plan covers all peoples in the world, regardless of race and ideology.

Citizenship

The concept of citizenship is critical to the success and effectiveness of people who have adopted new homelands. Historically, it indicates the privileges of members who enjoy equal status in collective decision-making as well as rights as a political community.[29] In most cases, the right to vote marks democratic citizenship; however, pairing democracy and citizenship can be problematic.[30] Citizenship remains complex and hard to navigate, as it is derived "from manifold sources, influences, and needs."[31] Whether it is national, dual/transnational, corporate, or global, three interweaving themes are evident: relationship, responsibility, and reciprocity.

First, no one moves to a gaping society where social systems and networks do not exist. Even in the most economically depressed societies, there are always places where relationships could be formed, valued, and expanded. The depth and scope of relationships are contingent on one's outlook and resolve and the degree of access that local governments afford to new residents. Relationships vary—for example, they can be social, cultural, political, religious, professional, institutional, educational, ideological, or economic.

Second, established relationships are expressed in and cultivated by responsibilities, both explicit and implicit. As people move, they soon discover the necessity to participate in their adopted societies no matter the difficulty and degree of strangeness; they can never be *not* part of them. Some may create enclaves for their ethnolinguistic groups, like Chinatowns, Koreatowns, or Indiantowns, but they will always face the reality of needing to interact with pluralistic communities. Active participation in societal affairs is inherent in people's lives, both for host communities and for migrants. When people move, they are expected to behave responsibly and follow the laws of the land. All social and political institutions set ethical behavior rules for community members, and they apply to diasporic people, whether their stay is temporary or permanent.

Third, the demand for reciprocity is latent in the concept of citizenship. As people of diasporas move into new neighborhoods, their societies provide them with environments in which to be productive and opportunities to fulfill individual dreams. Soon, diaspora children begin attending local schools, joining sports clubs, enjoying outdoor community activities, receiving internship offers, participating in community services, and most importantly, establishing friendships with new acquaintances. To varying degrees, host societies strive to make all these accessible, convinced, perhaps, that *all* residents need to have avenues for success. In return, the people reciprocate the kindnesses with taxes, voluntary services, charitable donations, professional services, cultural and religious celebrations, and so on. The reciprocity principle is embedded in the notion of citizenship regardless of one's race, ethnicity, socioeconomic status, political affiliation, religious beliefs, and cultural heritage.

Scripture speaks of a type of citizenship that applies particularly to God's covenant people and is unapologetically heavenly and spiritual (Heb 11:16). God's people are pilgrims and sojourners who are simply passing through this physical earth (1 Pet 2:11). This concept of heavenly citizenship is crucial to diaspora missiology for at least five reasons.[32]

First, *heavenly citizenship provides spiritual grounding to the pilgrim status of believers.* As global diasporas move from one place to another, so do God's covenant people. Like the rest of the body of Christ, Christian diasporas are concurrently spiritual pilgrims; they are sojourners of the faith who are in constant motion—always mobile, always on the go. In missiological parlance, the starting point of all these movements, both geographically and spatially, is God's act of *sending* his people as witnesses in the world.[33]

Second, *heavenly citizenship does not absolve God's covenant people of earthly responsibilities.* The followers of Christ in diasporic locations are expected to be active participants in their adopted lands without compromising their Christian integrity. "Thus, we are sojourners," Amos Yong asserts, "continuously living in a diasporic existence, thrust into a world that is in some ways, not our home. At the same time, the goal is not merely to escape from the world, as we anticipate a transformation of the present world and its remaking as a new one fit for the presence of God and the new city of God."[34]

Third, *heavenly citizenship reminds believers of their limited stay on earth and that their journeys will end one day.* Their geographic and spatial mobility could be permanent, but their faith journey and pilgrimage remain temporal as the "eschatological people of God."[35] To this effect, the urgency of their task as the missional people of God gets stronger by the day. As Richard R. De Ridder observes, "The Church's diaspora is being sent out by Christ. The gathered ones go out to gather yet others. The significance and purpose of the Christian diaspora is to be found in its mission dimension."[36] This journey has a climax presupposed by the brevity of life.

Fourth, *heavenly citizenship does not offer God's covenant people immunity to the ills and troubles of this world.* The journey of faith can sometimes be hard, complicated, and risky. Spiritual pilgrims have to fend off daily the attacks of the spiritual forces on every side. This eschatological community has to hold fast to its mission as the light and salt of the earth, "with a heroic refusal to compromise with a system it sees as aligned with the forces of sin and death."[37] Although pilgrims have already set their sights on their destination, persecutions can be life-threatening, suffering can be rampant, trials can be real, and temptations and distractions can lurk everywhere. Heavenly citizenship is not a guarantee of continuing a trouble-free journey.

Fifth, *heavenly citizenship provides the people of God with the hope they need as they deal with adversities and with confidence in times of uncertainty.* No matter how difficult the journey is, divine provisions are sufficient to endure and persist through troubling times. The march toward the throne of God is long, and sufferings abound, but divine grace is sufficient for all pilgrims of God.

Transnationalism

Transnationalism intersects with ideas of nations and citizenship, especially when identity is at stake. Geographic mobility and border crossing serve as trajectories for transnationalism and, consequently, *identity modification.* There are interweaving existential realities in the dispersions of people globally as follows: original ethnic identity based on the concept of nations, citizenship acquired through structured processes and expressed in varied terms, and transnational identity formation as a construct of several significant factors.

Transnationalism or "flexible citizenship" refers to "the cultural specificities of a global process, tracing the multiplicity of the uses and conceptions of culture."[38] The focus is human agency and contemporary behavior and imagination that have been defined or changed in the process of movements across geographic lines, time, space, and the logic of culture. The matrix of transnationalism has three components: (1) "transnationalization," which refers to "the processes involving transnational ties and practices, including the cross-border transactions of goods, services, capital and ideas and the movement of people"; (2) "transnational spatial spaces," which are social formations out of the "transactions of migrants and other agents across borders," including "kinship groups, circuits, and communities"; and (3) "transnationality," which points to "the degree of connectivity between migrants and non-migrants across national borders."[39] These complexities make transnational identity a paradox. From a linguistic and educational perspective, transnationalism interfaces with alternative frames and practices that "build connections, crossings, and spaces between the existing national, ethnic, racial, and linguistic boundaries."[40]

Many immigrants hold dual or multiple identities, which makes transnationalism latent in diasporic conditions and situations. This preference does not make migrants less Asian, for example, as they strive to maintain strong ties with their national heritage and simultaneously establish presumably beneficial alliances in their host societies. Dual or multiple identities have disadvantages, especially among the 1.5 and second generations. Not all succeeding generations are committed to a *transnational existence*, although they may retain a *transnational identity* through their bloodline, ethnic heritage, or generational association.[41] Many do not live outside their birthplace, but they establish ties with friends and relatives overseas through social or economic networks courtesy of parents or members of extended families. Retaining their ethnic identities remains a challenge for many diasporic people. Their idealized homelands fade despite some lingering residue. For others, the memories of the first generation may still be sedimented and etched in the psyche, which also suffers from lapses during trying times away from home. In many cases, though, they opt for a transnational existence to fend off discrimination, racism, and inequality.[42]

Pyong Gap Min found that ethnic identity is constructed primordially, structurally, and socially.[43] The *primordial construct* portrays shared characteristics that bind a group in terms of the members' language, culture, religion, political ideology, physical features, or historical background. The *structural construct* includes aspects related to the people's settlement, education, socioeconomic status, employment, and experiences of racial prejudice and discrimination. It is challenging to live in a society where identity is imposed and controlled by the majority, especially for those who were born in their parents' host countries. The *social construct* of ethnicity results from interactions with others, which make diasporic people active participants in their host societies, as they struggle to define their identities over against ones that are being imposed on them by others. They try to fend off criticism, creatively respond to racial discrimination and ethnic prejudice, and offer a more positive view of who they are.

Perceptions vary on the value of holding dual/multiple or even well-defined transnational identities. The first generation finds it reassuring and comfortable to retain a single identity because of factors like linguistic difficulties, cultural differences, or gaps in worldviews. The 1.5 and second generations embrace multiple identities to succeed in their parents' adopted societies. Those of transnational diasporas find support in *multilinguality*, religious communities, and the laws of host countries that are favorable to them. Others emphasize "the fluid and artificial boundaries and diverse modes of representation in human communication."[44]

The importance of forming, retaining, and enhancing one's ethnic identity in the diaspora community cannot be understated.[45] A good case in point is the second-generation children of diaspora parentage. Although these children are born in their parents' adopted countries, many remain to live in homes where their ethnic cultural heritage is strong and protected. I have seen how the cultures of parents continue to bear influence on the second generation, although many of them have never visited their parents' homelands. Self-concept among the children of first-generation immigrants remains a perennial issue and struggle. The fusion of ethnic identities, including those from the host cultures, is not always a pleasant experience among younger generations. Sam George, reflecting on the Indian diaspora experience, calls them the "coconut generation" and offers ways to overcome this struggle of having evolving identities. He aptly writes, "Who we really are changes with the context; our true identity can be seen as a shifting shadow. The danger of relativism, pluralism and compartmentalization is real with plural self."[46]

Diasporic people always struggle with complex cultural experiences, as integration into their adopted countries remains challenging. The host societies expect new settlers to assimilate and integrate, which is burdensome for the first generation, as the amalgamation process takes a long time. First, they contend with the intricacies of *cultural identification*. It requires great effort to *fit in*, and many diasporic people try to hide their heritage, though their accents, physical features, and cultural traits give them away. Others change their names (Santiago to James, Junjun to Johnny, or Shanti to Shelly). Second, they learn the dynamics of *cultural appropriation*. It requires energy and time to appropriate cultural forms and practices with the hope that their host societies will accept them as "insiders." To blend in, some dye their hair (from black to blond) or switch to local fashions (from a saree to blue jeans), and others simply ditch curry for hamburgers or pizza. Third, they tread the slippery slope of *cultural assimilation.* As new settlers absorb local cultural standards and practices, they create pathways for integration into their host societies. There is a risk of migrants losing their heritage when they succumb to naive cultural adaptation. Fourth, they are cautious about the degree of *cultural accommodation.* People of diasporas are constantly plagued by the issue of adopting some of the social ethos and mores of the host cultures at the expense of their ancestral homelands' morals and ethical ideals. The hazards are obvious when they begin to adapt to cultural practices that are not their own, though there are benefits. The extent of accommodating the cultural forms and practices of their hostlands depends on how much the people are willing to give up the cultures of their homelands.

The inability to integrate causes "identity distress," which, if not addressed properly, results in violence or vulnerability. The diaspora youths are prone to identity crisis when they cede to whoever or whatever provides social structures and meaning to their lives, including drug dealing, gang violence, prostitution, and terrorism.[4] The painful experiences of displacements, coupled with the absence of a collective identity, make the youths easy targets of predators who could provide a sense of belonging no matter how destructive. There exist negative and positive aspects of displacements. As Miriam Adeney observes, "Displacements can bring non-Christians into contact with the gospel and with loving Christian communities, sometimes for the first time. Displacements can drop a new mission field right into a neighborhood of comfortably settled Christians. Displacements can introduce believers of wildly different backgrounds to each other, where each can learn from the other. Displacements can uproot our false sense of security until we have to sink our roots deeper into God. There is much pain in displacement, but there are also blessings."[48]

In both conditions of changing identity and disrupted belongingness, *connectivity* is vital to *transnational functionality*, involving identity, efficiency, settlement, employment, religion, advocacy, ethnicity, and race. Nowadays, transnational identity is more defined with advanced technology through the internet and social media. Digital connectivity strengthens the bond between immigrants and loved ones back home. It deals with security issues in host countries and homelands, improves the quality of life in diasporic conditions, and makes significant contributions to the socioeconomic growth of immigrants' homelands through regular remittances. Their integration into their host societies becomes easier "when diasporans (members of diasporas) have opportunities to express their hybrid identities (a sense of self that is neither wholly of the homeland nor explicitly exclusive of the hostland) collectively."[49] Digital technology highlights the potential of diasporas in international affairs and globalization.

Transnationalism, therefore, makes sense as a solution to the tussle between identities. Settling in a place away from one's native land can be tantamount to experiencing either a second birth or an ethnocide. Attempting to retain their ethnic heritage, diasporic people struggle with integrating into their receiving societies. The tension between *exclusivity* (preserving their inherited identities) and *inclusivity* (assimilating into their host societies) is acute. Some succeed in accommodating; others fail in assimilating. Achieving both can be daunting and confusing because displacement "necessitates an adaptation to new culture and language, new friends, neighborhoods, and schools, as well as novel social and recreational activities."[50]

Nevertheless, transnational identity is not without concerns. The first relates to *loyalty*. To what extent are the transnationals devoted to their adopted countries? They may be naturalized citizens, but to what degree are they able to identify themselves with their receiving societies? Will they die for their host nations as they would for their homelands? The second concerns *responsibility*. This involves corporate citizenship, a more dominant issue for those who hold dual or multiple citizenships. How do they fulfill duties as the legal citizens of two competing countries? The third deals with *patriotism*. Can transnationals claim equal love for two or more nations simultaneously? How will they straddle their love for their ancestral homelands and fascination for their adopted countries? This implies Christian migrants who wrestle with their *residential* identities and *ecclesiastical* identities.[51]

Conclusion

The interlocking concepts of nations, citizenship, and transnationalism are important to diaspora missiology. When people move, part of their nations move with them as their identities change and civic responsibilities are curtailed or expanded. Corporate citizenship paves the way for diasporic people to be responsible members of their adopted nations as they seek to actively participate in and contribute to the advancement of their receiving societies. They embrace a transnational existence to maintain strong ties to their homelands and ethnic heritage while engaging their host countries intentionally. Transnationalism offers flexible citizenship to them, from which dual or multiple identities can emerge, and though it has a complex dynamic, it holds much promise. They suffer from disrupted belongingness, but resources to overcome this can be identified. The eschatological community is part of the global migration flow; however, as sojourners and pilgrims, their scattering is earthly, but their ultimate citizenship remains heavenly.

Notes

1 The Global Diaspora Network defines diaspora missiology as "a missiological framework for understanding and participating in God's redemptive mission among people living outside their place of origin." Lausanne Movement and Global Diaspora Network, *Scattered to Gather: Embracing the Global Trend of Diaspora*, rev. ed. (Vernon Hills, IL: Parivar, 2017), 28.

2 Duane L. Christensen, "Nations," in *The Anchor Bible Dictionary*, ed. David Noel Freedman, vol. 4 (New York: Doubleday, 1992), 1037.

3 Terence L. Donaldson, "Nations," in *The New Interpreter's Dictionary of the Bible*, ed. Katherine Doob Sakenfeld, vol. 4 (Nashville: Abingdon, 2009), 232.

4 Christensen, "Nations," 1037.

5 David Watson, *I Believe in the Church* (London: Hodder & Stoughton, 1978), 67.

6 Watson, 66.

7 L. A. Hoedaker, "The People of God and the Ends of the Earth," in *Missiology: An Ecumenical Introduction*, ed. F. J. Verstraelen (Grand Rapids, MI: Eerdmans, 1995), 168.

8 Douglas R. A. Hare, *Matthew, Interpretation* (Louisville, KY: Westminster John Knox, 1993), 289.

9 See Richard R. De Ridder, *Discipling the Nations* (Grand Rapids, MI: Baker, 1979), 184.

10 See Kenneth Scott Latourette, *A History of Christianity* (New York: Harper & Row, 1953), 703–1000; Herbert J. Kane, *A Concise History of the Christian World Mission: A Panoramic View of Missions from Pentecost to the Present* (Grand Rapids, MI: Baker, 1982), 73–75; Johannes Verkuyl, *Contemporary Missiology: An Introduction*, trans. Dale Cooper (Grand Rapids, MI: Eerdmans, 1978), 18–25; Ho-Jin Jun, "Reformation and Mission: A Brief Survey of the Missiological Understanding of the Reformers," *ACTS Theological Journal* 5 (June 1994): 160–78.

11 For further discussion, see David Bosch, *Transforming Mission: Paradigm Shifts in Theology of Mission* (Maryknoll, NY: Orbis, 2011), 248–57.

12 Martin Luther, *Luther's Works*, vol. 12 (Minneapolis: Lutherans in All Lands, 1907), 25–26, 183–84, 214–16.

13 John C. Thiessen, *A Survey of World Missions* (Chicago: InterVarsity, 1955), 18.

14 Kane, *Concise History*, 76.

15 See Tereso C. Casiño, "Is Diaspora Missions Valid?," in *Scattered: The Filipino Global Presence*, ed. Luis Pantoja, Sadiri Joy Tira, and Enoch Wan (Manila: LifeChange, 2004), 123–48.

16 For varying positions, see Joachim Jeremias, *Jesus' Promise to the Nations* (Naperville, IL: Alec R. Allenson, 1958), 19, 39; Johannes Blauw, *The Missionary Nature of the Church* (New York: McGraw-Hill, 1962), 85; Donald Senior and Carroll Stuhlmueller, *The Biblical Foundations of Mission* (Maryknoll, NY: Orbis, 1983), 252.

17 For the relationship between Matt 10 and Matt 28, see Roger Hedlund, *Mission to Man in the Bible* (Madras, India: Evangelical Literature Service, 1985), 196–206. Joachim Gnilka, "Der Missionsauftrag

des Herrn nach Matthaus 28 und Apostelgeschicte I," *Bibel und Leben*, 1968, 1–9, cited in Verkuyl, *Contemporary Missiology*, 106.

18 See Douglas R. A. Hare and Daniel J. Harrington, "Make Disciples of All the Gentiles (Matt. 28:19)," *Catholic Biblical Quarterly* 37, no. 3 (1975): 359–69; cf. Delos Miles, *Introduction to Evangelism* (Nashville: Broadman, 1983), 128.

19 De Ridder, *Discipling the Nations*, 188.

20 See John P. Meir, "Nations or Gentiles in Matthew 28:19?," *Catholic Biblical Quarterly* 39, no. 1 (January 1977): 95–102.

21 Vincent J. Donovan, *Christianity Rediscovered* (Maryknoll, NY: Orbis, 1978), 29–30.

22 Donald A. McGavran, *Understanding Church Growth*, rev. ed. (Grand Rapids, MI: Eerdmans, 1980), 22, 56. Vinay Samuel and Chris Sugden dismiss the people group idea, claiming it to be an invention of multi-national agencies that seek to bypass the national church. Vinay Samuel and Chris Sugden, "Mission Agencies as Multinationals," *International Bulletin of Mission Research* 7, no. 6 (October 1983): 152.

23 William Dyrness, *Let the Earth Rejoice* (Eugene, OR: Wipf & Stock, 1998), 149.

24 Pierce Beaver, "The Apostolate of the Church," in *The Theology of the Christian Mission*, ed. Gerald H. Anderson (New York: Abingdon, 1961), 264.

25 See Sadiri Joy Tira and Tetsunao Yamamori, eds., *Scattered and Gathered: A Global Compendium of Diaspora Missiology*, rev. ed. (Cumbria, UK: Langham, 2020).

26 See Robin Cohen, *Global Diasporas: An Introduction*, 2nd ed. (New York: Routledge, 2008).

27 For further discussion, see Tereso C. Casiño, "Why People Move: A Prolegomena to Diaspora Missiology," *Torch Trinity Journal* 13, no. 1 (May 2010): 19–44.

28 Seok-Hwan Kim, *Disciple's Bible Study—Stage 3* (Seoul: Disciples, 1994), 11.

29 Richard Bellamy, *Citizenship: A Very Short Introduction* (Oxford: Oxford University Press, 2008), 1.

30 For further discussion, see Étienne Balibar, *Citizenship* (Cambridge: Polity, 2015), 1–6.

31 Derek Heather, *What Is Citizenship?* (Malden, MA: Polity, 2008), 3.

32 Daniel Rodriguez asserts, "An important step for missiologists and leaders in the worldwide mission of God is to embrace and actively promote our identity as resident aliens whose true citizenship is in heaven (Phil 3:20–21)." See Daniel Rodriguez, "From the Promised Land to Egypt: Immigration, Transnationalism, and Mission among Hispanic Evangelical Churches in North America," in *Churches on Mission*, ed. Geoffrey Hartt, Christopher R. Little, and John Wang (Pasadena, CA: William Carey Library, 2017), 228.

33 David D. Ruiz, "The Pilgrim Church," in *The Church in Mission: Foundations and Global Case Studies*, ed. Bertil Ekstrom (Pasadena, CA: William Carey Library, 2016), 59.

34 Amos Yong, "From Every Tribe, Language, People, and Nation: Diaspora, Hybridity, and the Coming Reign of God," in *Global Diasporas and Mission*, ed. Chandler H. Im and Amos Yong (Oxford: Regnum, 2014), 260.

35 Michael W. Goheen, *A Light to the Nations: The Missional Church and the Biblical Story* (Grand Rapids, MI: Baker Academic, 2011), 180.

36 De Ridder, *Discipling the Nations*, 217.

37 Sung Chul Hong, "The Missiological Understanding of the Book of Revelation," *Korea Journal of Theology* 3 (2002): 376–77.

38 Aihwa Ong, *Flexible Citizenship: The Cultural Logics of Transnationality* (Durham, NC: Duke University Press, 1999), 4.

39 See Thomas Faist, Margit Fauser, and Eveline Reisenauer, *Transnational Migration* (Malden, MA: Polity, 2013), 2.

40 Xiaoye You, introduction to *Transnational Writing Education: Theory, History, and Practice* (New York: Routledge, 2018), 2.

41 See Peggy Levitt, "Transnational Migrants: When 'Home' Means More Than One Country," MPI, October 1, 2004, https://www .migrationpolicy.org/article/transnational-migrants-when-home -means-more-one-country.

42 Ji-hoon Jamie Kim, "Transnational Identity Formation of Second-Generation Korean Americans Living in Korea," *Torch Trinity Journal* 13, no. 1 (May 2010): 74.

43 See Pyong Gap Min, ed., *The Second Generation: Ethnic Identity among Asian Americans* (Walnut Creek, CA: AltaMira, 2002), 1–18.

44 You, introduction, 5.

45 Min, *Second Generation*, 7.

46 Sam George, *Understanding the Coconut Generation: Ministry to the Americanized Asian Indians* (Niles, IL: Mall, 2006), 61.

47 For a comprehensive treatment, see Seth J. Schwartz, ed., *Identity around the World: New Directions for Child and Adolescent Development* (San Francisco: Jossey-Bass, 2013).

48 Sam George and Miriam Adeney, eds., *Refugee Diaspora: Missions amid the Greatest Humanitarian Crisis of Our Times* (Littleton, CO: William Carey, 2018), 169.

49 Jennifer M. Brinkerhoff, *Digital Diasporas: Identity and Transnational Engagement* (New York: Cambridge University Press, 2009), 2.

50 Sidney L. Werkman, "Coming Home," in *Cross-Cultural Reentry: A Book of Readings*, ed. Clyde N. Austin (Abilene, TX: Abilene Christian University Press, 1986), 9.

51 Myles Werntz, "Addressing Migration among Christian Audiences: A Modest Proposal," *Review & Expositor* 115, no. 3 (August 2018): 317.

Bibliography

Balibar, Étienne. *Citizenship*. Cambridge: Polity, 2015.

Beaver, Pierce. "The Apostolate of the Church." In *The Theology of the Christian Mission*, edited by Gerald H. Anderson, 258–268. New York: Abingdon, 1961.

Bellamy, Richard. *Citizenship: A Very Short Introduction*. Oxford: Oxford University Press, 2008.

Blauw, Johannes. *The Missionary Nature of the Church*. New York: McGraw-Hill, 1962.

Bosch, David. *Transforming Mission: Paradigm Shifts in Theology of Mission*. Maryknoll, NY: Orbis, 2011.

Brinkerhoff, Jennifer M. *Digital Diasporas: Identity and Transnational Engagement*. New York: Cambridge University Press, 2009.

Casiño, Tereso C. "Is Diaspora Missions Valid?" In *Scattered: The Filipino Global Presence*, edited by Luis Pantoja, Sadiri Joy Tira, and Enoch Wan, 123–148. Manila: LifeChange, 2004.

———. "Why People Move: A Prolegomena to Diaspora Missiology." *Torch Trinity Journal* 13, no. 1 (May 2010): 19–44.

Christensen, Duane L. "Nations." In *The Anchor Bible Dictionary*, edited by David Noel Freedman, 1037–1049. Vol. 4. New York: Doubleday, 1992.

Cohen, Robin. *Global Diasporas: An Introduction*. 2nd ed. New York: Routledge, 2008.

De Ridder, Richard R. *Discipling the Nations*. Grand Rapids, MI: Baker, 1979.

Donaldson, Terence L. "Nations." In *The New Interpreter's Dictionary of the Bible*, edited by Katherine Doob Sakenfeld, 231–238. Vol. 4. Nashville: Abingdon, 2009.

Donovan, Vincent J. *Christianity Rediscovered*. Maryknoll, NY: Orbis, 1978.

Dyrness, William. *Let the Earth Rejoice.* Eugene, OR: Wipf & Stock, 1998.

Faist, Thomas, Margit Fauser, and Eveline Reisenauer. *Transnational Migration.* Malden, MA: Polity, 2013.

George, Sam. *Understanding the Coconut Generation: Ministry to the Americanized Asian Indians.* Niles, IL: Mall, 2006.

George, Sam, and Miriam Adeney, eds. *Refugee Diaspora: Missions amid the Greatest Humanitarian Crisis of Our Times.* Littleton, CO: William Carey, 2018.

Gnilka, Joachim. "Der Missionsauftrag des Herrn nach Matthaus 28 und Apostelgeschicte I." *Bibel und Leben,* 1968, 1–9.

Goheen, Michael W. *A Light to the Nations: The Missional Church and the Biblical Story.* Grand Rapids, MI: Baker Academic, 2011.

Hare, Douglas R. A. *Matthew, Interpretation.* Louisville, KY: Westminster John Knox, 1993.

Hare, Douglas R. A., and Daniel J. Harrington. "Make Disciples of All the Gentiles (Matt. 28:19)." *Catholic Biblical Quarterly* 37, no. 3 (1975): 359–369.

Heather, Derek. *What Is Citizenship?* Malden, MA: Polity, 2008.

Hedlund, Roger. *Mission to Man in the Bible.* Madras, India: Evangelical Literature Service, 1985.

Hoedaker, L. A. "The People of God and the Ends of the Earth." In *Missiology: An Ecumenical Introduction,* edited by F. J. Verstraelen, 157–171. Grand Rapids, MI: Eerdmans, 1995.

Hong, Sung Chul. "The Missiological Understanding of the Book of Revelation." *Korea Journal of Theology* 3 (2002): 347–377.

Jeremias, Joachim. *Jesus' Promise to the Nations.* Naperville, IL: Alec R. Allenson, 1958.

Jun, Ho-Jin. "Reformation and Mission: A Brief Survey of the Missiological Understanding of the Reformers." *ACTS Theological Journal* 5 (June 1994): 160–178.

Kane, Herbert J. *A Concise History of the Christian World Mission: A Panoramic View of Missions from Pentecost to the Present*. Grand Rapids, MI: Baker, 1982.

Kim, Ji-hoon Jamie. "Transnational Identity Formation of Second-Generation Korean Americans Living in Korea." *Torch Trinity Journal* 13, no. 1 (May 2010): 74.

Kim, Seok-Hwan. *Disciple's Bible Study—Stage 3*. Seoul: Disciples, 1994.

Latourette, Kenneth Scott. *A History of Christianity*. New York: Harper & Row, 1953.

Lausanne Movement and Global Diaspora Network. *Scattered to Gather: Embracing the Global Trend of Diaspora*. Rev. ed. Vernon Hills, IL: Parivar, 2017.

Levitt, Peggy. "Transnational Migrants: When 'Home' Means More Than One Country." MPI, October 1, 2004. https://www .migrationpolicy.org/article/transnational-migrants-when-home -means-more-one-country.

Luther, Martin. *Luther's Works*. Vol. 12. Minneapolis: Lutherans in All Lands, 1907.

McGavran, Donald A. *Understanding Church Growth*. Rev. ed. Grand Rapids, MI: Eerdmans, 1980.

Meir, John P. "Nations or Gentiles in Matthew 28:19?" *Catholic Biblical Quarterly* 39, no. 1 (January 1977): 95–102.

Miles, Delos. *Introduction to Evangelism*. Nashville: Broadman, 1983.

Min, Pyong Gap, ed. *The Second Generation: Ethnic Identity among Asian Americans*. Walnut Creek, CA: AltaMira, 2002.

Ong, Aihwa. *Flexible Citizenship: The Cultural Logics of Transnationality*. Durham, NC: Duke University Press, 1999.

Rodriguez, Daniel. "From the Promised Land to Egypt: Immigration, Transnationalism, and Mission among Hispanic Evangelical Churches in North America." In *Churches on Mission*, edited by

Geoffrey Hartt, Christopher R. Little, and John Wang, chap. 11. Pasadena, CA: William Carey Library, 2017.

Ruiz, David D. "The Pilgrim Church." In *The Church in Mission: Foundations and Global Case Studies*, edited by Bertil Ekstrom, 59–66. Pasadena, CA: William Carey Library, 2016.

Samuel, Vinay, and Chris Sugden. "Mission Agencies as Multinationals." *International Bulletin of Mission Research* 7, no. 6 (October 1983): 152.

Schwartz, Seth J., ed. *Identity around the World: New Directions for Child and Adolescent Development*. San Francisco: Jossey-Bass, 2013.

Senior, Donald, and Carroll Stuhlmueller. *The Biblical Foundations of Mission*. Maryknoll, NY: Orbis, 1983.

Thiessen, John C. *A Survey of World Missions*. Chicago: InterVarsity, 1955.

Tira, Sadiri Joy, and Tetsunao Yamamori, eds. *Scattered and Gathered: A Global Compendium of Diaspora Missiology*. Rev. ed. Cumbria, UK: Langham, 2020.

Verkuyl, Johannes. *Contemporary Missiology: An Introduction*. Translated by Dale Cooper. Grand Rapids, MI: Eerdmans, 1978.

Watson, David. *I Believe in the Church*. London: Hodder & Stoughton, 1978.

Werkman, Sidney L. "Coming Home." In *Cross-Cultural Reentry: A Book of Readings*, edited by Clyde N. Austin, 5–17. Abilene, TX: Abilene Christian University Press, 1986.

Werntz, Myles. "Addressing Migration among Christian Audiences: A Modest Proposal." *Review & Expositor* 115, no. 3 (August 2018): 317.

Yong, Amos. "From Every Tribe, Language, People, and Nation: Diaspora, Hybridity, and the Coming Reign of God." In *Global Diasporas and Mission*, edited by Chandler H. Im and Amos Yong, 253–262. Oxford: Regnum, 2014.

You, Xiaoye. Introduction to *Transnational Writing Education: Theory, History, and Practice*, 1–30. New York: Routledge, 2018.

4

**_Motus Dei_
(The Move of God)**

A Theology and Missiology
for a Moving World

Sam George

God is on the move. God is moving in the lives of men and women across the street and around the world. The message of the kingdom of God is going forth remarkably these days, and God's reign is advancing in unexpected ways. God is powerfully moving among people who are on the move. Migrants, displaced peoples, and diaspora communities are at the forefront of God's mission in the world today. Migration is one of the megathemes of the biblical narratives, and the trajectories of salvation history and the church worldwide have been reshaped repeatedly by people on the move.

This chapter delves into Christian doctrines to introduce (to some) and develop the concept of *motus Dei* by arguing that the God of the Bible is one who is continually on the move and beckons his followers to come alongside to see what God is doing in the world. Thus, the mission is all about moving with God to see all things made new as we harmonize our wandering steps to be in sync with a moving God. The mission is following, moving in, and catching up with God in many different cultural and geographical spaces all over the world to grow in our appreciation of God's work in, though, and around us as we move about. Within the confines of this chapter, I briefly venture into the domains of theology (proper), anthropology, soteriology, pneumatology, and eschatology while constructing a new theology and missiology for a world in motion. It draws from the rich resources of Christian theology to understand God and God's work in a world of unprecedented human mobility and consequent societal and global transformations wrought about by what is now considered an age of migration.

Moving God:
Creation and the Trinity

The God of the Bible is a missionary God because God is always on the move, and God is on the move because God is a living being.[1] The divine attributes of omnipresence, immutability, and impassibility should not lead us in the direction of viewing God as rigid, static, immovable, and stationary. God cannot be confined in space or time yet sovereign over spatial and chronological realms. After closely examining the history of Israel given in the sermon of the first Christian martyr, Stephen, in the book of Acts, John Stott concludes that the "God of the Old Testament was the living God, a God on the move and on the march, who was always calling his people out to fresh adventures, and always accompanying and directing them as they went."[2]

First of all, in the very beginning, in the creation account immediately after the opening statement about God creating the cosmos, we read, "The Spirit of God was hovering over the waters" (Gen 1:2 NIV), where we observe God's movement over the earth, which is without form, empty, and dark. Even before God speaks creation commands in Genesis 1:3 and thereafter, we see God moving over the earth. Before the illuminating, life-creating, and order-making creative work of God, we see a moving God. Some translations use words such as *blowing, soaring, sweeping over*, or *moving* in place of *hovering* and could be compared with the word *hover* mentioned in Deuteronomy 32:11, which renders the imagery of an eagle brooding over its nest. The Hebrew noun for God in Genesis 1:1 is plural, which establishes the Trinitarian foundations from the very beginning, and Pentecostal theologians have affirmed the role of the Spirit in the creation using Genesis 1:2.[3] One may argue that the divine utterances of creation resulted from the divine movement and in response to it.

Moreover, in the creation account, the formless and empty earth (Gen 1:2) was "separated" and "gathered" by God on days one to three to establish a form, and God's "making" and "filling" occurred on days four to six to remove the emptiness. Likewise, scattering and gathering could be seen as megathemes of divine action throughout to establish God's reign in the created order. The creation mandate to "be fruitful and multiply, and fill the earth and subdue it" (Gen 1:28) charges human beings to be corulers over the creation on God's behalf, and its scope covers the whole earth, requiring humanity to move from place to place.

Unlike the Creator, who is not confined by space, is sovereign, and is found moving about, the creatures have to navigate beyond their spatial subjectivities to establish the divine reign on earth. This mandate encompasses humans' destiny to be communal beings in order to inhabit and shape social life as well as the natural world. The fall is portrayed as alienation and expulsion from the garden (a form of forced displacement) and sets the stage for an eventual redemption, which could be conceived as moving back to a state of restored communion and proximity to the Divine Being, thus requiring soteriology to be articulated afresh in locational and relational terms.

God moves within Godself and outside of Godself. The Trinitarian nomenclature of the three persons of the Godhead as coindwelling, coinhering, and interpenetrating "allows the individuality of the person to be maintained while each person shares in the life of the other two."[4] God moves because God is the Trinity—both monotheistic and tritheistic ideations make the Godhead motionless, while the polytheistic notion of god makes them territorial. The conceptualization of Trinitarian relationality and the dance of perichōrēsis require kinematic imagination, as it cannot be grasped solely in a static state. The Trinity provides the basis of ontological foundations for understanding human personhood and interpersonal relations, polycentric and symmetrical reciprocity of the many.[5]

The relationality of the Trinity allows the persons of the Godhead to move toward one another and together move into the created order and the entire cosmos: "God goes forth from God, God creates the world, God suffuses its history and dwells within it, redeeming the world from within."[6] Such a model of the Trinitarian God has many implications for theological anthropology. For this chapter, such intrinsic sociality of human beings requires mobility, without which a creature is not fully alive or social. Another important way in which humans relate is through language and being in communication with other human beings, which is closely tied to the idea of being in motion. The etymology of the word *migrate* is instructive and related to *commute, commune, communication,* and other similar words. Kevin Vanhoozer writes, "Humans are like God in their capacity to go out of themselves and enter into personal relations through a communicative agency."[7] The history of innovations in trade, transportation, and communication has a symbiotic relationship with the history of human migrations.

In contrast to a living and moving God, idols cannot move about and need to be carried from place to place (Jer 10:5). Idols and territorial spirits are bound within geographical confines and keep devotees chained to their locales. John Calvin expounds the second commandment (that representing God in images is forbidden) because people are confined to their physical surroundings when they create images of deities, they are distracted from God's true spiritual being, and to some degree, the deities are conceived in some corporeal way.[8] In developing a theology of idolatry, G. K. Baele asserts that we become what we worship—as without mouths, eyes, ears, hands, or feet—based on the psalmist's claim that "those who make them [idols] will become like them" (Ps 115:8), and we resemble what we revere, either for ruin or for restoration.[9] In other words, idolatry makes us motionless and fastens us to geography like dead people. A static view of God turns the Divine Being and the created humanity into lifeless, immobile, and sterile figures. The insular nature of idolatrous societies stems from their provincialism, which in turn makes their religions less transportable and missionary. Their parochial tendencies restrict the territorial dominion of evil and demonic spirits, as they are not omnipresent or omniscient like the God of the Bible. The beliefs and practices of ancestral worship and mediation to guardian spirits point to territorial bondage and ethnic elitism, and they remain imprisoned in their localities. These gods, spirits, and ancestors reside in particular objects or territories and protect people who dwell within their vicinities. Their powers do not extend beyond those areas, and when people travel to distant places, they are no longer under the protection of their gods and are expected to change their allegiance to a stronger god of their new regions and serve him. In contrast to tribal deities, "Jehovah declared himself not to be a territorial god but the God of the universe."[10]

When the physicality of the temple occupied a more overbearing place for the Israelites and considerable superficiality, corruption, and ritualism took over, God allowed it to be destroyed by the invading armies, resulting in the exile of the Israelites. The tabernacle was more archetypal of a moving God than the sedentary God of the Jerusalem temple. The disciples' response to the transfiguration of Jesus was to "put up three shelters" (Mark 9:5 NIV), as they wanted to erect tents to memorialize or establish a shrine at that place. The divine corrective to the disciples affirmed the Sonship of Jesus and called them to obey him. Likewise, Jesus resolved the dilemma faced by the Samaritan woman about the true place of worship—between Mount Gerizim for Samaritans and Jerusalem for Jews—by exhorting her that it is neither here nor there, but true worshipers "must worship in spirit and truth" (John 4:24 NIV). The place was deemed inconsequential, and Jesus broke through the human tendency to domesticate God and bind the infinite boundless Spirit within cultural and geographical particularities.

The Japanese theologian Kosuke Koyama compares Mount Fuji—the cosmological center of the world, according to Japanese imperial ideology—with Mount Sinai, the place of divine epiphany and where the Law was given to the Israelites. Because of the image of a mobile God, the people did not acknowledge Mount Sinai as a place of worship, and their imagination of God was not bound to a place. Instead, God himself "symbolize[d] the center of salvation. The center symbolism travel[ed] with the people."[11] Koyama further contends that centrality, whether of an individual, a race, a nation, an institution, or an empire, is always open to abuse and exploitation by destructive ideologies.

Created to Move:
Human Beings and the Fall

Second, a doctrine of humanity needs to be articulated in motile terms to understand our innate propensity toward peripatetic wanderings. Here I contend that movability is a characteristic feature of human beings, since we are created in the likeness of God (Gen 1:26 NIV), similar to the notions of human rationality, relationality, dignity, identity, solidarity, freedom, worth, and other dominant interpretations of the image of God in classical theological texts. We are created to move because we bear the image of a moving God, and it is high time to reimagine theological anthropology and mission theology kinesiologically.

"I move, therefore I am" (*moveo ergo sum*) is more pertinent in the age of migration than Descartes's dictum.

Augustine speaks of human life as ever on the move: "You have made us *toward* yourself, and our hearts are restless until they rest in you."[12] Andrew F. Walls argues that the history of humanity is "determined by the movements of peoples,"[13] and Daniel Groody claims that the theme of migration is intrinsic to our biological and spiritual genes.[14] We are created to move about, and only when we move are we fully alive and do we exhibit our likeness to our Creator. An inability to move denies personhood to and utterly dehumanizes a person. Being created in the image of God is not a state or condition but a movement with a goal.[15] Such a directional teleology can aid the development of a more nuanced construal of the doctrine of the fall as alienation or falling away using biblical narratives of the expulsion from the garden, the call of Abraham, the exodus, the exile, and other texts. This will help reconceive the soteriological task as a moving experience "passed from death into life" and "out of darkness into his marvelous light" (1 John 3:14; 1 Pet 2:9 NIV). Contemporary urban nomadism and migration across national borders only prove that we are truly *homo mobilis*.

In his Areopagus sermon, the apostle Paul quotes the seventh-century BCE Cretan poet and philosopher Epimenides from his work *Cretica*—"In him we live and move and have our being" (Acts 17:28)—and uses it to talk about a God who made the world and everything in it, in contrast to pantheistic Stoicism. He goes on to confront the idolatry of the Athenians, introduce Jesus, and call his listeners to repentance. At the heart of this comparison is the belief that human existence and our very being are intricately linked to our capacity for motion, and all of it is derived from the Divine Being, who is not a mere lifeless and immotile idol crafted by human hands. We move in response to God, who is on the move incessantly. And this moving nature not only is a sign of being alive but lies at the very core of our identity. This also presents the fact that created human beings are totally and continually dependent on the Creator for their existence, sustenance, abilities, and activities. All living creatures, especially human beings, are brought to life by the divine breath (Gen 2:7), and in the second of the four speeches Elihu makes to Job, he states, "If he [God] should take back his spirit to himself, and gather to himself his breath, all flesh would perish together, and all mortals return to dust" (Job 34:14–15). Paul believes that "[God] himself gives everyone life and breath and everything else" (Acts 17:25 NIV). Jesus tells his disciples that "the Son can do nothing on his own, but only what he sees the Father doing" (John 5:19) and "apart from me you can do nothing" (John 15:5).

Later in the same sermon, Paul quotes the Cilician poet Aratus (ca. 315–240 BCE) from his *Phaenomena*—"We are [God's] offspring" (Acts 17:28b NIV)—and finds a common anthropological and theological ground with the audience using pagan literature. Paul suggests that the unknown god of the Athenians was the God of Jesus Christ and finds a mutually tenable platform to engage his heathen listeners evangelistically without alienating them. He is more inclusive and tries to identify with his interlocutors without creating a division of "us versus them." Earlier, he had claimed that from one man God had made every nation inhabiting the whole earth and thus argued that the whole of humanity has a common ancestry. Amos Yong uses this passage to renew his vision for a pneumatological missiology of the Spirit for the pluralistic context of the twenty-first century.[16] As migration brings people closer to others who are unlike themselves and hold different belief systems, theological anthropology in terms of mobile, familial kinship and mutuality of human diversity without compromising the core Christian convictions is required to provide a credible witness to the gospel.

In the Athenian discourse, the apostle Paul also claims the sovereignty of God over human dispersion, saying God "determined allotted periods and the boundaries of their dwelling place" (Acts 17:26 ESV). Beyond the economic, sociological, legal, and political dimensions of human migration, we see a divine origin at work as people change their domiciles across borders. Paul explicates the reason why God moves people—"so that they . . . seek him" (Acts 17:27 NIV)—and underscores the spiritual consequences of migration. Though God is not distant from them, the migrants come near to God after moving to new places. Displacement makes people seek after God in new ways by testing the validity of their past beliefs in new contexts while being open to other alternatives and spiritual experiences. They compare and contrast the worlds they are exposed to while striving to seek the ultimate truth claims. No wonder migration is considered "a theologizing experience."[17]

Christians are more likely to travel beyond the places of their birth, since they are not bound to any locale, and their peripatetic encounters with foreign cultures and languages lead to new endeavors in adapting the tenets of their faith and practices in new contexts. Some opine that "if you are a Christian, you will travel, and if you travel, you will become a Christian." On the contrary, Hinduism is considered a geographically imprisoned religion because of its scriptures' prohibition against traversing large expanses of water, its dietary restrictions, its views of pollution, its purification rituals upon returning home, its beliefs about demotion in the social hierarchy if one travels, and the people's fear of dying in a foreign land. Hindus are expected to live and die in places close to where they were born, and most remain largely bound within specific lands and cultures.[18] Their destinies are determined by their places of birth, within the confines of both geography and the caste hierarchy. The only way they can escape Karmic fatalism is by migrating out of the territorial boundaries of such provincial gods and changing their allegiance to a more benevolent and universal God. Likewise, Islam is also a rooted religion on account of its pilgrimages, prayers uttered while facing a particular place, and untranslatable scriptures.[19] Lamin Sanneh succinctly juxtaposes Islam and Christianity by alleging the "Muslim *hijrah* bequeathed a legacy of geographical and linguistic orthodoxy while the Christian Pentecost created the reverse, an abandonment of the idea of divine territoriality."[20]

Moving to Save:
The Incarnation and Salvation

Third, *incarnation* means "take on," "become," or "enter into flesh." It refers to the Christian doctrine that the preexistent Son of God became a man in Jesus.[21] The birth of Jesus can be understood as a move of God into an alien world to become a human being within a particular sociocultural and historical setting yet without losing his divinity. Thus, through the incarnation, God in the person of Jesus crossed the divide between the divine self and the created order. The New Testament does not use static or metaphysical concepts to explain the mystery of the incarnation; rather, it is seen in terms of a dynamic movement. The Johannine Gospel describes the enfleshment of the incarnation as follows: "The Word became flesh and made his dwelling among us" (John 1:14 NIV), where God is portrayed as moving into our neighborhood or pitching his tent next door. The imagery is closely linked to the Old Testament idea of the Tent of Meeting, which was filled by the glory of God (Exod 40:34–35), and the portable sanctuary of God during the wilderness period, which later became the model for the temple in Jerusalem (Exod 25). God was moving with his people, and his presence was visible in the form of a cloud by day and fire by night that assured the people on their journey to their promised land.

Likewise, the apostle Paul speaks of the incarnation of Jesus, the Second Person of the Trinity, in terms of an emptying (kenosis) of himself in becoming a human being and finally of exaltation in the resurrection (Phil 2:6–11). This hymn depicts the incarnation as a descent and lowering to become nothing. The mystery of the incarnation of Jesus, who did not give up his deity but laid aside his glory, being fully man and fully God, is explained using kinetic terms, such as "being poured out," "lowered," "exalted," "highest place," "above all," and so on. Such a Christology starts from above, descends to the level of a human being, and ascends again to the divine plane. On the contrary, in the Acts of the Apostles, we have a Christology from below, starting with the human life of Jesus Christ and the ascension and the angelic assurance to the disciples about the second coming of Jesus (Acts 1:10 and 11). These verses are loaded with directional and motional words, such as "look up," "sky," "stood beside," "here," "above," "going," "taken from," "come back," "go into," and so on. The New Testament accounts focus on the functional aspects of Christ—his life, teachings, and redemptive activities—while in later centuries, theologians took a metaphysical approach to understand his being as two natures (divine and human) united in one person.

The Aristotelian concept of the "unmoved Mover" had a significant influence on Christian metaphysics and notions of the attributes of God's divinity, such as God's immutability and impassibility. However, Jürgen Moltmann believes that the biblical experience of God more likely corresponds to a "self-moved Mover" because "God moves out of God-self and loves the being God has created."[22] The belief is that what is divine is not subjected to change over time or change brought about by an external force. But the attribute of immutability deprives a divine being of its vitality, and those of unchangeability and immovability portray God as a dead rather than a living and active being. In "coming down" to deliver his people out of the hands of slave masters in Egypt, God is "moved by compassion" after seeing the affliction of his people and having heard their cry (Exod 3:7–8). God descends for their sake—to liberate them from their bondage and suffering in Egypt—and leads them to the promised land by going before them. Viewing these depictions as anthropomorphism does not take the human subject's likeness to God seriously, while viewing God as immovable and incapable of love or suffering makes the Godhead less divine.

Soteriology can be conceived not only as acquittal, expiation, justification, atonement, and redemption from sin and death, as commonly done in Western theological writings, but also in relational, religious, and motile terms such as *reversal of estrangement*, *alienation*, *ostracization*, and *contamination* using conceptual ideations like *brought near*, *reconciliation*, *purification*, and *restoration*. Generally, the effect of the fall is traced to the inherited guilt or corruption of humanity, for which salvation is presented as a gift of grace through Christ's death. The finished work of Jesus on the cross offers not only substitutionary atonement but also wholeness and fullness through soul cleansing, adoption into the family of God, and the restoration of a broken relationship. Shame- and honor-based communitarian cultures require a more holistic and multidimensional stance on Christian salvation.

The ultimate salvation for Christians is their eschatological vision of the future, which helps them pivot their present predicaments in light of eternity and live with their eyes set on the Savior and eternal life. The eschatological kingdom is the ultimate goal of all missionary work, and mission is all about witness to the reign of God, which *has come* in Jesus Christ and is *yet coming*.[23] Christians move, whether in the form of missionaries or migrants, across cultural and geographical boundaries, and in the process of uprooting and transplanting, they become strangely aware of the moving of God in their lives and new locations. Many become Christians after moving to new places, whether for economic opportunities, for educational prospects, or as a result of forced displacement because of famine, wars, or persecution. Faith in a moving God becomes an indispensable resource for people on the move, and they become natural evangelists and cultural translators over time, exerting missional influence on the places of their origin, sojourn, and settlement. During their earthly peregrine lives, the pilgrim people of God have no abiding city on earth but look forward to the city with a foundation whose maker and builder is God (Heb 11:10). They have no fixed abode on earth; their earthly home is *paroikia* (dwell beside or among), a temporary residence, and they have their eyes fixed on their eternal abode.[24] Their eschatological hope propels them to live each day faithfully with a divine sense of a grander purpose for their transitory lives to participate in the mission of God. Thus, the displaced immigrants serve a missionary function, just as the functional missionaries are culturally displaced migrants.

Mission in Motion: Migration and Movements

Finally, at its core, the Christian faith is a diasporic missionary faith. If it remains captive to a culture, people, or geography, it will turn into a religion like any other and be deprived of its innate dynamism. Much of the Bible was written in diasporic contexts, and a common thread that runs throughout its pages is the select people and nation that God displaced in a different epoch of history to advance God's reign in the world. Salvation history is framed within migratory wanderings, and much of Christian expansion and transformation over the last two millenniums has ensued in diverse diasporic contexts. The expansion of Christianity has occurred along the trajectories of human dispersions, as they become conduits for the reinvigoration and cultural diffusion of the gospel from one group of people to another, and it has now reached every geopolitical entity while becoming the most global, dispersed, and diverse faith in the world.

In developing a radically new Christian theological framework by reversing the order of theological formulation for the increasingly charismatic form of spirituality, the diversity of global Christianity, and its missionary character since its beginning, Yong concludes that "Christianity was a transportable religion. Arguably its mobility lay in its capacity to accommodate itself to many different cultures, languages, and people groups."[25] It was the mobility of its adherents that took early Christians to the fringes of the Roman Empire—on account of religious persecution as well as the socioeconomic conditions stemming from Pax Romana—and that spread Christianity throughout the Mediterranean rim and beyond. About the early history of Christianity, Adolf Harnack notes that "the apostles as well as many of the prophets travelled unceasingly in the interest of their mission. Paul . . . [and] his fellow workers and companions were also continually on [the] move."[26] Christians are mobile people, since they get unhinged from the geographical, sociocultural, fiscal, and political bondages to particular localities. The second-century anonymous *Epistle to Diognetus* notes, "For Christians are no different from other people in terms of their country, language or customs. . . . They live in their countries but only as resident aliens; they participate in all things as citizens, and they endure all things as foreigners. For every foreign territory is a homeland for them, every homeland foreign territory."[27]

The nature of the Christian faith is that its center lies outside the circumference, which continually pivots itself with new people and new centers. In establishing the nature of the church for the reign of God, Gustavo Gutiérrez contends, "Its [the church's] existence is not 'for itself' but rather 'for others.' Its center is outside itself; it is in the work of Christ and his Spirit."[28] So the mission is pivoting the message of the gospel of the risen Jesus outside the walls of the church with an eschatological orientation and pneumatological empowerment. No wonder the ancient Greek mathematician Archimedes came out with the principle of the lever and fulcrum that is widely used in common gadgets and engineering applications; he claimed that he could "move the Earth if he had a place to stand outside of it and a lever long enough."[29] The Christian faith is translatable and continually engaged in tweaking its scriptural interpretation and practices for those outside its fold. Lamin Sanneh claims that vernacular translations of the Bible have played central catalytic roles in the spread of the Christian faith.[30] The Christian message can be expressed in any language and interpreted into any culture. The Christian faith is at home in any culture, and it cannot be bound within any culture or geography, for its very nature makes it diffuse across cultural lines. The translatability factor helped it spread to new cultures across many regions of Africa, Asia, and Latin America in the last few centuries. I argue that it is the mobility that results in its translatability, as displacement creates the need to bridge the linguistic divide. It is evident from the Great European Migration and the modern missionary movement that people who had richly benefited from the scriptural translations in their native tongues became exceptional champions for the cause of translating the Bible into the vernacular languages of the people and places to which those missionaries went.

Several new theologies of mission have taken *journey, sojourner, pilgrim, hospitality, migration, alien,* and *exile* as major theological motifs to understand the contemporary Christian mission for a world that is in perpetual motion.[31] Some have maintained that *journey* does not offer a helpful analytical concept for describing Paul's missionary praxis, since he lived and worked in Corinth and Ephesus for two years each.[32] However, I argue that the detailed accounts of Paul's travels, ministry, and writings have emerged because he was a product of the Jewish diaspora, his work began with diasporic settlers, and his distinctive conceptualization of the gospel from a diasporic vantage point liberated it beyond Jewish captivity into the broader gentile world.[33] An apt metaphor for doing mission in the age of migration is "shooting a moving target." Our theologies and strategies for mission engagement have to be completely reinvented in the context of global migration. Many unreached people groups are no longer confined within the 10/40 Window or any particular geographical region but have now relocated to other nations. As in archery, strategies to shoot a fixed target and a moving target are poles apart, and archers are trained to shoot not where the target is at present but where it will be when the arrow reaches it. This requires anticipating where the target is going, creative and quick thinking, mastering one's equipment, taking into account the environment, and being prepared for high failure rates.

A major development at the turn of the twenty-first century was the move (or shift) of "the center of gravity of Christianity" in the world from the Global North to the Global South, first noted by Andrew F. Walls, and subsequently, many have examined it at length only to confirm the trend and its far-reaching repercussions.[34] Christianity has a universal savior and is now more global, geographically dispersed, and diverse than it has ever been in its entire history—closer to "the full stature of Christ" (Eph 4:13). This Ephesian moment holds tremendous potential for increased momentum in mission but also poses many new challenges. Christians from other cultures and regions of the world can enrich our understanding of the faith, remedy our mistakes, enlarge our parochial perspectives, and help us gain a fuller perspective of God's moving work among all peoples of the world.

Undoubtedly, one of the major theological innovations of the last century is the notion of *missio Dei*, understanding mission as God's mission.[35] Based on a Barthian conceptualization, mission is no longer perceived as an activity of the church but an attribute of God derived from the very nature of God and framed within the context of the doctrine of the Trinity, not based on ecclesiology or soteriology. Mission is seen as a movement from God to the world, and the church is viewed as an instrument of that mission. Such a movement is not limited to a particular incident or age, but God is continually moving toward the world and his creation to recreate them and establish his reign. The development of missional ecclesiology further emphasizes the sending nature of God and the church.[36] However, it fortifies the critical role of the sending bodies, the sociocultural and economic disparity between senders and receivers, the reproduction of sending institutional cultures, unhealthy dependencies, a lopsided power structure, and a form of neocolonialism.[37] The sending model is incongruous for reimagining the work of God in a postcolonial, post-Western, post-Enlightenment, post-Christendom, and postmission era.[38] The contemporary mission praxis is from everywhere to everywhere, is multilateral, is multidirectional, involves sending as well as receiving, and has a polycentric meshed network requiring it to be conceived as having a polycentrifugal and polycentripetal flow. Multidirectional scattering and gathering are helpful motifs to understand the contemporary moving of God in the world.

Conclusion

Christianity is a missionary faith par excellence, since it is a faith that was born to travel. In fact, the mobility of its adherents and the moving nature of God are what make the Christian faith a transportable and translatable faith, as it continually transcends borders of all kinds over time. The movement of people is of utmost significance to the Christian faith, as displaced people have reconfigured the contours of its growth and expansion throughout its history. Since its inception, Christianity has diffused across cultural and geographical lines repeatedly, and many different people in varied places have been the chief representatives of Christianity. The Christian faith cannot be bound to a location or domesticated by any people because its nature is to break free of the prisons we enshrine it in. It must move from one place to another continually because it is a quintessential missionary, translatable, and mobile faith. Seeing God as a moving person and his ongoing work as a result of the moving of God is a helpful way to develop a theology and missiology for a moving world. A fresh formulation using *motus Dei* can help in this regard, and it is consistent with the biblical, historical, and ongoing work of God in the world.

Notes

1 John Stott, "Living God Is a Missionary God," in *Perspectives on the World Christian Movement: A Reader*, ed. Ralph Winter and Steve Hawthorne (Pasadena, CA: William Carey, 2013), 3–9; Christopher Wright, *The Mission of God: Unlocking the Bible's Grand Narrative* (Downers Grove, IL: InterVarsity Academic, 2006), 71–74.

2 John Stott, *The Message of Acts*, Bible Speaks Today Series (Downers Grove, IL: InterVarsity Academic, 1994), 131.

3 Amos Yong, *The Missiological Spirit: Christian Mission Theology in the Third Millennium Global Context* (Eugene, OR: Cascade, 2014);

Wonsuk Ma and Julia Ma, *Mission in the Spirit: Toward a Pentecostal/Charismatic Missiology* (Oxford: Regnum, 2011); Craig Keener, *Spirit Hermeneutics: Reading Scripture in Light of Pentecost* (Grand Rapids, MI: Eerdmans, 2017).

4 Alister McGrath, *Christian Theology: An Introduction* (Malden, MA: Blackwell, 2011), 325.

5 See John D. Zizioulas, *Being as Communion: Studies in Personhood and the Church* (London: Darton, Longman & Todd, 1985); Miroslav Volf, *After Our Likeness: The Church as the Image of the Trinity* (Grand Rapids, MI: Eerdmans, 1998), 217.

6 Catherine LaCugna, *God for Us: The Trinity and Christian Life* (San Francisco: Harper, 1993), 353.

7 Kevin Vanhoozer, "Human Beings: Individual and Social," in *Cambridge Companion to Christian Doctrine*, ed. Colin Gunter (New York: Cambridge University Press, 1997), 177.

8 John Calvin, *Commentaries on the Last Four Books of Moses* (Grand Rapids, MI: Eerdmans, 1964), 116–17.

9 G. K. Baele, *We Become What We Worship: A Biblical Theology of Idolatry* (Carol Stream, IL: InterVarsity, 2008), 44–49.

10 Paul G. Hiebert, *Transforming Worldviews: An Anthropological Understanding of How People Change* (Grand Rapids, MI: Baker Academic, 2008), 117. See Jehu J. Hanciles, *Migration and the Making of Global Christianity* (Grand Rapids, MI: Eerdmans, 2021), 130.

11 Kosuke Koyama, *Mount Fuji and Mount Sinai: A Critique of Idols* (Maryknoll, NY: Orbis, 1985), 88.

12 Augustine, *Confessions*, trans. Rex Warner (New York: Mentor, 1963), 1.1.1 (emphasis and translation mine).

13 Andrew F. Walls, "Towards a Theology of Migration," in *African Christian Presence in the West: New Immigrant Congregations and Transnational Networks in North America and Europe*, ed. Frieder Ludwig and Kwabena Asamoah-Gyadu (Trenton, NJ: Africa World, 2011), 407–17.

14 Daniel Groody, "Homebound: A Theology of Migration," *Journal of Catholic Social Thought* 9, no. 2 (Summer 2012): 409–24.

15 Daniel Migliore, *Faith Seeking Understanding: An Introduction to Christian Theology* (Grand Rapids, MI: Eerdmans, 1991), 128.

16 Yong, *Missiological Spirit*, 129–31.

17 Timothy L. Smith, "Religion and Ethnicity in America," *American Historical Review* 83, no. 5 (1978): 1181.

18 Sam George, "Crossing *Kala Pani*: Overcoming Religious Barriers to Migration," in *Diaspora Christianities: Global Scattering and Gathering of South Asian Christians*, ed. Sam George (Minneapolis: Fortress, 2018), 69–83.

19 Sam George, "Diaspora Mission and North American Muslims," *Evangelical Missions Quarterly* 56, no. 3 (July–September 2020): 35–37.

20 Lamin Sanneh, *Translating the Message: The Missionary Impact on Culture*, 2nd ed. (Maryknoll, NY: Orbis, 2009), 262.

21 Walter A. Elwell, *Evangelical Dictionary of Theology* (Grand Rapids, MI: Baker, 1984), 555.

22 Jürgen Moltmann, *The Living God and the Fullness of Life* (Geneva: World Council of Churches, 2015), 26. See also Jürgen Moltmann, *The Crucified God* (Minneapolis: Fortress, 2015).

23 Craig Ott, Stephen Strauss, and Timothy Tennent, *Encountering Theology of Mission* (Grand Rapids, MI: Zondervan, 2010), 90. See writings on *missio Dei* by Karl Hartenstein, Karl Barth, Leslie Newbigin, Darrel Guder, Alan Hirsch, and others.

24 See Jürgen Moltmann, *Theology of Hope* (Minneapolis: Fortress, 1983).

25 Amos Yong, *Renewing Christian Theology: Systematics for a Global Christianity* (Waco, TX: Baylor University Press, 2014), 2.

26 Adolf Harnack, *The Expansion of Christianity in the First Three Centuries* (London: Williams & Norgate, 1904), 463.

27 Bart D. Ehrman, trans. and ed., *The Apostolic Fathers*, vol. 2, Loeb Classical Library (Boston: Harvard University Press, 2003), 139, 141.

28 Gustavo Gutiérrez, *Theology of Liberation* (Maryknoll, NY: Orbis, 1973), 260.

29 Quoted by Plutarch in *Marcellus*, written in 75 CE. http://classics.mit.edu/Plutarch/marcellu.html.

30 Sanneh, *Translating the Message*.

31 See Charles Van Engen, *Mission on the Way: Issues in Mission Theology* (Grand Rapids, MI: Baker, 1996); Michael Frost, *Exiles: Living Missionally in a Post-Christian Culture* (Grand Rapids, MI: Baker, 2006); Gemma T. Cruz, *Pilgrim in the Wilderness: An Intercultural Theology of Migration* (Leiden: Brill, 2010); Christine Pohl, *Making Room: Recovering Hospitality as a Christian Tradition* (Grand Rapids, MI: Eerdmans, 1999); Michael Stroope, *Transcending Mission: The Eclipse of a Modern Tradition* (Downers Grove, IL: InterVarsity Academic, 2017); John Flett, *The Witness of God: Missio Dei, Karl Barth and the Nature of Christian Community* (Grand Rapids, MI: Eerdmans, 2010); Craig Bartholomew and Fred Hughes, eds., *Explorations in a Christian Theology of Pilgrimage* (London: Routledge, 2016); and others.

32 Eckhard Schnabel, *Early Christian Mission*, vol. 2, *Paul and the Early Church* (Downers Grove, IL: InterVarsity Academic, 2004), 1445.

33 See John M. G. Barclay, *Pauline Churches and Diaspora Jews* (Grand Rapids, MI: Eerdmans, 2016).

34 Andrew F. Walls, *The Cross-Cultural Process in Christian History: Studies in the Transmission and Appropriation of Faith* (Maryknoll, NY: Orbis, 2002), 45–47. See writings on "Christendom" by Philip Jenkins, *The Next Christendom: The Coming of Global Christianity* (New York: Oxford University Press, 2002); Jehu J. Hanciles, *Beyond Christendom: Globalization, African Migration, and the Transformation of the West* (Maryknoll, NY: Orbis, 2008); Orlando Costas; Ogbu Kalu; and others.

35 David Bosch, *Transforming Mission: Paradigm Shifts in Theology of Mission* (Maryknoll, NY: Orbis, 2001), 390. See also J. Andrew Kirk, *What Is Mission? Theological Exploration* (Minneapolis: Fortress,

2000); Henning Wrogemann, *Theologies of Mission* (Downers Grove, IL: InterVarsity, 2018); Ott, Strauss, and Tennent, *Encountering Theology of Mission*; Charles Van Engen, *Transforming Mission Theology* (Pasadena, CA: William Carey Library, 2017).

36 Darrell Guder, *Missional Church: A Vision for the Sending of the Church in North America* (Grand Rapids, MI: Eerdmans, 1998). Also see the writings of Leslie Newbigin, Ross Hasting, Alan Hirsch, etc.

37 See Stroope, *Transcending Mission*; Flett, *Witness of God*, 201; John Flett and David Congdon, eds., *Converting Witness: The Future of the Christian Mission in New Millennium* (Lanham, MD: Lexington, 2019); Anthony Gittins, *Ministry at the Margins: Strategy and Spirituality for Mission* (Maryknoll, NY: Orbis, 2002); Christopher Wright, *The Mission of God's People: A Biblical Theology of the Church's Mission* (Grand Rapids, MI: Zondervan Academic, 2010); Allen Yeh, *Polycentric Missiology: Twenty-First Century Mission from Everyone to Everywhere* (Downers Grove, IL: InterVarsity Academic, 2016).

38 Amos Yong, *Mission after Pentecost: The Witness of the Spirit from Genesis to Revelation* (Grand Rapids, MI: Baker Academic, 2019); Samuel Escobar, *The New Global Mission: The Gospel from Everywhere to Everyone* (Downers Grove, IL: InterVarsity Academic, 2003); Stroope, *Transcending Mission*, 2017.

Bibliography

Augustine. *Confessions*. Translated by Rex Warner. New York: Mentor, 1963.

Barclay, John M. G. *Pauline Churches and Diaspora Jews*. Grand Rapids, MI: Eerdmans, 2016.

Bartholomew, Craig, and Fred Hughes, eds. *Explorations in a Christian Theology of Pilgrimage*. London: Routledge, 2016.

Beale, G. K. *We Become What We Worship: A Biblical Theology of Idolatry.* Carol Stream, IL: InterVarsity, 2008.

Bosch, David. *Transforming Mission: Paradigm Shifts in Theology of Mission.* Maryknoll, NY: Orbis, 2001.

Calvin, John. *Commentaries on the Last Four Books of Moses.* Grand Rapids, MI: Eerdmans, 1964.

Cruz, Gemma T., *Pilgrim in the Wilderness: An Intercultural Theology of Migration.* Leiden: Brill, 2010.

Ehrman, Bart D., trans. and ed. *The Apostolic Fathers.* Vol. 2. Loeb Classical Library. Boston: Harvard University Press, 2003.

Elwell, Walter A. *Evangelical Dictionary of Theology.* Grand Rapids, MI: Baker, 1984.

Engen, Charles Van. *Transforming Mission Theology.* Pasadena, CA: William Carey Library, 2017.

Escobar, Samuel. *The New Global Mission: The Gospel from Everywhere to Everyone.* Downers Grove, IL: InterVarsity Academic, 2003.

Flett, John. *The Witness of God: Missio Dei, Karl Barth and the Nature of Christian Community.* Grand Rapids, MI: Eerdmans, 2010.

Flett, John, and David Congdon, eds. *Converting Witness: The Future of the Christian Mission in New Millennium.* Lanham, MD: Lexington, 2019.

Frost, Michael. *Exiles: Living Missionally in a Post-Christian Culture.* Grand Rapids, MI: Baker, 2006.

George, Sam. "Crossing *Kala Pani*: Overcoming Religious Barriers to Migration." In *Diaspora Christianities: Global Scattering and Gathering of South Asian Christians*, edited by Sam George, 69–83. Minneapolis: Fortress, 2018.

———. "Diaspora Mission and North American Muslims." *Evangelical Missions Quarterly* 56, no. 3 (July–September 2020): 35–37.

Gittins, Anthony. *Ministry at the Margins: Strategy and Spirituality for Mission.* Maryknoll, NY: Orbis, 2002.

Groody, Daniel. "Homebound: A Theology of Migration." *Journal of Catholic Social Thought* 9, no. 2 (Summer 2012): 409–424.

Guder, Darrell. *Missional Church: A Vision for the Sending of the Church in North America.* Grand Rapids, MI: Eerdmans, 1998.

Gutiérrez, Gustavo. *Theology of Liberation.* Maryknoll, NY: Orbis, 1973.

Hanciles, Jehu J. *Beyond Christendom: Globalization, African Migration, and the Transformation of the West.* Maryknoll, NY: Orbis, 2008.

———. *Migration and the Making of Global Christianity.* Grand Rapids, MI: Eerdmans, 2021.

Harnack, Adolf. *The Expansion of Christianity in the First Three Centuries.* London: Williams & Norgate, 1904.

Hiebert, Paul G. *Transforming Worldviews: An Anthropological Understanding of How People Change.* Grand Rapids, MI: Baker Academic, 2008.

Jenkins, Philip. *The Next Christendom: The Coming of Global Christianity.* New York: Oxford University Press, 2002.

Keener, Craig. *Spirit Hermeneutics: Reading Scripture in Light of Pentecost.* Grand Rapids, MI: Eerdmans, 2017.

Kirk, J. Andrew. *What Is Mission? Theological Exploration.* Minneapolis: Fortress, 2000.

Koyama, Kosuke. *Mount Fuji and Mount Sinai: A Critique of Idols.* Maryknoll, NY: Orbis, 1985.

LaCugna, Catherine. *God for Us: The Trinity and Christian Life.* San Francisco: Harper, 1993.

Ma, Wonsuk, and Julia Ma. *Mission in the Spirit: Toward a Pentecostal/ Charismatic Missiology.* Oxford: Regnum, 2011.

McGrath, Alister. *Christian Theology: An Introduction.* Malden, MA: Blackwell, 2011.

Migliore, Daniel. *Faith Seeking Understanding: An Introduction to Christian Theology.* Grand Rapids, MI: Eerdmans, 1991.

Moltmann, Jürgen. *The Crucified God.* Minneapolis: Fortress, 2015.

———. *The Living God and the Fullness of Life*. Geneva: World Council of Churches, 2015.

———. *Theology of Hope*. Minneapolis: Fortress, 1983.

Ott, Craig, Stephen Strauss, and Timothy Tennent. *Encountering Theology of Mission*. Grand Rapids, MI: Zondervan, 2010.

Pohl, Christine. *Making Room: Recovering Hospitality as a Christian Tradition*. Grand Rapids, MI: Eerdmans, 1999.

Sanneh, Lamin. *Translating the Message: The Missionary Impact on Culture*. 2nd ed. Maryknoll, NY: Orbis, 2009.

Schnabel, Eckhard. *Early Christian Mission*. Vol. 2, *Paul and the Early Church*. Downers Grove, IL: InterVarsity Academic, 2004.

Smith, Timothy L. "Religion and Ethnicity in America." *American Historical Review* 83, no. 5 (1978): 1155–1185.

Stott, John. "Living God Is a Missionary God." In *Perspectives on the World Christian Movement: A Reader*, edited by Ralph Winter and Steve Hawthorne, 3–9. Pasadena, CA: William Carey, 2013.

———. *The Message of Acts*. Bible Speaks Today Series. Downers Grove, IL: InterVarsity Academic, 1994.

Stroope, Michael. *Transcending Mission: The Eclipse of a Modern Tradition*. Downers Grove, IL: InterVarsity Academic, 2017.

Van Engen, Charles. *Mission on the Way: Issues in Mission Theology*. Grand Rapids, MI: Baker, 1996.

Vanhoozer, Kevin. "Human Beings: Individual and Social." In *Cambridge Companion to Christian Doctrine*, edited by Colin Gunter, 158–188. New York: Cambridge University Press, 1997.

Volf, Miroslav. *After Our Likeness: The Church as the Image of the Trinity*. Grand Rapids, MI: Eerdmans, 1998.

Walls, Andrew F. *The Cross-Cultural Process in Christian History: Studies in the Transmission and Appropriation of Faith*. Maryknoll, NY: Orbis, 2002.

———. "Culture and Coherence in Christian History." *Scottish Bulletin of Evangelical Theology* (Spring 1985): 1–10.

———. "Towards a Theology of Migration." In *African Christian Presence in the West: New Immigrant Congregations and Transnational Networks in North America and Europe*, edited by Frieder Ludwig and Kwabena Asamoah-Gyadu, 407–417. Trenton, NJ: Africa World, 2011.

Wright, Christopher. *The Mission of God: Unlocking the Bible's Grand Narrative*. Downers Grove, IL: InterVarsity Academic, 2006.

———. *The Mission of God's People: A Biblical Theology of the Church's Mission*. Grand Rapids, MI: Zondervan Academic, 2010.

Wrogemann, Henning. *Theologies of Mission*. Downers Grove, IL: InterVarsity, 2018.

Yeh, Allen. *Polycentric Missiology: Twenty-First Century Mission from Everyone to Everywhere*. Downers Grove, IL: InterVarsity Academic, 2016.

Yong, Amos. *The Missiological Spirit: Christian Mission Theology in the Third Millennium Global Context*. Eugene, OR: Cascade, 2014.

———. *Mission after Pentecost: The Witness of the Spirit from Genesis to Revelation*. Grand Rapids, MI: Baker Academic, 2019.

———. *Renewing Christian Theology: Systematics for a Global Christianity*. Waco, TX: Baylor University Press, 2014.

Zizioulas, John D. *Being as Communion: Studies in Personhood and the Church*. London: Darton, Longman & Todd, 1985.

5

Diaspora, Origins, and Asian American Theology

Daniel D. Lee

Contemporary diaspora studies have dispelled myths of essentialized identities and eternal homelands by revealing the complexities of concrete lives.[1] These complexities exist whether referring to the Jewish community, the etymological ground zero of "diaspora," or migration communities throughout history, including numerous Asian diasporic communities around the world. Three conceptual categories—"heterogeneity, hybridity, multiplicity"—mark the Asian American experience and respectively refer to the internal diversity of Asian Americans, cultural intermixing for survival under domination, and the locations within multiple axes of power. Lisa Lowe, in a provocative essay, uses the above lens to study the negotiation of ethnic and pan-ethnic racial identities necessitated by sociopolitical pressures and expediencies.[2]

The internal and contextual differences of Asian Americans mean that there is also an "ideological heterogeneity" of self-understanding among various Asian American communities.[3] Are Asians living in America with their hearts back in the motherland, forever foreigners in the United States? Or are they Americans of Asian descent with 170 years of history and struggle as marginalized racial minorities? Is being yellow/brown people living as model minorities or in peril two sides of the same otherizing coin? Or are Asian Americans part of the Third World subalterns in solidarity, transcending the discrete boundaries of nation-states?

In this chapter, bringing these theoretical abstractions to the ground, I offer a typology of various Asian American origins.[4] This typology can be used to analyze how an individual or a community understands Asian American identity and what the Christian faith means in light of that understanding. The four types of Asian American origins are *personal* history, *ethnic* history, *racial* history, and *postcolonial* history. For each, I explain how the origin and homeland are understood and provide a corresponding Asian American historiography and discuss its implications for the task of Asian American theology. Each type has its uses and limitations, although some are more problematic than others, especially in light of theological adequacy.

Four Types of Asian American Origins and Theology

The origins and the corresponding theology of Asian Americans emerge out of what I have observed in studies and theological literature as well as Asian American Christians whom I have interacted with over the last two decades. As stated above, not only do the experiences of Asian Americans vary significantly, but their level of critical contextual awareness also ranges widely. While this typology, like any other, possesses theoretical deficiencies, such as putting real-life transgressive complexities into seemingly clear-cut discrete categories, it can still serve as a diagnostic tool to discern the theological and contextual substructures of Asian American Christian spiritualities.

Personal History

The first type understands Asian American origins narrowly in terms of one's personal or familial history. This type can be labeled a nonhistory of Asian American origins in the sense that it lacks a historical consciousness of Asian American identity. In this individualistic venue, Asian American history began with one's family coming to the United States. Any history before that belongs to Asia. This connection back to Asia, however, is tenuous because what matters is a personal experience, and with each passing year, this connection diminishes. The homeland is directly connected to one's personal history (birthplace and childhood home). *Asian America* is simply a descriptor for a conglomerate of various peoples from Asia or of Asian descent.

There are numerous reasons why many hold this view of Asian American identity and origins. Personal experiences are distinct depending on the historical period and ethnic community. The sufferings that resulted from the Chinese Exclusion Act of 1882 were registered differently from the relief experienced from the Refugee Act of 1980. The personal emphasis can be understood as an expression of the enormous diversity of Asian American experiences. When commonality seems tenuous, the personal becomes more salient. The erasure of Asian Americans, along with other minorities, from the white normative vision of US history results from their absence in public education curricula and the lack of a broader public consciousness about them. Historically, white nationalism has rejected Asian Americans as perpetual or forever foreigners, never to be accepted as true Americans unless they fully assimilate and leave behind their Asianness, which they can never completely do. The white dominance and assimilation pressures also function under the guise of color blindness.[5] Inculcated with and internalizing this dominant white narrative, many Asian Americans lack a historical sense of their origins or any sociopolitical consciousness, ultimately rejecting the very idea of a social identity.

Such an ahistorical view is common even among highly educated Asian Americans. For example, in Eric Liu's *The Accidental Asian*, he questions the notion of Asian American identity while affirming his Chinese family roots. Without understanding race or history, Liu lists various personal preferences and characteristics that make him "white."[6] Though he experiences racism personally, he fails to see its roots beyond himself in a broadly systemic and societal purview. His concerns about racial tokenism and essentialism are valid because a pan-ethnic political identity can result in another form of invisibility and marginality through ethnic monopolization by one group over the whole. For example, brown South Asian Americans protest the yellow dominance of East Asian American identity. Nevertheless, Liu misses the nature of racial forces that face all Asian Americans and, thus, unite them as a political community.

Theologically, American Christianity is part and parcel of American white normativity. The Pentecostal theologian Amos Yong summarizes the white evangelical theological outlook as "a-historical, a-cultural, and even a-contextual."[7]

Many Asian American pastors and ministries espouse a similar outlook. Besides these theological features, individualism is deeply entrenched in American Christianity, especially evangelicalism, and tends to steer toward an ahistorical and individualistic conception of Asian Americanness.[8] The white normative faith that passes itself as universal offers a color-blind Christian identity in exchange for a socially cumbersome Asian American identity. Being "in Christ" signifies a disembodied reality where earthly particularities cease to be relevant. The pastor and speaker Francis Chan is a good example of this kind of theology, as the Chinese/Asian aspects of his identity are merely decorative at best, having little to no relevance to his color-blind ministry or faith.

In a doctrinal evaluation, this theology that claims acontextual universality suffers from Docetism. The God revealed in Christ is not an abstract spiritual principle or theistic ideal, eternal and aloof, but rather covenantal, encountering and engaging creation in concrete particularities in time and space.[9] When this covenantal God is abandoned, no longer to be sought and encountered in living freedom, a tamed and abstract set of doctrines, morals, or philosophical concepts fill the divine absence. This naked divinity, replacing the fleshed God revealed in the first-century Palestinian Jewish Jesus, allows ethereal discipleship that is blind to the sociopolitical plight of neighbors and ethical struggles beyond categorical imperatives.

The gospel's reach is total, meaning Christ's rule is personal, familial, communal, societal, and cosmic. Thus, personal and familial histories need to be fully owned and taken up spiritually and theologically. However, Asian American Christians with a narrow individualistic idea of their sociohistorical origins struggle to engage in informed and significant political activism because they lack historical and structural awareness. While Christian discipleship and ministry should not be reduced to politics, gospel faithfulness cannot be otherworldly quietism either. Whether regarding the Black Lives Matter movement or the migration crisis, the gospel according to these Asian American Christians offers little guidance in living out kingdom witness either as individual Christians or as the corporate faith community.

Ethnic History

The second type of Asian American origins is ethnic history. The focus is on one's ethnic and cultural heritage, not race or structural racism. Culture and ethnicity in this narrow sense are attractive to conservative Christianity, with its strong convictions about global missions and mission history. Asian American Christians who hold such a narrow ethnic-cultural understanding of their Asian Americanness focus on cultural contextualization. Depending on how white normative their theological outlook is, the contextualizing agenda might be the task of identifying cultural encroachments on pure biblical faith or a more progressive redeeming of cultural heritage. Their homeland is either in Asia or in transition from Asia to the United States, and they become American in the process.

From this perspective, Asian American history is received and understood as the histories of the myriad of Asian immigrants who eventually became "Americans" like all other immigrants. Consider Ronald Takaki's *Strangers from a Different Shore*, which captures the history of Asian Americans and alludes to John Higham's *Strangers in the Land*, which covers the nativism experienced by Italian, Jewish, Irish, and other European immigrants as they slowly but surely became part of American society.[10] Takaki addresses racialization but more as an expression of why nativism and exclusion continue, and inclusion remains a challenge for Asian Americans. Takaki's agenda is to prove the Americanness of Asian Americans, and the idea of the United States as a multicultural nation of immigrants serves as its basis. The Asian American movement as a pan-ethnic development is noted clearly, but the chronological narration of Asian American history questions how later Asian immigrant groups can adopt this movement, which is rooted in Chinese and Japanese communities, as their own. Moreover, the national framing glosses over the history of American imperialism in Asia, a history that locates Filipino American history as well as that of Pacific Islanders.

With a long-standing history of violence, oppression, and wars in Asia, it is challenging for Asian Americans of one ethnic heritage to incorporate the history of a different ethnic group. Japanese American incarceration as the experience of racially oppressed Americans is quite removed from Japanese imperialism in Asia, but the cultural connection can be disconcerting for many Korean Americans and Chinese Americans. Any political solidarity of Indian Americans with Pakistani Americans is historically overladen. Since no pan-Asian identity exists in Asia given the nationalistic divisions, a pan-ethnic Asian American identity is a hurdle, especially for recent immigrants.

Erika Lee's *The Making of Asian America*, with its stress on the ethnic plurality of Asian American histories, can be read in a similar fashion, where the pan-ethnic movement is mistakenly relegated to a singular historical moment. To be clear, what I am arguing is that Takaki and Lee can be erroneously and reductively read that way when the American archetype of individualism is renounced because ethnic diversity is stressed over racial solidarity in their chronological presentations of Asian American history. The reason for this misreading is that the radical politics of the Third World Liberation Front (TWLF) of 1968, with Marxist underpinnings, are unpalatable to many Asian Americans with a historical memory of Communist atrocities in Asia as well as to Asian American Christians who recall Marxist atheism. Properly incorporating the TWLF and its critical insights into Asian American history is fundamental because it defined and catalyzed the Asian American movement. As we will see in the next two types of origins, the decisive question will be where the Asian American movement should be located in narrating Asian American history because before the TWLF, *Asian American* did not exist.

Many Asian American ministry resources such as *Following Jesus without Dishonoring Your Parents* or *Growing Healthy Asian American Churches* fall under this type, framing the spiritual issues as ethnic or cultural. Asian cultural heritage persists in Asian American life and is passed down to later generations embedded within values and practices and through family system dynamics and transgenerational epigenetics. To name this cultural heritage and to theologically engage it is vital for the work of discipleship, allowing the gospel to deeply transform the whole person, working below superficial religious compliance to white spirituality. However, when the Asian American experience is only understood from this cultural perspective, Asian American identity and features can easily be pathologized because the societal forces that Orientalize these elements remain largely invisible without structural critiques. Some examples of such structural critiques include exposing the racism embedded in American immigration and naturalization laws or Asian American misrepresentation or nonrepresentation in American mass media and its impact on Asian American minds and hearts.[11] With white normativity within their Christianity unquestioned, the only path remaining is to problematize Asianness. While Asian cultural values are indeed fallen and in need of redemption like all others, this approach ends up unduly singling them out with accusations of syncretism and cultural encroachment.

Many Asian American Christians with this ethnic conception of their origins are political quietists like those of the first type. Those who do engage in political activism do so either detached from their acontextual faith or as honorary whites who are learning from Black theological traditions. I have seen Asian Americans in progressive spaces disparage "Asian Americans" as a whole for their collective ignorance and compliancy without any reference to the broader and historic Asian American movement. While the Black liberation tradition has much to offer, there is an Asian American tradition as well, which will help locate the specificity of the Asian American perspective and struggle more accurately. Grasping only ethnic identity and with personal experience limited to their conservative churches, these Asian American Christians are eluded by the broader history of Asian American pan-ethnic racial identity and activism.

Racial History

The third type of Asian American origins involves the TWLF, understood as bringing about the beginnings of ethnic studies and "Asian American" pan-ethnic identity formulated for political activism. As Frank H. Wu explains, Asian Americans are "made, not born," self-inventing "collectively and individually in the United States" with no true physical place of origin on a map.[12] The homeland under this type is the United States, where Asian American identity was created through the process of racialization in the crucible of racism. Later generations of Asian Americans often do not consider their ethnic cultural heritage as impactful as their racial identities. Thus, the idea of solidarity with other minoritized Americans becomes most salient as they seek out a helpful rubric for social engagement.

In terms of Asian American historiography, the radical and political agenda of Shelley Sang-Hee Lee's *A New History of Asian America* is qualitatively different from that of Ronald Takaki or Erika Lee.[13] Instead of presenting Asian Americans as part of immigrant America in a progressive chronological manner, Shelley uses "the salience of race" from the Asian American perspective as a programmatic linchpin. From chapter 1 onward, she maintains this focus on race, starting the narration from early European Orientalism, and throughout her book, she keeps the pan-ethnic racial Asian American identity as a clear interpretative rubric even when taking up ethnic-specific historical episodes. Her work allows no wiggle room to circumvent the radical roots of Asian America for a lighter history of ethnic immigrants—no way to miss the shared racial lot of Asian Americans of all ethnic heritages.

Jung Young Lee's *Marginality* and Sang Hyun Lee's *From a Liminal Place* come close to this racial orientation for organizing their Asian American theologies.[14] For them, Asian Americans exist at the margins of both Asia and America in "coerced liminality" and present a Christ who resists the hegemonic powers of the centers. However, these works focus on mostly personal experiences of racism, missing the larger history and structures of racism in the United States, as Shelley addresses. A more robust Asian American theology from this racial angle would target the dismantling of America's racialist foundations from the particular lens of Asian American history and experience. In this vein, Soong-Chan Rah's *The Next Evangelicalism* grasps the larger narrative of racism better, although its Asian American aspect is quite weak, limited to Korean Americans.

This racial origin connects Asian American Christians with the kind of historical knowledge and depth about the United States as a nation to resource and develop their political activism qua Asian Americans, not as Asians in America or as honorary whites. Racism as America's original sin, as part of the powers and principalities that rule this world, is named in order to resist the faithful witness of God's kingdom. The limitation of this type is that race as a totalizing category ends up homogenizing all Asian Americans, ignoring internal diversity, and further marginalizing those with underrepresented ethnic heritages. Also, this narrow racial thinking can dismiss ethnic-cultural remnants still residing deep below the surface.

Postcolonial History

The final and fourth type of Asian American origins again finds its inception with the TWLF but this time understood as the beginning of Third World studies and an anti-imperial, anti-colonial movement beyond the national racial dynamics in the United States. Asian America began with Western desire and imperialism in Asia, since "Asians did not go to America; Americans went to Asia."[15] Instead of the narrative of America as a nation of immigrants, we move beyond the boundaries of modern nation-states to interrogate hegemonic forces of imperialism and colonialism.

According to Gary Y. Okihiro, the idea of ethnic studies is a reductive miscarriage of what student protests sought in the late 1960s. Rather than separating out Asian Americans as a racial group, the TWLF members understood their fate as joined with the subalterns of the Third World. Their agenda was bound not by national racial polities but rather by transnational dynamics of empires and capitalism, eradicating oppression resulting from social formations. Along a similar trajectory as Shelley Sang-Hee Lee, Okihiro's *American History Unbound* moves nationally and transnationally to situate the United States as a nation among nations contra its exceptionalism. Using world-systems theory to expose the capitalism and imperialism and the idea of ocean worlds to recover the significance of islands along with the so-called continents, this innovative work reorganizes conventional narrations of Asian American history and beyond.[16] One of its many benefits is the full inclusion of the often-marginalized Pacific Islanders and their peoples within Asian American history. Unseating Chinese and Californian exceptionalism within Asian American historiography, Okihiro offers a more robust basis for the pan-ethnic solidarity as well as the significance of Asian Americans in the world.

Roy Sano compiled the earliest Asian American theological work, following closely from the TWLF protests.[17] It employs the faith of Asian Americans to make sense of the revolutionary and liberation fervor that they saw around them. However, when Third World studies became ethnic studies, radical liberation understandings gave way to cultural concerns or even communal or personal ones, especially as later immigrants of the 1980s subscribed to a more conservative Christianity and politics, similar to that seen in the first two types above. PANAAWTM (Pacific, Asian, and North American Asian Women in Theology and Ministry) shares similar transnational and radically liberative sensitivities.[18]

With this "Third World" understanding of Asian American origins, the scope of political activism for Asian American Christians would be much broader or more radical. One example involves better perceiving the role of the United States as an empire. In what ways did confessing that "Jesus Christ is Lord" subvert and confront the Roman Empire and its emperor in the early church? What is the cost of discipleship and witness in contemporary American society, with its rampant nationalism, nativism, and racism? Another example entails critiquing and rejecting the evils of capitalism. Rejecting the script of the model minority myth, what does seeking God's kingdom for economic justice globally look like personally and communally?

In sum, the first type of Asian American origins—personal history—affirms immediate experience in its particularity, lacking a historical understanding of Asian American origins. This type is unacceptable, since it lacks adequate contextual awareness and understanding. Its acontextual theology fails to address the covenantal God of revelation faithfully. However, this type is useful in the identification and analysis of those who hold it in real life. The last three complement one another while playing specific roles. As the second type, ethnic history highlights the need to identify and engage Asian cultural heritage. By itself, it is open to Orientalist societal manipulations, but if it is accepted along with the last two, the focus on ethnicity serves an important purpose in terms of theology and ministry. The third type, racial history, is crucial for Asian America to be properly understood, especially its radical and liberation roots. For Asian Americans to be activists, they must be fully aware of historical and structural racism and actively resist its reductive and oppressive powers. To comprehend the social location of Asian Americans, this type must be incorporated. At the same time, ethnic history can ensure that political representation is not advanced at the cost of internal diversity. Last, the fourth type, postcolonial history, situates Asian Americans globally and protects the racial understanding from becoming provincial and nationalistic. While conceptually sophisticated and analytically impressive, its weakness is that its high-level perspective can feel too abstract for the everyday experiences of Asian Americans.

Conclusion

This chapter presented a typology of Asian American origins and their corresponding historiographies and theologies. Deep contextual awareness is vital for theology because it is in our particularities that we hear God's word and are called to follow our particular vocations. Just like Moses, Esther, Daniel, and others in Scripture who were living under the shadow of empires and had their own spiritual and ethical callings from God, in like manner, Asian American Christians are called to bear a particular witness to such a time as this.

Notes

1 Jana Evans Braziel and Anita Mannur, eds., *Theorizing Diaspora: A Reader* (Malden, MA: Blackwell, 2003).

2 Lisa Lowe, "Heterogeneity, Hybridity, Multiplicity: Marking Asian American Differences," *Diaspora: A Journal of Transnational Studies* 1, no. 1 (1991): 24.

3 Viet Thanh Nguyen, *Race and Resistance: Literature and Politics in Asian America* (New York: Oxford University Press, 2002), 6–7.

4 I am indebted to Justin Tse for this insight regarding the plurality of Asian American historiography.

5 Ian Haney López, *White by Law: The Legal Construction of Race*, 10th ed. (New York: New York University Press, 2006).

6 Eric Liu, *The Accidental Asian: Notes of a Native Speaker* (New York: Vintage, 1998), 33–34.

7 Amos Yong, *The Future of Evangelical Theology: Soundings from the Asian American Diaspora* (Downers Grove, IL: InterVarsity, 2014), 114.

8 See Soong-Chan Rah, *The Next Evangelicalism: Freeing the Church from Western Cultural Captivity* (Downers Grove, IL: InterVarsity, 2009).

9 Daniel D. Lee, *Double Particularity: Karl Barth, Contextuality, and Asian American Theology* (Minneapolis: Fortress, 2017), 69.

10 See Ronald Takaki, *Strangers from a Different Shore: A History of Asian Americans*, rev. ed. (Boston: Little, Brown, 1998); John Higham, *Strangers in the Land: Patterns of American Nativism, 1860–1925* (New Brunswick, NJ: Rutgers University Press, 1955).

11 See López, *White by Law*; Kent A. Ono and Vincent N. Pham, *Asian Americans and the Media* (Malden, MA: Polity, 2009).

12 Frank H. Wu, *Yellow: Race in America beyond Black and White* (New York: Basic, 2002), 306.

13 Shelley Sang-Hee Lee, *A New History of Asian America* (New York: Routledge, 2014).

14 Jung Young Lee, *Marginality: The Key to Multicultural Theology* (Minneapolis: Fortress, 1995); Sang Hyun Lee, *From a Liminal Place: An Asian American Theology* (Minneapolis: Fortress, 2010).

15 Gary Y. Okihiro, *Third World Studies: Theorizing Liberation* (Durham, NC: Duke University Press, 2016), 9.

16 Gary Y. Okihiro, *American History Unbound: Asians and Pacific Islanders* (Oakland: University of California Press, 2015).

17 Roy Sano, ed., *The Theologies of Asian Americans and Pacific Peoples: A Reader* (Berkeley, CA: Asian Center for Theology & Strategies, 1976).

18 Rita Nakashima Brock et al., *Off the Menu: Asian and Asian North American Women's Religion and Theology* (Louisville, KY: Westminster John Knox, 2007).

Bibliography

Braziel, Jana Evans, and Anita Mannur, eds. *Theorizing Diaspora: A Reader*. Malden, MA: Blackwell, 2003.

Brock, Rita Nakashima, Jung Ha Kim, Kwok Pui-lan, and Seung Ai Yang, eds. *Off the Menu: Asian and Asian North American Women's Religion and Theology*. Louisville, KY: Westminster John Knox, 2007.

Higham, John. *Strangers in the Land: Patterns of American Nativism, 1860–1925*. New Brunswick, NJ: Rutgers University Press, 1955.

Lee, Daniel D. *Double Particularity: Karl Barth, Contextuality, and Asian American Theology*. Minneapolis: Fortress, 2017.

Lee, Erika. *The Making of Asian America: A History*. New York: Simon & Schuster, 2015.

Lee, Jung Young. *Marginality: The Key to Multicultural Theology*. Minneapolis: Fortress, 1995.

Lee, Sang Hyun. *From a Liminal Place: An Asian American Theology*. Minneapolis: Fortress, 2010.

Lee, Shelley Sang-Hee. *A New History of Asian America*. New York: Routledge, 2014.

Liu, Eric. *The Accidental Asian: Notes of a Native Speaker*. New York: Vintage, 1998.

López, Ian Haney. *White by Law: The Legal Construction of Race*. 10th ed. New York: New York University Press, 2006.

Lowe, Lisa. "Heterogeneity, Hybridity, Multiplicity: Marking Asian American Differences." *Diaspora: A Journal of Transnational Studies* 1, no. 1 (1991): 24–44.

Nguyen, Viet Thanh. *Race and Resistance: Literature and Politics in Asian America*. New York: Oxford University Press, 2002.

Okihiro, Gary Y. *American History Unbound: Asians and Pacific Islanders*. Oakland: University of California Press, 2015.

———. *Third World Studies: Theorizing Liberation*. Durham, NC: Duke University Press, 2016.

Ono, Kent A., and Vincent N. Pham. *Asian Americans and the Media*. Malden, MA: Polity, 2009.

Rah, Soong-Chan. *The Next Evangelicalism: Freeing the Church from Western Cultural Captivity*. Downers Grove, IL: InterVarsity, 2009.

Sano, Roy, ed. *The Theologies of Asian Americans and Pacific Peoples: A Reader*. Berkeley, CA: Asian Center for Theology & Strategies, 1976.

Takaki, Ronald. *Strangers from a Different Shore: A History of Asian Americans*. Rev. ed. Boston: Little, Brown, 1998.

Wu, Frank H. *Yellow: Race in America beyond Black and White*. New York: Basic, 2002.

Yong, Amos. *The Future of Evangelical Theology: Soundings from the Asian American Diaspora*. Downers Grove, IL: InterVarsity, 2014.

6

From Reverse Mission to Diaspora Mission

Narry F. Santos

Reverse mission is now considered a significant phenomenon and an "increasingly popular view by some scholars and church leaders" on Christian mission.[1] This growing trend is also called *reverse flow* or *mission in reverse* because of its association with the "relationship between Western former Christian mission-sending centers and former colonial mission fields."[2] Reverse mission is also seen as reevangelism because "the enterprise is aimed at re-evangelizing regions that were once the heartlands of Christianity and the heartlands of missionary movements."[3]

This chapter presents an overview of missiological studies on reverse mission, including its definitions, contributing factors, implications, and difficulties. Then it relates reverse mission studies to the Filipino global mission experience and summarizes the past Western missions to the Philippines and the present influx of Filipinos to Canada. Finally, it gleans lessons learned by the Greenhills Christian Fellowship (GCF) in Canada, started by the church planting vision of a church in the Philippines, which in turn was started by an

American missionary back in 1978. This revolves around the notion of a shift from reverse mission to diaspora mission that is missional, multiracial, multicultural, multidirectional, and multigenerational ministry.

Overview of Reverse Mission

To grasp the significance of reverse mission, it is important to begin with its definition. Matthews Ojo defines it as the "sending of missionaries to Europe and North America by churches and Christians from the non-Western world, particularly Africa, Asia, and Latin America, which were at the receiving end of Catholic and Protestant missions as mission fields from the sixteenth to the late twentieth century."[4] Afe Adogame views it as the "rediscovery of the entire geographical context, the former heartlands of Christianity, as a new mission field."[5] Rebecca Catto sees it as denoting a change in the direction of mission between the Global North and the Global South.[6] In short, reverse mission is a geographical inversion in mission direction that Catto describes as "from the rest to the west" and Paul Freston describes as mission "from below."[7]

The reverse mission idea took off around the early 1980s and rapidly gained momentum in the 1990s. The founding of the Third World Mission Association in 1989 helped create momentum to build the capacity of mission-sending agencies in Africa, Asia, and Latin America and transform the non-Western world into a global mission force. By the mid-1990s, the non-Western world was sending missionaries, most of them nonprofessionals, to reevangelize Europe. A notable example is the Overseas Filipino Workers (OFWs), representing a portion of the Filipino global diaspora. Ojo considers the OFWs "one of the most successful diaspora Evangelical missionary movements in the Middle East, Europe, and North America."[8]

Several factors have contributed to the increase of reverse mission, the foremost of which is Christianity's growth in the Global South and its decline in the Global North.[9] The number of Christians in Latin America, Africa, and Asia is growing at a faster rate than in other regions. Thus, the center of gravity of Christianity has shifted from the Western nations to the Southern Hemisphere.[10] In fact, Philip Jenkins notes that the "era of Western Christianity has passed within our lifetimes and the day of Southern Christianity is dawning. The fact of change itself is undeniable: it has happened and will continue to happen."[11] Christianity has been quickly transformed from a European religion to a global one.[12]

Another factor causing reverse mission is global migration. Socioeconomic changes in the South are generating new pressures to migrate to the North.[13] A major reversal of the missionary enterprise is underway, one significantly tied to the fact that the direction of the global migratory flow is now primarily south to north and east to west.[14] About the reversal of migration, Andrew F. Walls comments, "The great new fact of our time and it has momentous consequences for mission that the migration has now gone in reverse . . . from the non-Western to the Western world."[15] This migratory reversal is causing a massive number of non-Western Christian migrants in Western countries to take missionary action. Samuel Escobar observes that "travelers from poor countries who migrate for economic survival bring the Christian message and missionary initiative with them. Moravians from Curacao have gone to Holland, Baptists from Jamaica emigrated to Central America and to England, Christian women from the Philippines work in Muslim countries, Haitian believers have gone to Canada, and Latin American missionaries are going to Japan, Australia, and the United States. This missionary presence and activity have been significant."[16]

Another factor in the increase of reverse mission is the growing desire and passion for mission in the Global South. New missionary "sending countries" have emerged, including South Korea, Brazil, the Philippines, India, South Africa, Ghana, Nigeria, and Guatemala.[17] In addition, there is an increased number of committed young people willing and able to travel, wishing to evangelize the "dark continent of Europe" and "give back."[18] "The rationale for the reverse mission," Adogame finds, "is anchored on claims to the divine commission to spread the gospel."[19] Jenkins foresees the results of these three contributing factors to reverse mission (Christianity's increase in the Global South and its decrease in the Global North, global migration, and the growing missionary zeal in the Southern Hemisphere): The "immigrant Christians represent a potent cultural and religious force. Even if we accept the most pessimistic view of the faith of Christianity among Europe's old-stock white populations, these thriving new churches represent an exciting new planting, even potentially a kind of re-evangelisation."[20]

The five major implications of African-led reverse mission for European and global Christianity are the following:[21] First, reverse mission has brought a major shift in mission understanding, providing better sensibilities to and appreciation of the multicultural nature of Christianity in the twenty-first century. Second, new definitions of mission are emerging in which traditional "mission fields" now form "mission bases" of renewed efforts to reevangelize Europe and North America. Mission has changed from being unilateral to multilateral and from a cultural export to a contextualized ministry. The number of itinerant missionaries has increased, and many short-term mission projects have emerged. Third, Western, particularly European, churches are declining in attendance and missionary significance, and non-Western missionaries hope to revive Christianity in Europe. Fourth, this trend helps deconstruct and demystify the ecclesiastical paternalism that characterized global Christianity. Fifth, there is a proliferation of priests and missionaries from the two-thirds world to fill a spiritual and administrative vacuum that is caused by the dearth of European clergy.

However, there are concerns regarding reverse mission. Is it a reality or mere rhetoric or myth?[22] African-initiated and Pentecostal-charismatic churches in Europe have mostly Black congregations, with no or very few Caucasian members, which makes the reverse flow argument untenable.[23] "African Mission to Europe is not yet a success unless the Europeans who are being re-evangelized are reached and converted. . . . Nigerian churches in western territories do not necessarily indicate mission in the diaspora."[24] "White converts" form a "negligible percentage" in Europe, and African Pentecostal churches must reach out to white European populations before they can lay claim to any success in reverse mission.[25] Moreover, the host nations are suspicious of migrants exploiting their economic systems or compassion. Immigrant pastors lack the skills to reach people in the host societies and are kept busy with the struggles of immigrant communities. Immigrant Christians are unwilling to give up their homeland ethos to reach the host societies, and being adept in one cultural form of Christianity makes them ineffective in others.

Recognizing that evidence can be marshaled for and against reverse mission, this issue is saddled with much-disputed baggage, proselytization, colonial connotations involving ministry, and an inversion of previous relations.[26] Alternatively, "from everywhere to everywhere" has been proposed, which avoids the boundary drawing and power imbalance implicit in the term *reverse mission.*[27] It may indicate a shift in attitude and practice, but it may not be very analytically useful: "If mission is now simply 'from everywhere to everywhere,' then how do we draw distinctions, make comparisons, and investigate relationships (paralleling critique of globalization theory)?"[28]

The Past Western Missionary Work in the Philippines

The Philippines is an archipelago of over seven thousand islands, and Filipinos belong to the Malay race and were originally animistic in religion. Before the arrival of the Spanish conquerors, the Filipinos traded with and had cultural influences from China and India. Islam came to the southern Philippines and Manila via Indonesia. The Spanish came in the middle of the sixteenth century and introduced Catholicism to the Philippines. The Christianization was "intimately related to the entire process of establishing Spanish civil rule in the colony. . . . As missionaries, the friars worked within the system of the Spanish colonial policies. They were agents of the State as well as servants of the Church."[29]

The early friars (Augustinians, Franciscans, Jesuits, and Dominicans) showed missionary zeal, learned the language of the people, emphasized instruction, and encouraged

Indigenous religious forms. As a result, these missionaries saw phenomenal success in actual conversion. In addition, the timing of the Spanish arrival is seen as providential because it counteracted the advance of Islam. Arthur L. Tuggy writes, "If the islands had gone to Islam, the whole history of missions in this area would have been different, and evangelization immensely more difficult."[30] However, the later missionaries obtained properties and consolidated power by not allowing native clergy, which eventually set the stage for the great revolt against the friars at the end of the nineteenth century. The cruelty, corruption, and political abuse and oppression played major roles in the Philippine Propaganda Movement (1872–92), which called for reforms, and in the ensuing Revolutionary Movement (1892–96), which called for revolt, after more than three centuries of Spanish domination.[31]

With the American occupation of Manila came American missionaries who introduced Protestantism to the Filipinos. The missionaries (Presbyterian, Methodist, United Brethren, Christian and Missionary Alliance, YMCA, and Bible Societies) formed the Evangelical Union of the Philippine Islands to "unite all the evangelical forces in the Islands to secure comity and effectiveness in their missionary operations."[32] The beginning of the Protestant mission was marked by great enthusiasm on the part of the missionaries and the responsiveness of the people. However, the fragmentary nature of the Philippine society and the American character of the introduced Protestantism hindered any large-scale movement into Protestant churches.[33]

Aside from missionary initiatives by Spain and America in the Philippines, Canada was engaged in Protestant evangelization in Asia. According to the Canadian Legation in Tokyo, by the early 1930s, Canada had more missionaries (including French-Canadian Roman Catholic fathers and sisters) in the Japanese Empire—metropolitan Japan, Korea, and Taiwan—than had any other single country.[34] At that time, only in China did the Canadian missionary movement have fewer numbers: "For sixty years from the mid-1890s, East Asian countries were the setting for the most significant, sustained Canadian overseas endeavor anywhere in the world . . . the largest organized and stable Canadian presence abroad."[35]

Global Migration and Filipino Diaspora in Canada

The trend of migration has spread so widely that it is now called the age of migration, and the year 2015 was dubbed the "Year of the Migrants."[36] Canadian immigration has been dramatically influenced by the global diasporas. From 2011 to 2016, the Canadian population increased by 1.7 million (5 percent), two-thirds of which was the result of migration.[37] These statistics indicate that migrants have arrived at Canadians' doorsteps and are having an impact on Canadian society. Canada has opened up more opportunities for diaspora and reverse mission in a multicultural milieu.

The multicultural face in Canada continues to become visible as the minority population surges. In 1981, minorities composed 4.7 percent of the total population, which jumped to 32.3 percent in 2021 (projected to cross 40 percent by 2036). The 2016 Canadian census found that 48 percent of the foreign-born population came from Asia. Out of the 1,212,075 new immigrants who settled in Canada from 2011 to 2016, the largest share (188,805) was from the Philippines.

As of 2016, the total number of Filipinos in Canada was 851,405, and Filipinos form the third-largest Asian group after Indians and Chinese. These growing numbers point to the insight that global and reverse missions can further expand through the Filipino diaspora. Philip Jenkins writes, "In Canada as in Europe, immigrant groups have slowed the general decline in churchgoing. . . . The effects of immigration can be seen across the denominational spectrum. . . . It is obvious that new interests in Christianity and Christian faith in Canada has been rekindled and kept alive by the efforts of immigrant churches."[38]

The GCF Canada Reverse Mission Experience and Church Planting Lessons

The following reverse mission story comes from my experience as a pastor and church planter (sixteen years in the Philippines and nine years in Canada) through the GCF. The GCF was started by an American missionary to the Philippines in 1978, and after growing the church to more than a thousand members in fifteen years, he passed the baton to a Filipino pastor who previously had served in America and Canada as a church planter, pastor, and Bible college professor for fifteen years. His thrust on church planting left a legacy of twenty-three GCF churches across the Philippines in eighteen years.[39]

I started the first GCF church plant south of Manila (GCF South Metro) in 1997 and also helped plant three other GCF churches. On our tenth year at GCF South Metro, the church leadership sensed that God's mission was nothing less than global and sent my family and me to plant a church in Canada in 2007. We knew that it was time for us to leave our comfort zone and be a blessing in Western contexts. From this mission journey to plant a church in Toronto, I present three major lessons on diaspora and reverse mission.

The first lesson we learned is about Global South and Global North partnerships. When we started GCF Toronto in 2007, we needed to be part of a bigger family in Canada who knew who we were, our dreams, and our needs. We affiliated with the Canadian Baptists of Ontario and Quebec, which later became the family for GCF Peel and GCF York (other churches in eastern Canada). Three years later, GCF churches in Vancouver, Calgary, and Winnipeg joined with the Canadian Baptists of Western Canada. We saw how this Global South and Global North partnership forged a relationship of trust.

When GCF Toronto sensed a need to equip our church leaders in doing diaspora mission, God opened a training and coaching relationship with the Tyndale Intercultural Ministries Centre (TIM Centre) in Toronto. The TIM Centre creatively offered a two-year certificate program called "Missional Ministry and Church Leadership" to twenty GCF leaders. This program has now served more than four hundred students and continues to be a model of an ongoing partnership in mission.

Another lesson is about missional ministry through hospitality. Amos Yong argues that the study of a missional hermeneutic should include a theology of hospitality: "Christian hospitality is grounded in the hospitable God who through the Incarnation has received creation to himself and through Pentecost has given himself to creation."[40] Hospitality and welcoming strangers must become ways of life—acts of love and expressions of faith. Our hospitality reflects and anticipates God's welcome.[41] To inculcate the value of hospitality, GCF Toronto went through a six-part sermon series called "AT HOME," which was an acronym for six ways to show hospitality: (1) acceptance with a warm welcome; (2) turning guests into friends; (3) hearty service for the new and needy; (4) open homes, open hearts; (5) making room for others; and (6) extravagant and untamed hospitality.

GCF Toronto sought to connect with international students in our community. At that time, we were meeting on Sundays at a college. I inquired with the college official about how we could help the more than two hundred international student residents there. She willingly opened doors for us to help the students feel at home. She asked our church to help the new students carry their luggage from the parking lot to dorm rooms. Later, she permitted us to host a thanksgiving dinner, a luncheon on the Family Day weekend, and a special event on Good Friday. She welcomed our effort to invite a Christian lawyer to talk with the graduating students about the immigration process.

What I find encouraging in this ministry of hospitality is that the director, after seeing our efforts to serve the international students, told me, "Your church has been doing these things for the students, and you have not asked us for anything back." She offered a free room every week, and we conducted a weekly Tuesday night gathering called "Chips and Chow." During this fun and relaxed time with the international students, we provided free pizza, hot dogs, and chips. The students could practice their English and watch short videos on relevant topics. We also partnered with a couple of staff from an international student ministry in Canada to coach us on how to serve the students well.

The implication of missional ministry through hospitality for diaspora is that it allows us to get to know our neighbors, to be aware of their needs and interests, and to add value to our communities. It opens more doors to engage our neighbors in loving deeds of kindness. Thus, the good news becomes adorned with good works that lead the diasporic people to be attracted to the Jesus whom we know, love, and serve.

The third lesson is about multicultural ministry. We needed to learn how to reach beyond the Filipino diaspora, and it came the hard way. Upon our arrival at the Toronto airport in April 2007, the church leader who came to pick us up told me, "Pastor, you cannot start a Filipino church in Toronto." I had left a thriving ten-year church ministry in the Philippines; uprooted my family from the comfort and safety of a Christian church, their school, and their friends; and traveled halfway around the globe. I was taken aback at his remark, but I managed to ask, "Why not?" In the back of my mind, I knew I was in trouble because that is what I knew how to plant—a Filipino church. He replied, "It does not make sense to plant a Filipino church in one of the most multicultural cities of the world." After being a full-time pastor for thirteen years at that time, I had to unlearn what I knew and afresh learn how to plant a church in a Canadian context, which was extremely challenging. With the initial core team of leaders of GCF Toronto, we began a process of discernment and exploration. We asked God, "What kind of church do you want us to be in Canada?"

We landed on our 3M ethos: (1) missional, (2) metropolitan, and (3) multicultural. By "missional," we meant that we were committed to being on mission with God by intentionally multiplying churches and incarnationally adding value to the community where we belonged by serving the people there. By "metropolitan," we meant that we were committed to intentionally going where the people were flocking and strategically ministering in the urban centers. By "multicultural," we meant that we were committed to intentionally reaching out to the different diaspora groups and host Canadians. To help fulfill this multicultural value, the TIM Centre provided resources and training. There were two words that the director of the TIM Centre told me to describe this kind of ministry: "difficult" and "slow," which were contrary to our preferred style of ministry.

Our diaspora mission story continues with GCF's "Vision 2024," which includes planting seven new churches in Canada in the next seven years and developing a Next Generation Summit to equip young leaders so that the current leaders (the Moses generation of GCF leaders) can pass the spiritual leadership baton to the 1.5 and second generations (the Joshua generation). GCF Canada believes that the way for the GCF churches to thrive in the future is to prepare the next generations' leaders now and develop an effective path toward a multicultural ministry through Generation Y and Generation Z. The hope and prayer of the GCF Canada leaders is that our diasporic mission story will lead to an intentional missional, multicultural, and multigenerational ministry that benefits Filipino Canadians, other ethnic groups, and host nations in the coming decades.

Notes

1 See Matthews Ojo, "Reverse Mission," in *Encyclopedia of Mission and Missionaries*, ed. Jonathan Bonk (London: Routledge, 2007), 280;

Dele Jemirade, "Reverse Mission and the Establishment of Redeemed Christian Church of God (RCCG) in Canada," *Missionalia* 45, no. 3 (2017): 263; Claudia Wahrisch-Oblau, "Getting Ready to Receive? German Churches and the New Mission from the South," Lausanne World Pulse, 2008, http://www.lausanneworldpulse.com/themedarticles.php/971/07-2008?pg=all.

2 Rebecca Catto, "The Church Mission Society and Reverse Mission: From Colonial Sending to Postcolonial Partnership and Reception," in *Religion on the Move! New Dynamics of Religious Expansion in a Globalizing World*, ed. Shobana Shankar and Afe Adogame (Leiden: Brill, 2013), 82.

3 Ojo, "Reverse Mission," 380.

4 Ojo, 380.

5 Afe Adogame, *The African Christian Diaspora: New Currents and Emerging Trends in World Christianity* (London: Bloomsbury, 2013), 173.

6 Rebecca Catto, "Reverse Mission: From the Global South to Mainline Churches," in *Church Growth in Britain: 1980 to the Present*, ed. David Goodhew (Surrey, UK: Ashgate, 2012), 92.

7 Rebecca Catto, "From the Rest to the West: Exploring Reversal in Christina Mission in Twenty-First Century Britain" (PhD thesis, University of Exeter, 2008); Paul Freston, "Reverse Mission: A Discourse in Search of Reality," *Pentecost Studies* 9, no. 2 (2010): 155.

8 Ojo, "Reverse Mission," 381.

9 See Lamin Sanneh and Joel Carpenter, eds., *The Changing Face of Christianity: Africa, the West, and the World* (New York: Oxford University Press, 2005); Philip Jenkins, *The New Faces of Christianity: Believing in the Bible in the Global South* (New York: Oxford University Press, 2006).

10 Rosalind Hackett, "Revisiting Proselytization in the Twenty-First Century," in *Proselytization Revisited: Rights Talk, Free Markets and Culture Wars*, ed. Rosalinda Hackett (Oakville, ON: Equinox, 2008), 16.

11 Philip Jenkins, *The Next Christendom: The Coming of Global Christianity*, rev. ed. (Oxford: Oxford University Press, 2007), 3.

12 Lamin Sanneh, *Translating the Message: The Missionary Impact on Culture* (Maryknoll, NY: Orbis, 1989); Kwame Bediako, *Christianity in Africa: The Renewal of a Non-Western Religion* (Maryknoll, NY: Orbis, 1995).

13 Stephen Castles and Mark Muller, *The Age of Migration: International Population Movements in the Modern World* (New York: Guilford, 1998), 139.

14 Jehu J. Hanciles, "Migration and Mission: Some Implications for the Twenty-First-Century Church," *International Bulletin of Mission Research* 27, no. 4 (2003): 149.

15 Andrew F. Walls, "Mission and Migration: The Diaspora Factor in Christian History," *Journal of African Christian Thought* 5, no. 2 (2002): 6.

16 Samuel Escobar, *Changing Tides: Latin America and World Mission Today* (Maryknoll, NY: Orbis, 2002), 163.

17 Paul Freston, "The Transnationalization of Brazilian Pentecostalism: The Universal Church of the Kingdom of God," in *Between Babel and Pentecost: Transnational Pentecostalism in Africa and Latin America*, ed. A. Corten and R. Marshall-Fratani (Bloomington: Indiana University Press, 2001), 196–215.

18 Catto, "From the Rest," 92.

19 Afe Adogame, "Reverse Mission: Europe—a Prodigal Continent," World Council of Churches, 2006, 1, http://www.wcc2006.info/fileadmin/files/edinburgh2010/files/News/Afe_Reverse%20mission.pdf.

20 Jenkins, *Next Christendom*, 118.

21 Adogame, *African Christian Diaspora*, 181–82.

22 Dele Jemirade, "Reverse Mission and the Establishment of Redeemed Christian Church of God (RCCG) in Canada." *Missionalia* 45, no. 3 (2017): 263.

23 Ogbu U. Kalu, ed., *African Pentecostalism: An Introduction* (New York: Oxford University Press, 2008), 283.

24 Dapo Asaju, "Colonial Politicization of Religion: Residual Effects on the Ministry of African Led Churches in Britain in Christianity,"

in *Africa and the African Diaspora*, ed. Afe Adogame, Rosswith Gerloff, and Klaus Hock (New York: Continuum, 2008), 285.

25 Afe Adogame, "Mapping Globalization with the Lens of Religion: African Migrant Churches in Germany," in *New Religions and Globalization*, ed. Armin Geertz and Margit Warburg (Aarhus, Denmark: Aarhus University Press, 2008), 210; Afe Adogame, "Who Do They Think They Are? Mental Images and the Unfolding of an African Diaspora in Germany," in *Christianity in Africa and the African Diaspora: The Appropriation of a Scattered Heritage*, ed. Afe Adogame, Rosswith Gerloff, and Klaus Hock (New York: Continuum, 2008), 260.

26 Catto, "Church Mission Society," 82.

27 Michael Nazir-Ali, *From Everywhere to Everywhere: A World View of Christian Mission* (London: Collins, 1991).

28 Rebecca Catto, "Reverse Mission," 103.

29 Arthur L. Tuggy, *The Philippine Church: Growth in a Changing Society* (Grand Rapids, MI: Eerdmans, 1971), 47–48.

30 Tuggy, *Philippine Church*, 67.

31 Teodoro A. Agoncillo, *History of the Filipino People*, 8th ed. (Quezon City, Philippines: C & E, 2012); Reynaldo C. Ileto, *Pasyon and Revolution: Popular Movements in the Philippines (1840–1910)* (Quezon City, Philippines: Ateneo University Press, 1979); Renato Constantino and Leticia R. Constantino, *A History of the Philippines: From the Spanish Colonization to the Second World War* (New York: Monthly Review, 1975).

32 Brown 1903, 188.

33 Tuggy, *Philippine Church*, 121.

34 Hamish A. Ion, *The Cross and the Rising Sun: The Canadian Protestant Missionary Movement in the Japanese Empire, 1872–1932*, vol. 1 (Waterloo, ON: Wilfred Laurier University Press, 1990), 2.

35 Margo Gewurtz and Peter Mitchell, "Canadians and East Asia: The Missionary Experience" (presentation at the China Missionary Project: Canadian Missionaries & East Asia Conference, University of Toronto, April 1981), 1.

36 Castles and Miller, *Age of Migration*, 5.

37 For the latest data on immigrants to Canada, see Statistics Canada, accessed June 2020, https://www.statcan.gc.ca.

38 Jenkins, *Next Christendom*, 114–15.

39 Narry F. Santos, "What's a Missionary Doing in Canada? The Story of Greenhills Christian Fellowship," in *Green Shoots Out of Dry Ground: Growing a New Future for the Church in Canada*, ed. John Bowen (Eugene, OR: Wipf & Stock, 2013), 97–110; see also Narry F. Santos, "'Diaspora Missions': Contemporary Missiological Significance of the People on the Move," in *Rejection: God's Refugees in Biblical and Contemporary Perspective*, ed. Stanley E. Porter (Eugene, OR: Pickwick, 2014), 191–208.

40 Amos Yong, *Hospitality and the Other: Pentecost, Christian Practices, and the Neighbor* (Maryknoll, NY: Orbis, 2008), 62.

41 Christine Pohl, *Making Room: Recovering Hospitality as a Christian Tradition* (Grand Rapids, MI: Eerdmans, 1999), 13.

Bibliography

Adogame, Afe. *The African Christian Diaspora: New Currents and Emerging Trends in World Christianity*. London: Bloomsbury, 2013.

———. "Mapping Globalization with the Lens of Religion: African Migrant Churches in Germany." In *New Religions and Globalization*, edited by Armin Geertz and Margit Warburg, 189–214. Aarhus, Denmark: Aarhus University Press, 2008.

———. "Reverse Mission: Europe—a Prodigal Continent." World Council of Churches, 2006. http://www.wcc2006.info/fileadmin/files/edinburgh2010/files/News/Afe_Reverse%20mission.pdf.

———. "Who Do They Think They Are? Mental Images and the Unfolding of an African Diaspora in Germany." In *Christianity in Africa and the African Diaspora: The Appropriation of a*

Scattered Heritage, edited by Afe Adogame, Rosswith Gerloff, and Klaus Hock, 248–264. New York: Continuum, 2008.

Agoncillo, Teodoro A. *History of the Filipino People*. 8th ed. Quezon City, Philippines: C & E, 2012.

Asaju, Dapo. "Colonial Politicization of Religion: Residual Effects on the Ministry of African Led Churches in Britain in Christianity." In *Africa and the African Diaspora*, edited by Afe Adogame, Rosswith Gerloff, and Klaus Hock, 279–292. New York: Continuum, 2008.

Bediako, Kwame. *Christianity in Africa: The Renewal of a Non-Western Religion*. Maryknoll, NY: Orbis, 1995.

Castles, Stephen, and Mark Miller. *The Age of Migration: International Population Movements in the Modern World*. New York: Guilford, 1998.

Catto, Rebecca. "The Church Mission Society and Reverse Mission: From Colonial Sending to Postcolonial Partnership and Reception." In *Religion on the Move! New Dynamics of Religious Expansion in a Globalizing World*, edited by Shobana Shankar and Afe Adogame, 81–95. Leiden: Brill, 2013.

———. "From the Rest to the West: Exploring Reversal in Christina Mission in Twenty-First Century Britain." PhD thesis, University of Exeter, 2008.

———. "Reverse Mission: From the Global South to Mainline Churches." In *Church Growth in Britain: 1980 to the Present*, edited by David Goodhew, 91–103. Surrey, UK: Ashgate, 2012.

Constantino, Renato, and Leticia R. Constantino. *A History of the Philippines: From the Spanish Colonization to the Second World War*. New York: Monthly Review, 1975.

Escobar, Samuel. *Changing Tides: Latin America and World Mission Today*. Maryknoll, NY: Orbis, 2002.

Freston, Paul. "Reverse Mission: A Discourse in Search of Reality." *Pentecost Studies* 9, no. 2 (2010): 153–174.

———. "The Transnationalization of Brazilian Pentecostalism: The Universal Church of the Kingdom of God." In *Between Babel* and Pentecost: Transnational Pentecostalism in Africa and Latin America*, edited by A. Corten and R. Marshall-Fratani, 196–215. Bloomington: Indiana University Press, 2001.

Gewurtz, Margo and Peter Mitchell. "Canadians and East Asia: The Missionary Experience." Presentation at the China Missionary Project: Canadian Missionaries & East Asia Conference, University of Toronto, April 1981.

Hackett, Rosalind. "Revisiting Proselytization in the Twenty-First Century." In *Proselytization Revisited: Rights Talk, Free Markets and Culture Wars*, edited by Rosalinda Hackett, 1–33. Oakville, ON: Equinox, 2008.

Hanciles, Jehu J. *Beyond Christendom: Globalization, African Migration, and the Transformation of the West*. Maryknoll, NY: Orbis, 2008.

———. "Migration and Mission: Some Implications for the Twenty-First-Century Church." *International Bulletin of Mission Research* 27, no. 4 (2003): 146–153.

Ileto, Reynaldo C. *Pasyon and Revolution: Popular Movements in the Philippines (1840–1910)*. Quezon City, Philippines: Ateneo University Press, 1979.

Ion, Hamish A. *The Cross and the Rising Sun: The Canadian Protestant Missionary Movement in the Japanese Empire, 1872–1932*. Vol. 1. Waterloo, ON: Wilfred Laurier University Press, 1990.

Jemirade, Dele. "Reverse Mission and the Establishment of Redeemed Christian Church of God (RCCG) In Canada." *Missionalia* 45, no. 3 (2017): 263–284.

Jenkins, Philip. *The New Faces of Christianity: Believing in the Bible in the Global South*. New York: Oxford University Press, 2006.

———. *The Next Christendom: The Coming of Global Christianity*. Revised ed. Oxford: Oxford University Press, 2007.

Kalu, Ogbu U., ed. *African Pentecostalism: An Introduction*. New York: Oxford University Press, 2008.

Nazir-Ali, Michael. *From Everywhere to Everywhere: A World View of Christian Mission.* London: Collins, 1991.

Ojo, Matthews. "Reverse Mission." In *Encyclopedia of Mission and Missionaries,* edited by Jonathan Bonk, 380–382. London: Routledge, 2007.

Pohl, Christine. *Making Room: Recovering Hospitality as a Christian Tradition.* Grand Rapids, MI: Eerdmans, 1999.

Sanneh, Lamin. *Translating the Message: The Missionary Impact on Culture.* Maryknoll, NY: Orbis, 1989.

Sanneh, Lamin, and Joel Carpenter, eds. *The Changing Face of Christianity: Africa, the West, and the World.* New York: Oxford University Press, 2005.

Santos, Narry F. "'Diaspora Missions': Contemporary Missiological Significance of the People on the Move." In *Rejection: God's Refugees in Biblical and Contemporary Perspective,* edited by Stanley E. Porter, 191–208. Eugene, OR: Pickwick, 2014.

———. "What's a Missionary Doing in Canada? The Story of Greenhills Christian Fellowship." In *Green Shoots Out of Dry Ground: Growing a New Future for the Church in Canada,* edited by John Bowen, 97–110. Eugene, OR: Wipf & Stock, 2013.

Tuggy, Arthur L. *The Philippine Church: Growth in a Changing Society.* Grand Rapids, MI: Eerdmans, 1971.

Wahrisch-Oblau, Claudia. "Getting Ready to Receive? German Churches and the New Mission from the South." Lausanne World Pulse, 2008. http://www.lausanneworldpulse.com/themedarticles.php/971/07-2008?pg=all.

Walls, Andrew F. "Mission and Migration: The Diaspora Factor in Christian History." *Journal of African Christian Thought* 5, no. 2 (2002): 3–11.

Yong, Amos. *Hospitality and the Other: Pentecost, Christian Practices, and the Neighbor.* Maryknoll, NY: Orbis, 2008.

7

A Window into the World of South Korean Protestant Missionaries

Chandler H. Im

Introduction

At a glance, the forty-year (1979–2019) history of the Protestant mission of South Koreans on the global stage appears to be a Cinderella story. By sovereign design and orchestration, the South Korean Protestant Church, located in a formerly destitute and missionary-receiving country, has grown exponentially to send out more missionaries to the rest of the world than any other country except the United States. The numbers of South Korean Protestant (SKP) missionaries have skyrocketed since 1979, when ninety-three people labored in twenty-six nations to advance the causes of God's mission.[1]

This chapter is composed of two parts. The first part strives to describe the present status of SKP missionaries: their numbers, their locations, the ministry/mission areas they are currently toiling in, their finances, their age groups, and "missionary kids" (MKs). The second part attempts to explain or analyze the five key areas of concern with respect to SKP missionaries and their missionary endeavors around the world.

Numbers

In December 2018, the Korean World Mission Association (KWMA) estimated that 27,993 SKP missionaries were serving in 171 nations around the world.[2] Those numbers are higher when taking into account all the other missionaries commissioned by smaller church denominations and individual churches not known to the KWMA. The numbers of SKP missionaries each year were as follows: 2006—14,896; 2007—17,697; 2008—19,413; 2009—20,840; 2010—22,014; 2011—23,331; 2012—24,742; 2013—25,745; 2014—26,677; 2015—27,205; 2016—27,205; 2017—27,436; and 2018—27,993.

Of the 190 mission agencies that are affiliated with the KWMA, the number of those who have ten or more missionaries under their care is approximately 130. The KWMA projects that in the future, SKP denominations—rather than individual churches—will commission more long-term missionaries overseas. Table 7.1 displays a steady growth of the SKP missionaries who belong to the KWMA's denominational mission agencies.

Table 7.1: The numbers of SKP missionaries (2012–18)

Year	2012	2013	2014	2015	2016	2017	2018
Number	11,024	11,482	11,764	11,930	12,192	12,374	12,686

Locations

Of the 171 countries in which SKP missionaries are currently laboring, the number of those where over five hundred are serving per country is thirteen.[3] The SKP missionaries in those thirteen countries, when added together, account for more than 50 percent of the total SKP missionary population (27,993). Table 7.2 shows the top ten countries where SKP missionaries are serving (as of December 2018).

Based on this table, 63.4 percent of SKP missionaries are currently working in different regions of Asia: Northeast

Table 7.2: The locations of SKP missionaries

	Country	Category	No. of mission agencies	No. of SKP missionaries
1	China	F1	142	3,549
2	United States	G2	75	2,590
3	Japan	F2	79	1,547
4	Philippines	G2	91	1,542
5	Thailand	F2	64	956
6	Unspecified	F3	64	847
7	Unspecified	F3	84	839
8	Cambodia	F2	82	829
9	Russia	F2	66	604
10	Vietnam	F2	70	564
Total SKP missionaries in the top ten countries (percentage)			13,867 (47.6)	
Total SKP missionaries globally			27,993	

Asia, Southeast Asia, South Asia, Central Asia, and the Middle East. In Asia, most SKP missionaries toil in animistic, Buddhist, Communist, Hindu, and Islamic contexts.

By the way, one might wonder, "Why are there many SKP missionaries in the United States?" A multitude of SKP workers are church planting for and ministering to Korean immigrants and Korean Americans. A large number of them also facilitate in specialized ministries such as multiethnic church planting, homeless ministries, and campus ministries (e.g., University Bible Fellowship and Korean Cru). Moreover, I have personally met with several SKP

Table 7.3: The regions of missionary service

Region	2014	2018
NE Asia	6,430	5,916
SE Asia	5,575	5,865
N. America	3,196	3,103
S. Asia	1,860	1,707
W. Europe	1,368	1,243
SE Africa	1,200	1,222
Latin America	1,222	1,166
Middle East	1,315	1,110
E. Europe	1,101	1,070
C. Asia	1,203	930
Oceania	951	918
N. Africa	611	441
W. & C. Africa	348	357
Caribbean	98	91

missionaries who were or are working with Native Americans on reservations in the United States and First Nations peoples in Canada.[4] Table 7.3 is a breakdown of various regions of the world in which respective SKP missionaries are stationed and indicates numerical changes from 2014 to 2018.

Ministry/Mission Areas

Table 7.4 indicates (1) various ministry/mission areas in which SKP missionaries are engaged, (2) the current numbers of the countries in which they work, and (3) the respective numbers of SKP missionaries involved.[5] An overwhelming majority (81.1 percent) of them are directly involved in church planting or discipleship ministries.

Table 7.4: The areas of missionary service

Ministry/mission area	No. of countries	No. of SKP missionaries involved
Church planting	153	14,624
Discipleship	141	9,663
Welfare/development	82	2,017
Campus	63	1,954
General education	79	1,671

Finances

Of the 273 SKP missionaries who responded to the Korea Research Institute for Mission's questionnaire in 2018, 54.2 percent received between $2,000 and $4,000 per month in mission support; 97.4 percent, under $4,000; and 2.6 percent, more than $4,000. In the last three years, 37.9 percent of SKP missionaries have experienced a decrease in mission support levels; 34.9 percent, an increase; and the rest, no change.[6] Also, 73.1 percent stated that they would not stop their mission work even in times of financial hardship.

Age Groups

According to the findings from the 2018 KWMA questionnaire, about 4,748 (17.3 percent) of SKP missionaries are estimated to be age sixty or above, approaching or having already reached retirement age.[7] As table 7.5 substantiates, this percentage of SKP missionaries aged sixty or older exceeds the total combined percentage (13.5) of SKP missionaries in their twenties and thirties. Moreover, more than two-thirds (69.3 percent) of SKP missionaries are in their forties and fifties.

Table 7.5: The ages of missionaries

Age group	20s	30s	40s	50s	60 or older
Percentage	2.9	10.6	35.3	34.0	17.3

Missionary Kids

As the numbers of SKP missionaries have increased in mission fields over the past forty years, so have the numbers of their children, who are commonly referred to as "missionary kids" (MKs), which is a misnomer because many of them are not "kids" but adults.[8] According to the KWMA's 2018 statistics, of the SKP missionaries who responded to the questionnaire, 4,595 MKs (52 percent) were nineteen or younger, and 4,220 (47 percent) were twenty or older. Furthermore, 4,817 MKs (56 percent) lived with their parents in mission fields, 2,656 (31 percent) in South Korea, and the rest (12 percent) in other countries attending schools, working, and so on. The number of Korean MKs dropped from 2017 to 2018. Thus, it would be worthwhile to keep an eye out in the future to see whether this drop was a onetime occurrence or the beginning of a downward trend.

Some Issues and Concerns

I begin the second part of this chapter with three caveats. First, even though countless SKP missionaries possess and display many good and positive qualities in their mission fields, I have decided to focus mainly on less discussed and more controversial areas that certain SKP missionaries

Table 7.6: The numbers of MKs (2006–18)

Year	2006	2009	2012	2015	2016	2017	2018
Number	10,433	13,868	16,586	18,543	18,810	19,661	18,372

(including myself as a Korean American missionary planting seeds of the gospel in Japan) need to improve on in the
future. These critical comments of mine on the five grave
areas are out of loving concern both as an "insider" and as
a third-party observer.

Second, my descriptions are by no means comprehensive. I have cherry-picked five issues and concerns that I
deem to be important. Due to limitations in space, I leave
other ones for other mission experts to explore and elucidate.
Third, the five ones I list are mainly gathered and derived
from (1) my interviews and interactions with hundreds of
SKP missionaries over the last twenty-plus years; (2) my
observations through personal visitations to numerous mission fields in two dozen countries in Africa, Asia, Europe,
North America, and South America; and (3) various Christian and mission-related publications.

Field Language Skills

Eugene Nida, a prominent Christian anthropologist, once
claimed the following while highlighting field language skills
that missionaries ought to acquire: "If locals say, your local
language is good, your language level is good. But it is still
not good enough. When they stop saying that your language
level is good, then it is finally good enough (as a missionary)."[9] In other words, missionaries must acquire language
proficiency until local native speakers pay very little attention
to the missionaries' language abilities.

One common trait among a majority of SKP missionaries whom I have known is a lack of field language skills.
Most of them cannot communicate in their field languages

at native or near-native levels. That reality causes miscommunications and misunderstandings with locals, including local and national Christian partners, and restricts their ministry spheres and influences as well. Western mission agencies generally require about one to two years of mandatory intensive language training before the field work and/or in the field before receiving a green light to commence local ministry. But numerous SKP missionaries forego or neglect vital language training in the early phase of their mission works. That carries a myriad of mission implications and complications in the present and for the future.

Instead of investing in the language acquisition process at the outset, some dive into local ministries prematurely, using or hiring local interpreters and translators. For instance, in the past, some SKP missionaries to China hired local Korean-Chinese workers, fluent in both Korean and Chinese, to serve as interpreters and translators for them. This language arrangement was and is not limited to SKP missionaries to China.

Ethnocentrism

The *Cambridge Academic Content Dictionary* defines the word *ethnocentrism* as "believing that the people, customs, and traditions of your own race or nationality are better than those of other races."[10] In other words, ethnocentric persons elevate their own culture (in this case, Korean) and look down on the local cultures in which they are ministering as inferior or less desirable. This ethnocentric attitude is another common denominator among some SKP missionaries, especially those who are serving in poorer and less "advanced" countries than South Korea, like in Africa, Asia, and Latin America. While numerous SKP missionaries are serving national partners and local people with true humility and modesty, some do not embody and exhibit Christlike, incarnational behavior in their mission fields when interfacing with them.

Some examples of Korean-centric behaviors and attitudes include but are not limited to the following: a sense of moral superiority, cultural insensitivity, racial discrimination against national partners, belittling of local customs and value systems, and unreasonable or imbalanced biases.[11] One specific Korean behavior that I, as a Korean-background individual, can mention as an example would be the Korean people's "hurry up" propensity—trying to do everything as quickly as possible and expecting others to do so as well. If and when others do not comply in a timely fashion as Koreans would do, the local leaders are perceived as lazy and not hardworking. In principle, it is a serious miscalculation and unbiblical notion to conceive that one's traditional ethical values and norms are superior to others' and to anticipate that one's cultural standards and practices can or should be applied in universal contexts, beyond one's cultural and national boundaries.

One main reason these SKP missionaries publicly show ethnocentrism is their monolingual and monocultural backgrounds from which they come. Most of them grew up and were nurtured in Korean language—and Korean culture—only settings before they set foot on foreign lands as missionaries. South Korea is one of the most ethnically homogeneous nations in the world.[12]

In response to ethnocentrism, Paul G. Hiebert urges missionaries to employ the attitudes of learners and offers three solutions: First, show respect to the host culture and its systems. Second, respond to various questions—cultural, philosophical, and religious—regarding cultural pluralism. Third, treat people of another culture as individuals, not as a homogeneous group.[13] Certain SKP field missionaries need to be reminded that God commissioned them to spread the love and message of the gospel and Jesus Christ, not Korean Christianity.

Contextualization

The lack of sufficient local language proficiency and Korean-centric attitudes subsequently lead to a lack of relevance and effective contextualization efforts and models. The low-level understanding of and very little appreciation for local languages, customs, values, religions, and worldviews often result in church models and ministry systems that are neither meaningful nor helpful to locals. In a similar vein, Indigenous expressions in various forms, like using traditional musical instruments during worship services and religious rituals, are not included or are even discouraged. Missionaries must critically examine multiple facets of their host culture through biblical, Christian contextualization lenses that are pertinent and well-balanced.

Moreover, SKP missionaries from theologically conservative traditions tend to undercontextualize the gospel in cross-cultural settings, in part for fear of being accused of condoning religious pluralism or allowing unbiblical theology and praxis. However, wrestling with challenging and contemporary issues (e.g., ancestor veneration customs and homosexual behavior) is a task every missionary must take on. As Eugene Nida claims,

"Biblical relativism is an obligatory feature of our incarnational religion, for without it we would either absolutize human institutions or relativize God."[14]

In their mission fields, during the contextualization process, it is imperative for missionaries to possess the wisdom to discern what is most important and urgent while having the ability to differentiate between essentials and nonessentials and between nonnegotiables and negotiables in Christian theology and practices. For instance, one South Korean missionary to Indonesia told me that in his Chinese-Indonesian church, wearing shoes inside it—a nonessential, negotiable cultural custom—became such a contentious issue that it almost divided the congregation. Stephen M. Davis asks, "How can Christian workers communicate the unchanging Gospel of Jesus Christ in the midst of a changing world?"[15] This is an indispensable contextualization question of our era that is worth pondering every day as missionaries.

Power Issues

In spring 2011, I had the honor of conversing privately with Andrew F. Walls, one of the most renowned Christian historians of the twentieth century. One of his questions to me was, "What do you think is the most important question in Christianity's two-thousand-year history?" I remained silent, with a pen in my hand, ready to write down whatever he was going to tell me. With a smile, he said, "Who's the boss?"[16] He did not elaborate on that answer. In retrospect, I surmise that Walls was asking, in simple English, Who is in control? Who has the power to hire and fire people? Who makes decisions and executes them? In human history, and in Christian history to an extent, those in power have often abused their authority to control, manipulate, and even persecute the marginalized and the weak.

Some SKP missionaries are known to have abused their powers in ministry spheres, particularly in the areas of decision-making, governance, finances, and ethical matters. For instance, in countless cases, SKP missionaries have failed to solicit, seriously consider, or give sufficient weight to local and national partners' voices and advice. In those cases, the relationship between SKP missionaries and local Christian leaders becomes one of paternalism, similar to the relationship between supervisors and subordinates, rather than a partnership of equal members in the body of Christ.

In Korean culture, *gapjil*—a Korean word for power abuse—refers to the abusive words and actions of those who have power over their subordinates. Robert Oh provides a working definition for this kind of patron-client relationship in mission fields: "The patron-client relationship, in both its formal and informal setting, is an arrangement between an individual of higher socio-economic status or some other personal resources (patron) who provides support to another person of lower socio-economic status (client) who gives assistance or service in return, which is mutually obligatory and beneficial."[17] Furthermore, certain SKP missionaries have been accused of verbal, physical, or sexual abuses in Cambodia, China, Japan, South Korea, Uganda, and various other places in the world. According to Ralph Winter, "A Christian missionary who was loved as an evangelist and liked as a teacher, may find himself resented as an administrator."[18] In applying that maxim to SKP missionaries, those who were once helpful as leaders might turn into obstacles by overexercising their influence and control, thereby hindering national and local

Christian leaders' progress toward administrative and financial autonomy in their respective ministry spheres.[19]

Retirement and Real Estate Issues

Another evolving and serious issue is the handling of real estate properties as SKP missionaries approach retirement. Certain SKP missionaries have intentionally left their mission agencies or severed ties with their mother churches or denominations for the sole purpose of "keeping" their properties registered under their names or their mission fields.

On one hand, this unethical action becomes especially tempting in mission fields where real estate prices have gone up significantly. To provide a couple of examples, (1) land prices in central Bangkok increased by 1,000 percent in thirty years, from 1988 to 2018, and (2) the prices of luxury houses in Phnom Penh, the capital of Cambodia, have skyrocketed by nearly 400 percent in less than seven years as of March 2019. As a direct result of elevated prices, the ways and means of handing over retiring and retired SKP missionaries' respective ministries and resources, including churches, schools, orphanages, buildings, houses, seminaries, and vacant land, have become thorny and legal issues between certain SKP missionaries and local leaders in some places and between SKP missionaries and their parent mission agencies.

On the other hand, it is worth noting that certain SKP missionaries resort to this unethical action for various reasons, not only because of greed. Some do not have a residence option after retirement because they lack sufficient funds to purchase or rent a home back in South Korea. Not enough retirement homes are offered in South Korea to accommodate the housing needs of all the returning retired SKP missionaries, especially those with insufficient funds. In some instances, no one would be available in South Korea to care for them in their retirement years, while others have to care for their aging parents. For some others, children stay back in mission field countries or move to other nations for studies or work, leaving none to care for them. For these reasons, in the present, certain SKP mission agencies are encouraging their missionaries to retire and remain in their mission fields. Besides, some SKP mission workers desire to retire, die, and have their bones buried in their mission fields, which are their new adopted homelands—sometimes at the request of local Christians.

Once again, due to the space limitations of this chapter, I have covered only five areas of concern. These are not exhaustive in any manner and require further analysis. I invite other missiologists to explore other crucial issues and concerns such as member care and retired and retiring missionaries' health care, retirement homes, and pensions; or how to provide support for the education, employment, and marriage of MKs; or how to reposition as missionaries after being expelled from countries where Buddhism, Communism, Hinduism, or Islam is a dominant religion; or the pros and cons of business as mission and the challenges of migration and diaspora peoples in mission fields as well as those migrating out of their mission fields.

Conclusion

Over the last forty years, God has abundantly blessed the Protestant churches of South Korea, and SKP missionaries are engaged all over the globe. In global mission circles, the Protestant Church in South Korea and SKP missionaries are known and respected for their emphasis on a fervent prayer life, tremendous interest in and passion for global mission works, sacrificial giving for the causes of God's kingdom, and other positive characteristics. However, there are more than a few areas of concern that SKP missionaries face and are criticized for, as discussed above.

It is evident that SKP churches and missionaries worldwide are encountering new challenges these days and will face newer issues in the coming decades. As Korean mission specialists have advocated over the past several years, it is about time that SKP churches, mission agencies, and missionaries focus more on the quality (e.g., How well are we doing out there?) of SKP missionary endeavors around the globe rather than heavily emphasizing quantity only (e.g., How many SKP missionaries are out there, and where?).

Without respecting, considering, and understanding local people, cultures, and languages, it is obvious that missionaries usually cannot expect to have meaningful relationships and fruitful ministries in mission fields. A well-known Korean proverb says, "After a tiger dies, a hide is left behind; after a person dies, a name is left behind." I end this chapter with my earnest prayer that after SKP missionaries leave or die in their mission fields, their good names (legacies) will be left behind, fulfilling the salvific vision the prophet Isaiah saw: "How beautiful . . . are the feet of those who bring good news, who proclaim peace, who bring good tidings, who proclaim salvation" (Isa 52:7 NIV).

Notes

1 Marlin Nelson, *Directory of Korean Missionaries and Mission Societies* (Seoul: Asian Theological Seminary, 1979), 44. Of the ninety-three SKP missionaries in 1979, twenty served in Japan, twelve in West Germany, nine in Indonesia, eight in Taiwan, six in the Philippines, and five in Brazil. See Todd Johnson, "Korean Christianity in the Context of Global Christianity," in *Korean Church, God's Mission, Global Christianity*, ed. Wonsuk Ma and Kyo Seoung Ahn, Regnum Edinburgh Centenary Series 26 (Oxford: Regnum, 2015), 72.

2 Most of the data in this section are derived from Korean World Mission Association (KWMA), *2018: An Annual Status Report on Korean Missionaries* [in Korean] (n.p.: KWMA, 2019). And Korea Research Institute for Mission (KRIM) reports show that the number of SKP missionaries in 2018 was 21,378 in 146 nations. It appears that the discrepancies between the KWMA and KRIM come in part from "double membership" missionaries—those who are counted twice because they belong simultaneously to denominational mission agencies and nondenominational mission agencies.

3 Data taken from KWMA, *2018*, 4–5.

4 Chandler H. Im and Amos Yong, eds., *Global Diasporas and Mission*, Regnum Edinburgh Centenary Series 23 (Oxford: Regnum, 2014), 145.

5 Data taken from KWMA, *2018*, 5.

6 Korea Research Institute for Mission, *2019: A Status Report on Korean World Mission* [in Korean] (n.p.: KRIM, 2019), 1.

7 KWMA, *2018*, 6.

8 KWMA, 5–6.

9 Eugene Nida, *God's Word in Man's Language* (Pasadena, CA: William Carey Library, 1973).

10 Paul Heacock, ed., *Cambridge Academic Content Dictionary* (Cambridge: Cambridge University Press, 2009), 314.

11 See S. Hun Kim and Wonsuk Ma, eds., *Korean Diaspora and Christian Mission* (Oxford: Regnum, 2011)

12 As of 2016, only 3.4 percent (1.76 million) of the South Korean population was foreign-born, whom the public views as outsiders and not "real" Koreans.

13 Paul G. Hiebert, *Anthropological Insights for Missionaries* (Grand Rapids, MI: Baker, 1985), 130–39.

14 Eugene Nida, *God's Word in Man's Language* (New York: Harper, 1952), 282.

15 Stephen M. Davis, "The Challenge of Missions in the Twenty-First Century," Lausanne World Pulse Archives, April 2008, https://www.lausanneworldpulse.com/perspectives-php/924/04-2008.

16 Andrew F. Walls, personal conversation with the author during the 20th Wheaton Theology Conference, Wheaton College, Wheaton, IL, April 2011.

17 Robert Oh, "Church Planting in Patronage Cultures: Aid Dependency Issues and Missional Implications" (PhD thesis, Oxford Centre for Mission Studies, 2018), 45–46.

18 Ralph D. Winter and Steve C. Hawthorne, *Perspectives on the World Christian Movement: A Reader* (Pasadena, CA: William Carey Library, 1999), 25.

19 Oh, "Church Planting," 192–93. See Gordon Marshall, "Patron-Client Relationship," in *Oxford Dictionary of Sociology* (New York: Oxford University Press, 1998), 555.

Bibliography

Davis, Stephen M. "The Challenge of Missions in the Twenty-First Century." Lausanne World Pulse Archives, April 2008. https://www.lausanneworldpulse.com/perspectives-php/924/04-2008.

Heacock, Paul, ed. *Cambridge Academic Content Dictionary*.
Cambridge: Cambridge University Press, 2009.

Hiebert, Paul G. *Anthropological Insights for Missionaries*. Grand
Rapids, MI: Baker, 1985.

Im, Chandler H., and Amos Yong, eds. *Global Diasporas and Mission*.
Regnum Edinburgh Centenary Series 23. Oxford: Regnum, 2014.

Johnson, Todd. "Korean Christianity in the Context of Global
Christianity." In *Korean Church, God's Mission, Global Christianity*,
edited by Wonsuk Ma and Kyo Seoung Ahn, 71–84. Regnum
Edinburgh Centenary Series 26. Oxford: Regnum, 2015.

Kim, S. Hun, and Wonsuk Ma, eds. *Korean Diaspora and Christian
Mission*. Oxford: Regnum, 2011.

Korean World Mission Association. *2018: An Annual Status Report on
Korean Missionaries*. [In Korean.] n.p.: KWMA, 2018.

Korea Research Institute for Mission. *2019: A Status Report on Korean
World Mission*. [In Korean.] n.p.: KRIM, 2019.

Marshall, Gordon. "Patron-Client Relationship." In *Oxford Dictionary
of Sociology*. New York: Oxford University Press, 1998.

Nelson, Marlin. *Directory of Korean Missionaries and Mission Societies*.
Seoul: Asian Theological Seminary, 1979.

Nida, Eugene. *God's Word in Man's Language*. Pasadena, CA: William
Carey Library, 1973.

Oh, Robert. "Church Planting in Patronage Cultures: Aid
Dependency Issues and Missional Implications." PhD thesis,
Oxford Centre for Mission Studies, 2018.

Winter, Ralph D., and Steve C. Hawthorne, eds. *Perspectives on the
World Christian Movement: A Reader*. Pasadena, CA: William
Carey Library, 1999.

8

The Future of English Ministry in Diaspora Chinese and Asian Churches

Andrew Y. Lee

From a historical perspective, immigrant churches are not unique. Prior generations of immigrants from European countries such as Germany, Poland, and Sweden relocated to the United States and formed churches in their native tongues. Ministries were established to serve the children of newcomers, and as the second generation became adults, many joined majority-culture congregations. As they assimilated into other local churches, the immigrant churches of their parents and grandparents began a slow death march toward extinction because they were no longer relevant to the younger generation. Are we seeing the same trend today among immigrant churches with differing skin tones? Anecdotal scrutiny from seasoned pastors on the West Coast suggests that English ministries are dominated by teens, as young adults leave the churches of their parents. Will this be the fate of English ministry for the majority of bilingual churches today?

There has been much conversation in recent years about the state of the "Nones," young adults who no longer affiliate with the institutional church. There is a cultural dissonance between the Nones and the traditional church. The chasm is greater in heritage churches, as marginalization is twofold—between the older generation and the younger generation and between Asian culture and Western culture. Helen Lee's landmark article on the Asian second generation and D. J. Chuang's recent work[1] find an outbound tide in Asian American churches. Chuang notes dropout rates between 55 and 90 percent. This means that the vast majority of children who grow up in their parents' churches are not retained, dimming the future hopes of these places.

This is not to say that all these young adults have necessarily abandoned their faith; they may be attending church elsewhere. What they have largely left behind is the immigrant church. The attrition rate is staggering, as ethnic Asian churches as a whole have lost the overwhelming majority of the young people who grew up in them.[2] What are some primary factors that have led to this exodus? What forces are at play in heritage churches? As Chinese compose the largest segment of the Asian American population and the annual immigration of Chinese to the United States continues in substantial numbers, what is the future of the bilingual Chinese church? What hope is there for English-language congregations in Asian American churches?

1. The Teen Experience

As children mature into their teen years, churches start worship services in English. A number of these churches segregate the teens into youth services, separate from the regular English adult services, in order to minister more effectively to this age group. Many keep the middle school and high school students together in their own Sunday worship services, whereas others only separate them in middle school. If the former is the practice, one unintended result is that teens have less contact with the adult population in settings where spiritual formation is planned. The Sunday worship services and Christian education and fellowship take place in age-segregated groups. The adults are not a population with whom the teens are well acquainted, so assimilation into this context after their college years is often awkward. This is true of churches in general in America due to the gap between the younger and older generations. The cultural disconnect in ethnic churches exacerbates this dilemma.

Without taking ethnicity into account, one longitudinal study tracked 2,500 young people for twelve years, from the time they were between thirteen and seventeen in age to when they became twenty-five to twenty-nine years old. The study concludes that interaction with nonparental adults, in both formal and informal relationships, had a profound, positive, and long-term impact on the retention of the faith of the teens.[3] Kara Powell of the Fuller Youth Institute finds that "one thing churches can do that really makes a difference is getting kids actively involved in the life of the church before they graduate. There is a strong link between kids staying in church after they graduate and their involvement in intergenerational relationships and worship."[4]

A study of Christian youth determines "intergenerational relationships in faith communities is crucial."[5] From a historical perspective, intergenerational worship and spiritual formation were characteristic of the church until the recent era of age segregation.[6] If relationships play a vital role in retaining the second generation, as these studies suggest, they become even more critical in bilingual churches. The dearth of English-speaking adults in immigrant churches inhibits the growth of the English congregation. The ability to speak English is insufficient as a criterion: these adult leaders must develop meaningful relationships with those raised in the United States. Locating appropriate role models with whom the teens can identify is an arduous task. When the teens move on to college, the experience of age-wise segmentation continues.

2. The Collegiate Experience

What shapes students as they leave their home churches and move to college campuses? What happens during their college years? Many national parachurch organizations have recognized the intersection of culture and faith in serving college students. InterVarsity has spawned Asian American IV, Cru (formerly Campus Crusades) has formed EPIC to appeal to Asian American students and faculty on campuses, and the Navigators has created an Asian American network. These Asian American campus fellowships consist of people of a similar ethnicity, age group, and stage of life. They can go to class together, study together, eat together, work out together, and read the Bible and fellowship together at all hours of the night. This is a continuation of the age-segmented church experience, and these collegiate organizations become home churches for students. While they may attend Sunday morning worship services elsewhere, few become involved in local churches. Their spiritual lives and growth center on mono-generational college fellowship.

While parachurch organizations are intended to walk alongside the church in ministry partnership, this is not the case with regard to the university fellowships. The students remain detached from local churches and become accustomed to spiritual communities that are oriented with practices targeted for their immediate contexts. However, these experiences make it more difficult to return to their home churches, where little, from their perspective, appears to have changed during their four-year sojourn to college. After graduation, many seek a church life that will extend their collegiate experience.

3. The Young Adult Experience

For young adults, returning to their immigrant churches has not proven to be an easy transition. While some certainly have successfully assumed leadership roles in the English congregations, perhaps even on a church level, a great majority have not. Some return for short periods, but ultimately, most withdraw from heritage churches. The blossoming of pan-Asian churches and English-speaking Chinese American and Korean American churches in recent years attests to the popularity and desire for churches that are largely monogenerational with members in their twenties and early thirties. Having benefited from monogenerational fellowships during their undergraduate years and in their youth groups, the young adult churches maintain the age segregation that the members experienced throughout their spiritual lives. One of the features of millennials is their privilege, and they self-describe themselves as "entitled." Narcissistic traits—including a lack of empathy, a self-absorbed interest in themselves, a need for admiration, and a sense of grandiosity—mark their passage through their young lives.[7]

Thus they seek churches that cater to their needs—people who are similar to themselves in their career trajectory, socioeconomic status, marital status, and cultural affinities. In selecting churches, they seek freedom from the restrictions of the first-generation immigrant leaders. If postmodernism stresses individualism and the power of self-expression, then the millennial generation seeks communities that match their desired experiences. Factors such as loyalty, allegiance, tradition, and duty are overlooked in the name of self-actualization. The boom in young adult, English-language, Asian church plants reflects their desire to seek church bodies that are consistent with their prior experiences, ones that are age segregated and Asian American in flavor. By associating with people who are close in age, have similar interests and experiences, and have a shared culture, doing life together as young adults prolongs and approximates their collegiate experience. These churches will not meet their needs when they approach midlife, which is not a major concern for many, as it looms on a distant horizon.

It is ironic that an Asian American background is a beacon that draws these believers into new church bodies, yet it is highly doubtful that they can articulate their faith as Asian Americans. Having been exposed to the mainstream American evangelical church in theology and practice, they desire similar experiences amid Asian faces. Most cannot verbalize the relationship between cultural heritage and faith. Whereas mainline churches teach the integration of Asian American identity with Christian identity, such is not the case with other churches. These theologically conservative worshippers separate their ethnic identities from their spiritual identities. Russell Jeung writes, "Christians must overcome their Asian American heritage to find their 'true' selves. This process of identity construction includes renunciation, affirmation, and discernment of calling."[8]

When I asked about his Asian American Christian identity, Frank, a millennial Chinese male, responded, "I am unsure of what it is to have an Asian American Christian identity. I understand what it is to have an Asian American identity because even if I [would] rather not think of myself as Asian, others do and therefore force me to think of myself as Asian." He explained his theology of culture: "I don't believe there is such a thing as [B]lack theology, feminist theology, liberation theology, etc. There is only Christian theology so perhaps there is only Christian identity."[9] Frank's theology is in line with prior studies that indicate a belief in a culture-blind theology among many evangelicals.[10]

Jackie Chan's plaintive cry in his movie of the same title, *Who am I?*, is not reflected in many Asian American churches or among young adults on American college campuses.[11] In reality, the practices of Asian American Christians often mirror dominant-culture theology. Soong-Chan Rah says, "We live under the reality of the oppression of the Western white captivity of the church. We may claim that our version of evangelicalism is culture-free. . . . But the reality of the situation is that Western, white culture dominates American culture and, in turn, dominates American evangelicalism."[12] If one were to attend a worship service with one's eyes closed in a typical pan-Asian church or the English ministry of an Asian church, it would be difficult to tell from listening that the setting is Asian or that the worship leaders are Asian. The worship music largely consists of popular songs played on Christian radio stations, and the Sunday format approximates that of many Western churches.

For example, Gary left his immigrant church to go to a pan-Asian church where a number of his friends attended. When asked what role identity played in his decision, Gary could not come up with an answer aside from the fact that attending a pan-Asian church was "comfy." Such a congregation appealed to his social identity. As for the worship style of the new church, Gary noticed that the Korean worship leader would at times speak English with a British accent, which he attributed to listening to the Australian worship music. The interconnections among spirituality, identity, and ethnicity seem tenuous at best for many young adults. There does not appear to be a conscious linkage, though many recognize the sociocultural dimension in their search for a church home. Asian identity is downplayed in evangelical spirituality, although it looms in the background. Thus Gary concluded, "When I left the immigrant church, I wasn't thinking of [it] as an immigrant church. I only saw it as a church."

4. Factors in Leaving or Staying

If there is a subconscious desire on the part of many to worship with Asian Americans, why do they continue to leave in large numbers? What are the factors that discourage these young adults from returning and staying? A survey asked this question to English ministry pastors in bicultural Chinese churches. Most of the respondents serve either on the West Coast or on the East Coast. Two questions were open ended so that pastors could answer as they wished, drawing from their experiences: "Excluding job relocation, list up to four reasons why young adults (Age 22–34) leave your church" and "List up to four reasons why young adults (Age 22–34) remain in your church."[13] The results are telling. The answers are consistent regardless of the geographic location and congregation size. To the question of leaving, at 58 percent, the top reason given by pastors is a lack of *community*. An additional 12 percent who did not answer with *community* note that members left to seek *marriage prospects*. Together, these reasons add up to 70 percent. By far, some aspect of community is perceived to be the overwhelming reason why members leave the heritage church.

A study on Asian American millennials affirms community as the primary reason church members leave.[14] The surveys of pastors and church members yield similar findings. *Culture* is cited by 31 percent of the respondents, and 25 percent view *intergenerational conflict* or *issues with leadership* as a problem. Together, these reasons amount to 56 percent. However, some cite both elements in their reasons for leaving. Eliminating the duplication, we are still left with nearly half (46 percent) who see either cultural conflict or leadership as problematic in their churches.

At 40 percent, *programming* is the next reason, especially in small congregations. However, the percentage giving this response is equivalent for those in churches with over one hundred in attendance as well as for those averaging fewer than one hundred on Sunday mornings. Programming is a factor regardless of the congregation size. Members are either satisfied or dissatisfied with what their churches offer. Moreover, 31 percent of those surveyed (in churches with fewer than one hundred and in those with over one hundred in attendance) think that programming as a reason for staying points in this direction. Some members are pleased by what their churches offer and remain, while others are not happy with the same programming and leave. Might these reactions to church programs, both positive and negative, be connected to the critical nature of millennials, given their entitlement mentality? They will stay if they concur with what is offered and leave if they differ. At 35 percent, *church focus/theology* lags slightly behind programming. There is dissatisfaction with the spiritual direction of the church leadership.

Megachurches, with multiple services and programs, become natural landing places for those dissatisfied with ethnic churches. The percentage of people who list *leaving for more popular churches* as a cause is 19 percent for both smaller and larger churches. The attraction of popular churches is not a major motivation for leaving, and not being able to find a community has emerged as the largest obstacle to retaining young adults. The latter is also the single most important reason why they stay. *Community* is cited as a reason for staying by 71 percent of the respondents. Only one pastor mentions *spouse* as the reason why members stay. Personal relationships are the primary factors why millennials either stay at or leave their immigrant churches.[15] The second reason cites *intergenerational family* (50 percent). Those who cherish intergenerational ties with the "uncles" and "aunties" of the church desire to maintain these relationships. Together, the factors of *community* and *intergenerational family* add up to an overwhelming 92 percent. *Church focus* is attributed by 37 percent of the respondents, and another 37 percent select *ministry opportunities*. Overall, the reasons for staying point to the communal atmosphere that was first experienced while growing up, and they have a burden to serve for the second generation.

5. Making the Bicultural Church More Attractive to Young Adults

Based on the above discussion, primary efforts toward retaining English-speaking young adults should include the following:

a. Develop a Strong Community

If community is the primary factor in leaving or staying, there needs to be a critical mass of young adults in order for this age group to flourish. If there are ten or fewer adults in the critical twenty-two to thirty-four age group, it can be classified as a small group rather than a true fellowship. A lack of peers is a prohibitive cause for people staying. When young adults graduate from college and return to their home churches, their friends are no longer there, so they quickly exit. From their perspective, the community circle is limited, prospects for marriage are diminutive, and those who remain are expected to shoulder the burden of caring for the next generation. Loyalty to the spiritual home that birthed them often is not a decisive factor for those considering leaving. The Western values of individualism and anti-institutionalism are extremely powerful.

The programs of bicultural churches typically target children and teens. The number of young adults often pales in comparison and might even be fewer than the number of older married adults in English ministry. While the immigrant generation recognizes the need to bring their children and teens to church, to care for them, and to marshal resources for these age groups so that there is a promise for the future, the ethnic church leaders are not as sensitive to the needs of young adults. They operate under the false assumption that young adults will naturally stay at their churches and will care for themselves and be role models for the next generation. They are correct that the presence of young adults is a welcome harbinger for the future of their churches. Millennials have been proposed as being the key generation that impacts the overall health of the church. Their presence, or absence, inordinately affects a church's future, as per a Hartford Institute report. While millennials compose 23 percent of the American populace, only 10 percent of churches have this representation. A critical mass of millennials is 15 percent for the health of a church, and a thriving millennial fellowship leads to a thriving congregation.[16]

Without a critical mass of young adults in attendance—and not just by the percentage in a congregation—fellowship meetings will remain small, discouragement will set in, newcomers will not be attracted, new leaders will not develop, those currently serving will grow weary, and future prospects will remain dim. Consequently, the temptation to leave for greener pastures is extremely inviting. Friendship circles are extremely important to this age group, as evidenced by the popularity of social media and networking sites. The spiritual and social elements are inescapably intertwined. Some young adults will stay for a period of time but then leave when they determine that prospects for change in the foreseeable future are limited.

As a rule, larger churches have more human resources so that there are more young adults to form a core group regardless of whether they have a critical mass of 15 percent or not. Young adult retention is a daunting task for smaller congregations. South Bay Bible Church in San Jose, California, made second-generation retention their focus and found that the parents who were bilingual and had to transition from a Chinese-language service to English worship continued fellowship groups in Chinese. This church retained many of the second generation because they made the shift to the English language. This strategy facilitated family relationships encouraging millennials to remain in their home church. Pouring more resources into reaching young adults and prioritizing them is critical for the future of the bilingual church.

b. Address Cultural and Intergenerational Conflict

This is a song that continues to be sung generation after generation. For decades, there has been a culture war between the first- and second-generation church leaders as well as conflict over leadership issues.[17] Furthermore, the trajectory of immigrant intergenerational churches has not changed for generations. The first-generation leadership remains entrenched, and English ministry leaders are considered to be "young people" even if they are married and have children. Differences with the first generation were a primary factor in the exodus of young adults from their immigrant churches because they found them to be "irrelevant, culturally stifling, and ill-equipped to develop them spiritually for life in the multicultural 1990s."[18] At times, the ethnic dimension of the churches overshadowed their spiritual nature.[19]

This description is accurate for Danielle's home church. Though she relocated to another state for career advancement, all her childhood friends have left their home church and worship in a racially diverse church with a large Asian population, where preaching and programs target the next generation. According to Danielle, her former church is too conservative. *Stodgy* is the term used by Ethan to describe his immigrant megachurch. Despite the numerous programs at his large English ministry, young adults continue to leave the conservative setting for a more open spiritual climate. Differences between Asian and Western approaches to worship, Christian education methods, evangelism and fellowship style, and format can be sources of the divide.

Aside from cultural relevancy, there are unresolved intergenerational conflicts in Ethan's church and in many others. Leaders from the first generation and those from the later generations do not share a common vision, nor do they share a common philosophy regarding how ministry is to take place. These disagreements cause many to leave. One study attempts to identify the factors that discourage English-language Chinese pastors and cause them to depart from ministry in the bicultural church. Not surprisingly, the reason most cited by these pastors is "cultural differences and demands."[20] The sociologist Rebecca Y. Kim argues that what makes the second-generation Korean Americans distinct is the experience of intercultural and intergenerational conflicts with the first generation.[21] Most immigrant church leaders do not understand why their children leave, nor do they desire to accept the reasons if informed. Many of the dynamics present today were detailed by the Fellowship of American Chinese Evangelicals (FACE) in newsletters published from 1979 to 2003. Launched in 1978 after the North America Congress on Chinese Evangelicals conference held in Toronto, FACE leaders gave voice to the second-generation conflicts experienced in bilingual churches.[22]

Enoch Wong's invaluable study of English-speaking believers in Chinese churches in Canada includes a number of recommendations for overcoming the cultural divide. Among his ten suggestions for retaining the English-speaking believers in Chinese churches are the following:

- *Move from Instructing to Journeying*—Mutual learning where the elderly and the young learn one from another. Discipleship becomes a two-way street.
- *Move from Rigidity to Fluidity*—Reimaging and redeploying images and symbols which means treading on sacred cows so that needed changes can take place.
- *Move from Hierarchy to Lower Power Differential*—Shifting the center of power from a top-down to a flatter decision-making structure where equality is highly valued. Authority is shared with the second generation.[23]

These directional actions reflect much-needed reform if English ministry is to flourish long term. It will require a change in the overall culture of a church. While these suggestions are sound, unless the organizational culture truly changes, these strategic proposals will fail. The key to Wong's action plan rests with the first-generation leaders, as they are the church's gatekeepers. The onus falls on them to take an active role in changing the existing culture, and a change in the organizational culture of a church may take a number of years.[24] Are young adults patient to play the long game in working toward organizational change? The majority of English ministry pastors have short tenures.

c. Give Young Adults a Voice

The transformation of the culture in an organization requires listening to the voices that advocate change. While bicultural churches seek representation from the second generation, there is an inherent problem in leadership representation. The few or lone English representatives are a minority on the church board. Their voices are drowned out by the strength of the first-generation board members. Without the support of the majority, whatever initiatives they bring to the table will be stillborn. Even if they are requested to serve on the church board, English-speaking members may decline due to the power dynamics in play.

It's been noted that having a voice to speak up is a characteristic of millennials.[25] When they are not heard, they will in all likelihood leave.[26] If they do not have a share of the leadership to direct ministry initiatives, they will depart. If they find themselves serving as workers, many will seek a new setting. For example, Beth grew up in an Asian church, and her family was active in church leadership. When she went away to college, she attended a large dominant-culture church. But her spiritual and social life revolved around the Chinese Christian campus fellowship. Following a graduate degree, marriage, and relocation, Beth and her husband had to decide about church membership and spent several weeks visiting various churches. The local Chinese church took a special interest in wooing them, as very few couples moved into the area. Ultimately, Beth chose to attend one of the popular college-town churches. This young couple concluded that if they had joined the Chinese church, they would have been immediately pressed into service and been expected to provide leadership beyond what they were prepared to do at that stage in their lives. They were of value to the church as workers to the English-speaking teens. Although Beth and her spouse both ultimately earned PhDs, their involvement in the church remained minimal.

d. Preach Biblically Relevant Sermons
This final recommendation lies outside the purview of the survey we conducted, probably because it is difficult for

pastors to make this evaluation of their own messages; however, it is identified as a significant retention factor by both Andrew Y. Lee and Stephen G. Quen in their respective studies.[27]

Conclusion

As long as the number of immigrants to the United States from Asia remains high, the need for bilingual churches will continue to exist. Asian immigrants are projected to become the largest foreign-born group by 2055.[28] The demand for English ministries to children and teens will continue to be a high priority in these churches. However, the observed pattern is that while some English-speaking adults will remain to serve this constituency, the vast majority will leave at some point unless conditions change. In communities where Asian immigrants compose a lower percentage of residents, they will have difficulty in retaining their adult children. The lack of third-generation English speakers in bilingual churches, much less the struggle to retain the second generation, attests to the historical failure of immigrant churches to provide a setting for the second generation to flourish. A proposal to break this deadlock is for the second generation to take the lead in planting English-speaking Asian American churches, a movement that is flourishing in many cities. They could then plant an immigrant congregation to reach the first generation, a reversal of the long-standing methodology that has been in place for creating bilingual churches in America.

Notes

1 See Helen Lee, "Silent Exodus: Can the East Asian Church in America Reverse the Flight of Its Next Generation?," *Christianity Today* 40 (1996): 50–53; D. J. Chuang, *MultiAsian.Church: A Future for Asian Americans in a Multiethnic World* (Los Angeles: CreateSpace, 2016).

2 D. J. Chuang, "Silent Exodus: Asian American Christians Leaving Churches," djchuang.com, December 8, 2017, https://djchuang.com/when-asian-american-christian-youth-go-to-college/.

3 Christian Smith, *Souls in Transition* (New York: Oxford University Press, 2009), 285.

4 Kara Powell, "Is the Era of Age Segmentation Over? An Interview with Kara Powell," *Leadership* 30 (Summer 2009): 44.

5 David Kinnaman, *You Lost Me* (Grand Rapids, MI: Baker, 2011), 203.

6 Holly C. Allen and Christine L. Ross, *Intergenerational Christian Formation* (Downers Grove, IL: InterVarsity, 2012).

7 Lindsay Miller and Annie Gabillet, "Everyone Thinks Millennials Are Entitled—Even Millennials," POPSUGAR, June 10, 2018, https://www.popsugar.com/news/Why-Millennials-Entitled-42873548. See also Jean M. Twenge, *Generation Me* (New York: Atria, 2006); Jean M. Twenge and W. Keith Campbell, *The Narcissism Epidemic* (New York: Atria, 2010).

8 Russell Jeung, "Evangelical and Mainline Teachings on Asian American Identity," in *Asian American Christianity Reader*, ed. Viji Nakka-Cammauf and Timothy Tseng (Castro Valley, CA: ISAAC, 2009), 211.

9 Andrew Y. Lee, "Should I Stay or Should I Go?" (unpublished manuscript, 2010), ISAAC Young Adult Primer.

10 See Andrew Y. Lee, "Reading the Bible as an Asian American: Issues in Asian American Biblical Interpretation," in Nakka-Cammauf and Tseng, *Asian American Christianity Reader*, 255–66.

11 Rudy V. Busto, "The Gospel according to the Model Minority: Hazarding an Interpretation of Asian American Evangelical College Students," *Amerasia* 22, no. 1 (1996): 140.

12 Soong-Chan Rah, *The Next Evangelicalism: Freeing the Church from Western Cultural Captivity* (Downers Grove, IL: InterVarsity, 2009), 200.

13 This survey was conducted by the writer in the fall of 2018. There were fifty-two respondents active in ministry, nearly all of whom currently serve as English ministry pastors in immigrant churches.

14 Stephen G. Quen, "Reaching and Retaining American-Born Asian Millennials at Bay Area Chinese Bible Church" (DMin diss., Biola University, 2018), 146. The top five reasons church members leave are related to community, sermons, church leadership, lack of life-stage transition ministries, and Chinese cultural identity.

15 Community is a crucial component that millennials seek, according to Richard Regan, "The 3 C's to Connecting with Millennials," govloop, February 17, 2017, https://www.govloop.com/community/blog/the-3-cs-to-connecting-with-millennials/.

16 Kristina Lizardy-Hajbi, *Engaging Young Adults* (Harford, CT: Faith Communities Today, 2015). See also Eric Swanson, "Millennials: The 'Keystone Species' to Your Church's Future," Leadership Network, August 24, 2017, https://leadnet.org/millennials-the-keystone-species-to-your-churchs-future/. The median number of young adults in the churches covered by this survey was twenty, comprising 33 percent of the congregations, and the median size of the English worship services was sixty.

17 The now defunct Fellowship of American Chinese Evangelicals (FACE) published years of newsletters detailing these struggles. FACE was formed in 1978 at the North America Congress of Chinese Evangelicals.

18 Lee, "Silent Exodus," 50.

19 Rebecca Y. Kim, "Second-Generation Korean American Evangeli-cals," in Nakka-Cammauf and Tseng, *Asian American Christianity Reader*, 219.

20 Justin Der, "ABC Pastor Discouragement and Dropout: A Study Based on the Responses of 64 Pastors," Scribd, June 6, 2001, http://www.scribd.com/doc/22821687/ABC-Pastors-Discouragement-and-Dropout.

21 Kim, "Second-Generation Korean," 226.

22 See FACE's history, ministry, and newsletters at "History of Fellow-ship of American Chinese Evangelicals (FACE)," open.djchuang.com, accessed April 15, 2022, https://open.djchuang.com/cache/history-of-face.

23 Enoch Wong et al., *Listening to Their Voices* (Toronto: CCCOWE Canada, 2018), 234–68.

24 See Gilbert R. Rendle, *Leading Change in the Congregation* (Lanham, MD: Rowman & Littlefield, 2007).

25 A characteristic of millennials is the desire to be heard. See John Kanelis, "Millennials Seek to Have Their Voices Heard," Panhandle PBS, January 5, 2016, http://www.panhandlepbs.org/blogs/public-view-john-kanelis/millennials-seek-to-have-their-voices-heard.

26 At one church leadership meeting discussing how to attract Chinese-speaking young adults, it was suggested to the leaders that they should meet with those in that age group to listen to them. The suggestion fell on deaf ears.

27 Lee, "Should I Stay?"; Quen, "Reaching and Retaining," 157–58.

28 See Abby Budiman, "Key Findings about U.S. Immigrants," Pew Research Center, August 20, 2020, http://www.pewresearch.org/fact-tank/2018/11/30/key-findings-about-u-s-immigrants.

Bibliography

Allen, Holly C., and Christine L. Ross. *Intergenerational Christian Formation*. Downers Grove, IL: InterVarsity, 2012.

Budiman, Abby. "Key Findings about U.S. Immigrants." Pew Research Center, August 20, 2020. http://www.pewresearch.org/fact-tank/2018/11/30/key-findings-about-u-s-immigrants.

Busto, Rudy V. "The Gospel according to the Model Minority: Hazarding an Interpretation of Asian American Evangelical College Students." *Amerasia* 22, no. 1 (1996): 140.

Chuang, D. J. *MultiAsian.Church: A Future for Asian Americans in a Multiethnic World*. Los Angeles: CreateSpace, 2016.

———. "Silent Exodus: Asian American Christians Leaving Churches." djchuang.com, December 8, 2017. https://djchuang.com/when-asian-american-christian-youth-go-to-college/.

Der, Justin. "ABC Pastor Discouragement and Dropout: A Study Based on the Responses of 64 Pastors." Scribd, June 6, 2001. http://www.scribd.com/doc/22821687/ABC-Pastors-Discouragement-and-Dropout.

Jeung, Russell. "Evangelical and Mainline Teachings on Asian American Identity." In *Asian American Christianity Reader*, edited by Viji Nakka-Cammauf and Timothy Tseng, 197–216. Castro Valley, CA: ISAAC, 2009.

Kanelis, John. "Millennials Seek to Have Their Voices Heard." Panhandle PBS, January 5, 2016. http://www.panhandlepbs.org/blogs/public-view-john-kanelis/millennials-seek-to-have-their-voices-heard.

Kim, Rebecca Y. "Second-Generation Korean American Evangelicals." In *Asian American Christianity Reader*, edited by Viji Nakka-Cammauf and Timothy Tseng, 217–228. Castro Valley, CA: ISAAC, 2009.

Kinnaman, David. *You Lost Me*. Grand Rapids, MI: Baker, 2011.

Lee, Andrew Y. "Reading the Bible as an Asian American: Issues in Asian American Biblical Interpretation." In *Asian American Christianity Reader*, edited by Viji Nakka-Cammauf and Timothy Tseng, 255–266. Castro Valley, CA: ISAAC, 2009.

———. "Should I Stay or Should I Go?" Unpublished manuscript, last modified 2010. ISAAC Young Adult Primer.

Lee, Helen. "Silent Exodus: Can the East Asian Church in America Reverse the Flight of Its Next Generation?" *Christianity Today* 40 (1996): 50–53.

Lizardy-Hajbi, Kristina. *Engaging Young Adults*. Harford, CT: Faith Communities Today, 2015. https://faithcommunitiestoday.org/wp-content/uploads/2018/12/Engaging-Young-Adults-Report.pdf.

Miller, Lindsay, and Annie Gabillet. "Everyone Thinks Millennials Are Entitled—Even Millennials." POPSUGAR, June 10, 2018. https://www.popsugar.com/news/Why-Millennials-Entitled-42873548.

Chuang, D. J. "History of Fellowship of American Chinese Evangelicals (FACE)." Accessed April 15, 2022. https://open.djchuang.com/cache/history-of-face.

Powell, Kara. "Is the Era of Age Segmentation Over? An Interview with Kara Powell." *Leadership* 30 (Summer 2009): 44.

Quen, Stephen G. "Reaching and Retaining American-Born Asian Millennials at Bay Area Chinese Bible Church." DMin diss., Biola University, 2018.

Rah, Soong-Chan. *The Next Evangelicalism: Freeing the Church from Western Cultural Captivity*. Downers Grove, IL: InterVarsity, 2009.

Regan, Richard. "The 3 C's to Connecting with Millennials." Govloop, February 17, 2017. https://www.govloop.com/community/blog/the-3-cs-to-connecting-with-millennials/.

Rendle, Gilbert R. *Leading Change in the Congregation*. Lanham, MD: Rowman & Littlefield, 2007.

Smith, Christian. *Souls in Transition*. New York: Oxford University Press, 2009.

Swanson, Eric. "Millennials: The 'Keystone Species' to Your Church's Future." Leadership Network, August 24, 2017. https://leadnet .org/millennials-the-keystone-species-to-your-churchs-future/.

Twenge, Jean M. *Generation Me*. New York: Atria, 2006.

Twenge, Jean M., and W. Keith Campbell. *The Narcissism Epidemic*. New York: Atria, 2010.

Wong, Enoch, Jonathan Tam, Kwing Hung, Tommy Tsui, and Wes Wong. *Listening to Their Voices*. Toronto: CCCOWE Canada, 2018.

9

Cross-Cultural Training of Missionary Candidates in the Global South

Paul Sungro Lee

Introduction

Christian mission is no longer from the West to the Rest, but it has increasingly become the task of many national churches and believers. Today, missionaries are being sent out from many nations to others of the world, and dozens of countries have emerged as mission-sending nations. Strategists had previously noted that Africa and Asia would emerge as key fulcra for world missions in the twenty-first century. The Lausanne Congress held in South Africa in 2010 confirmed it to be true.[1] With the unprecedented growth of Christianity in the Global South, the need for cross-cultural ministry and missionaries has skyrocketed. However, the missionary candidates have limited opportunities for mission training, let alone sound theological training. Joel A. Carpenter writes, "Outside North America and Western Europe, higher education is expanding at an astonishing rate, and the main crisis in higher education worldwide is how to meet the huge and growing demand for education with anything resembling university-quality teaching and learning."[2]

Christian missionaries from the Global North have played a major role in Great Commission endeavors in the last century. If the Macedonian man whom Paul encountered in a vision was from Asia or Africa, the Christian story would have unfolded very differently. It could have been the Global South that enjoyed the transformative aspects of blossoming Christian culture for centuries. It is a likely scenario that Global South missionaries must have propagated the gospel to the ends of the earth by the mid-twentieth century.[3] However, it was the Europeans and European settlers at large—the anthropologically rightful descendants of Japheth, one of Noah's three sons—who have been used by God as the brave forerunners of the world missions throughout history.

Unfortunately, the rise of colonization left the misconception that Christianity is a Western religion. It was somewhat confusing to differentiate those oppressed by colonizers of the past because they were explorers and often shared the same routes to enter new fields. It took incessant contextualization efforts by devout missionaries and local evangelists who assisted the national dissemination of the gospel and contextualization process to present the message to be faithful to its meaning but be flexible to its function. This effort served as an integral part of the growth of Christianity in the Global South and the growing number of church leaders raised within and missionaries sent out from the region. Missionary forces from both the Global North and the Global South are needed for the collaborative task of world evangelization.[4] They must overcome their differences and prejudices by promoting ethnorelativism rather than ethnocentrism and create partnerships for the church's common task of the Great Commission.[5] After all, neither can excel in world missions without the other.

The surge in the Third World mission movement is creating a crisis in missionary training, and global cooperation is crucial. Larry D. Pate asserts, "While there are some excellent examples of third-world missionary training institutions, many missionaries are sent to the field with little or no training, while others must wait months or even years for a training opportunity. But sending a missionary without training is like commissioning a carpenter without tools! With the number of Third World missionaries promising to multiply three and one-half times during this decade, this is a priority issue for Western and non-Western missionary leaders alike."[6]

In response to this growing crisis, this author and his colleagues have developed a missionary-training program with distinctive features to train the missionaries of the two-thirds world. The Evangelical Alliance for Preacher Training/Commission (EAPTC) operates training schools in Kenya, Tanzania, Malawi, the Philippines, China, South Korea, and Vietnam. The curriculum that was developed is called the Missionary Candidate Training (MCT) manual, and the course is offered online in cooperation with DCI Global Partnerships in the United Kingdom. The cross-cultural mission principles in this training manual are partially field-tested in parts of Africa, Asia, Oceania, and the Americas and are available in French, Spanish, Portuguese, Amharic, and Korean. Through this training, the EAPTC's work grew to nearly three hundred new church plants in fourteen countries of the world (as of April 2019).

One of the most critical components of missionary preparation is intercultural readiness. Leaving for overseas missionary services without enough chances to receive and get tested on cross-cultural preparedness to deal with the locals in the field may result in attrition, depression, and unfruitful services.[7] According to an exhaustive review of related literature, the four subdomain components that enhance one's intercultural readiness at the predeparture stage were found to be the following: (1) interpersonal relationships, (2) cultural adaptation, (3) family relationships, and (4) previous learning experiences.[8] An enhancement of interpersonal relationships is critical in missionary preparation. Poor interpersonal relationships result in ineffective missionary service. Being conversant with cultural issues helps missionaries be less stressed and more relational with the locals. Family support holds its members together through cultural transitions. This is true for those who immigrate to other countries for a job, education, marriage, or a better life. Life in an unfamiliar mission field is challenging, and it is wise to learn from past experiences and others who have lived in those cultures.

Conceptualization Elements of the MCT Program

Born in Korea and having spent about one-third of his life in Asia, America, and Africa, respectively, this author has experienced firsthand the difficulties of adjusting to new cultures. This study was born out of a quest for effective cross-cultural discipleship during my field studies in Kenya, Korea, and the Philippines while serving as a career missionary for twenty-three years. Intercultural readiness became my foremost concern to help anyone wishing to serve as a missionary in cross-cultural contexts. I have conducted missionary-training courses for missionary candidates in Africa and conducted advanced research in the field.

Robert W. Ferris identifies four characteristics that distinguish the programs of effective missionary-training centers. First, effective missionary-training centers are consciously and intentionally oriented toward character and skills development for cross-cultural ministry. Stress on character and faithfulness underlays the entire MCT program, from its orientation to the last lesson. Second, an effective missionary-training center is a community devoted to developing Christian graces and refining interpersonal skills. Small-group learning is mandatory in the MCT program regardless of the place and time. Third, effective missionary-training centers use informal and nonformal learning. From academic classes to practices, the MCT provides a well-researched teaching program. Fourth, an effective missionary-training center has training curricula appropriate to the trainees' tasks. The hands-on training is applied to assist them with cross-cultural preparation.[9]

The MCT lessons are based on a biblical worldview with an incarnational learning experience and run in a small community group of a minimum of five to a maximum of fifteen participants. The group experience develops critical thinking skills, and praxis components enable the spiritual growth of participants.[10] The training includes communal living and a blend of nonformal, informal, and formal education. After orientation, classes run for ten teaching sessions at flexible times and in flexible locations. Lessons are framed to suit any setting with or without a high-tech infrastructure. The MCT works with local congregations and facilitators to offer training as well as a hands-on internship in the areas where a participant needs more training. The MCT program deliberately runs in small groups to model the principles of discipleship exercised by the first disciples who spent time with Jesus. They heard what Jesus said and were under his supervision. Later, they did what Jesus did and reported back to him. They learned by hearing and by doing, and they learned the value of fellowship, teamwork, and accountability.[11] The EAPTC used this model in many countries without having to acquire a facility to convene classes, as it is easy to implement anywhere.

Non-Western Biblical Worldview Training

The MCT lessons are based on a non-Western biblical worldview learning model. David A. Noebel identifies six worldviews that are dominant today: (1) Christian theism, (2) Islamic theism, (3) secular humanism, (4) Marxism, (5) cosmic humanism, and (6) postmodernism.[12] Paul G. Hiebert finds that worldviews are transformed through two basic ways: "Normal change occurs when changes on the level of conscious beliefs and practices over time infiltrate and bring about change at the worldview level."[13] He sees the worldview transformation as a conversion and as a process of ongoing deep discipleship. The MCT can be adapted easily in local churches that wish to experience a biblical worldview transformation for those holding existing general worldviews, intentionally those of the two-thirds world distinctive. Figure 9.1 shows how one's worldview shifted as he was converted to Christ and matured as a disciple of Christ.

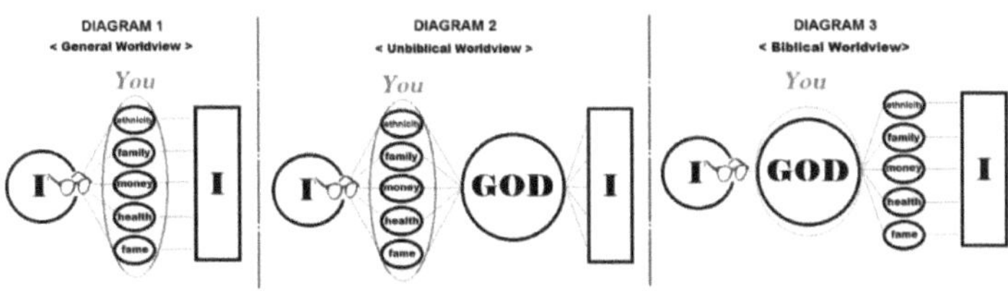

Figure 9.1. The MCT's model of progression for a shift in worldview

Missionary candidates either directly from the Global South or out of a diasporic background with a Global South heritage are encouraged to experience a transformative shift of worldview during their missionary training. Having offered the MCT mainly to those coming from a Global South background over the years, the EAPTC could not find many practical training curricula that were historically and biblically appropriate for the majority world. The training curriculum was written from a non-Western perspective and a biblical worldview. For instance, African missionaries bring an orientation to the supernatural; beliefs concerning the spirit world; the concepts of extended family relationships, care for the elderly, and hospitality; and the event versus time orientation.[14]

Denis Lane finds four advantages the two-thirds world missionaries have over their Western counterparts: (1) they are culturally similar to their target cultures, meaning less adjustment is required; (2) they are obtaining visas to similar countries, which is easier; (3) they are experienced in the educational needs, poverty, and difficult political situations of their target cultures; and (4) they lack a colonial background.[15] Besides, the worldviews of mission trainees from the non-Western world differ from the Western mission trainees', which expedited the development of the

MCT manual—and from the perspective of the two-thirds worldviews.

Incarnate Homogenization in Training

The MCT emphasizes the need to incarnate homogenization both in theory and in practice, vitally important for success in missions.[16] Today, it is no longer uncommon to witness Global South missionaries reevangelizing the secularized Europe. Responding sensitively to this trend, it is necessary to mention the importance of Christ's exemplary incarnational effort, which should be replicated regardless of the time and place. The gospel can only be effectively delivered when missionaries understand the people they are trying to reach and the world in which they live. Charles H. Kraft observes,

> Anthropology has said that in order to study people, we have to observe people by living with them and participating with them in their everyday life. We must live with them, learn their language, and do as much as we can to learn to look at the world from their point of view. We need to discover what their assumptions are concerning reality and ask ourselves questions such as, "If I assumed reality to be what they assume it to be, how would the world look to me? And if it looked that way to me, how would I behave?" On the basis of the understandings gained through seeking answers to such questions, applied anthropologists (including missionaries) have often been able to help people discover answers to problems they previously could not solve.[17]

Many different terms from various disciplines describe elements of "incarnational homogenization," including developmental psychology, sociology, and ethology. Terms such as *imprinting, bonding, attachment,* and *immersion* are used in developmental psychology, while terms such as *identification, role adaptation, bicultural community, incarnation,* and *attachment* are popular among missiologists. Each has a distinctive approach and a nuanced conceptual framework. For a detailed explanation, see the thesis of Evelyne Annick Reisacher and various reference works.[18]

The concept of incarnation has gained much attention during the last two decades. It was initiated by Kraft and was developed extensively by Sherwood G. Lingenfelter and Marvin K. Mayers.[19] It is based on Philippians 2:5–11: as Jesus became like us in order to communicate with us, missionaries must apply his example of the incarnation when they enter and live in the field concerning their lifestyles and attitudes.[20] Kraft sees the incarnational concept as God's strategy to aid the communication of his message more effectively to his receptors. God employed the most basic principle of effective communication—receptor-oriented communication.[21] Missionaries must learn and imitate this principle of personal participation in the lives of their receptors. The person (whether Jesus or a person) was the major component of the message conveyed in all life-changing communication.

Lingenfelter and Mayers explain that the incarnation of Jesus Christ could be used as a model for missionaries, instructing them to enter into, live in, and minister within the receptors' culture. Jesus left his home in heaven to live among and minister to people as a bonded belonger of a particular community, speaking the same language spoken by those living in Palestine at the time. In the same manner, the missionary is born, grows, and lives within the target community by going through the incarnational process. Christ's incarnation was God's way of meeting humans here on earth. Following his example, missionaries must learn to be at home in the new languages and cultures they enter—they must become bonded belongers.[22] Incarnation is akin to learning as if we are helpless infants and is necessary for intercultural ministry because culture is always learned and shared with others, and in this process, people begin to perceive and respond to one another in culturally conditioned ways.[23]

Missionary incarnation through bonding with local people opens the ultimate pathway to cross-cultural discipleship.[24] Incarnational ministry in this global age catalyzes respect, humility, and leadership through learning from brothers and sisters of different backgrounds and heritages.[25]

Over and beyond incarnational approaches, the sovereign work and grace of God cannot be ignored in this endeavor. They are the underlying ingredients of all God-used mission and evangelism efforts in church history. Matthew 24:14 tells us that the gospel of the kingdom *will* be preached in the whole world as a testimony to all nations, and then the end will come. The word *will* gives us a hint that this enterprise of world missions is going to eventually be the work of the Holy Spirit. To this end, the Lord often causes and orchestrates the movements of people and cultural groups to other geographic locations of the world, although their initial reasons for moving may vary. Acts 17:26 shows that it was *the Lord* who determined the nations' preappointed times and the boundaries of their dwellings. The sovereign work of the Spirit of the Lord is present in all successful cross-cultural discipleship. Therefore, total dependency on the leading of the Holy Spirit is an undeniable key for every successful cross-cultural disciple-making venture. This is the third conceptualization element of the MCT manual.

Missionary Longevity

Preparing missionary candidates with sufficient intercultural resilience is believed to be essential for longevity in mission fields.[26] While unpreventable departures of missionaries from the field might be unstoppable (e.g., retirement, death, loss of visa, and appointment to leadership in the mission agency), there are preventable causes that force missionaries to leave the field (e.g., work- or team-related reasons, dismissal, personal issues, and agency issues).[27] A study on missionary retention by the World Evangelical Alliance finds that the top four factors contributing the most to missionaries' effectiveness in their fields (as stated by seventy-five of the seventy-eight mission agencies in the United States) are the following: (1) the development of good relationships/teams (thirty-two agencies), (2) a commitment to the ministry (twenty-seven agencies), (3) effective leadership with good supervision and accountability (twenty-five agencies), and (4) clear objectives, goals, and expectations that were agreed upon (twenty-four agencies). When the same agencies were asked about factors that hindered missionaries the most from effectively attaining their tasks in the field, seventy-four of the seventy-eight agencies noted the top factors as (1) a lack of finances (thirty agencies), (2) family issues (twenty-eight agencies), and (3) relationship problems (twenty-seven agencies).[28]

The preventable causes of forced departure from mission fields, including interpersonal relationship conflicts and family discords, might be remedied if there were adequate training focusing on intercultural preparation provided before missionaries leave for the field.

Conclusion

Missionary training for the majority Christian world needs to be carefully designed to provide a small group-based learning environment to equip trainees with robust biblical and non-Western worldviews as well as incarnate homogenization in practical ways such that their intercultural readiness is increased in the following domains: interpersonal relationships, cultural adaptation, family relationships, and previous learning experiences. These domains play a critical role in missionaries' cross-cultural preparedness. The components of interpersonal relationships are well addressed in chapter 5 (cross-cultural communication), chapter 6 (developing leadership skills), and chapter 7 (the life and work of a missionary) of the MCT training manual. The components of cultural adaptation are well stressed in chapter 4 (the biblical cultures of the world), chapter 7 (the life and work of a missionary), chapter 9 (the multiplication of cross-cultural discipleship), and chapter 10 (homogenization and incarnation) of the MCT training manual. The components of family relationships are well tackled in chapter 6 (developing leadership skills) and chapter 7 (the life and work of a missionary) of the MCT training manual. The components of previous learning experiences are well addressed in chapter 6 (developing leadership skills) and chapter 7 (the life and work of a missionary) of the MCT training manual. All in all, the MCT was designed and developed to suit the above exclusive specifics to improve the intercultural readiness in one's missionary predeparture preparation. The purpose of eminence in intercultural preparation is for a sound and effective tenure in the mission field, with greater longevity and fruitful task performance in one's missionary service. Thus, there might be less crash and burn because of cultural differences.

Both the Global South and the Global North have a role to play in world missions today, increasingly doing them together. While the Lord is calling more missionaries from the churches in the Global South than the North, former mission-sending countries in the North have a new role in helping train more missionaries from the Global South and receive missionaries from other parts of the world in their countries. Northern churches could provide adequate training to new missionaries in the South for effective cross-cultural engagement and share their resources, including financial contributions. The churches of the Global North may need to overcome paternalistic approaches as they partner with missionary candidates of the South.[29] There are five forms of paternalism: (1) resource paternalism, (2) spiritual paternalism, (3) knowledge paternalism, (4) labor paternalism, and (5) managerial paternalism.[30]

Effective missionary training can be done at local churches and other cross-cultural mission agencies that provide predeparture mission training, which emphasizes communal learning, biblical worldviews, and incarnate homogenization. This training must also conduct assessments and develop missionary-training programs that are sensitive to tactile intercultural preparation for Global South missionary candidates. In the end, the work of sharpened missionary forces from the majority world will thrive and penetrate deeper when people are moving from everywhere to everywhere and when the gospel is going forth from everywhere to everywhere.

Notes

1 Rose Dowsett, *The Cape Town Commitment: A Confession of Faith and a Call to Action* (Peabody, MA: Hendrickson, 2012), 2.

2 Joel A. Carpenter, *Christian Higher Education: A Global Reconnaissance* (Grand Rapids, MI: Eerdmans, 2014), 8.

3 Robert Hall Glover, *The Bible Basis of Missions* (Chicago, IL: Moody, 1946), 190.

4 Larry D. Pate, *From Every People: A Handbook of Two-Thirds World Missions with Directory, Histories, Analysis* (Monrovia, CA: MARC, 1989).

5 Jay Moon, "Toward True Globalism in World Missions," *Lausanne Global Analysis* 8, no. 1 (January 2019), https://www.lausanne.org/content/lga/2019-01/toward-true-globalism-in-world-missions?fbclid=IwAR3QlIgHGe1rOuiPvrMhUel1Y45A-2n7ibIix98cq4fLfAMObR2d7g8HcBQ.

6 Larry D. Pate, "The Changing Balance in Global Mission," *International Bulletin of Mission Research* 15, no. 2 (1991): 56–61.

7 Sangkeun Kim, "Sheer Numbers Do Not Tell the Entire Story," *Ecumenical Review* 57, no. 4 (2005): 467–68.

8 See Paul Sungro Lee, "The Impact of Missionary Training on Intercultural Readiness in Seoul, Korea" (PhD diss., Oxford Graduate School, 2014).

9 Robert W. Ferris, ed., *Establishing Ministry Training: A Manual for Programme Developers* (Pasadena, CA: William Carey Library, 1995), https://weamc.global/archive/Ferris_Ministry-Training.pdf.

10 Myung Ho Kim, "The Dialogical Approach and Spiritual Growth: Discipleship Training in Korea" (PhD diss., Trinity Evangelical Divinity School, 2006).

11 See Bill Hull, *The Disciple-Making Church* (Old Tappan, NJ: F. H. Revell, 1990).

12 See David A. Noebel, *Understanding the Times: The Religious Worldviews of Our Day and the Search for Truth* (Eugene, OR: Harvest House, 1997).

13 Paul G. Hiebert, *Transforming Worldviews: An Anthropological Understanding of How People Change* (Grand Rapids, MI: Baker Academic, 2008), 319.

14 Paul Sungro Lee, *Missionary Candidate Training* (Merrifield, VA: Evangelical Alliance for Preacher Training Commission, 2008), 21–22.

15 Denis Lane, *Tuning God's New Instruments* (Singapore: World Evangelical Fellowship, 1990), 3.

16 For the importance of missionary incarnation, see Thomas V. Morris, "The Coherence of the Incarnation," in *Christian Apologetics: An Anthology of Primary Sources*, ed. Khaldoun A. Sweis and Chad V. Meiste (Grand Rapids, MI: Zondervan, 2012), 260–70.

17 Charles H. Kraft, *Anthropology for Christian Witness* (Maryknoll, NY: Orbis, 1996), 12.

18 See Evelyne Annick Reisacher, "The Processes of Attachment between the Algerians and French within the Christian Community in France" (PhD diss., Fuller Theological Seminary, 2001).

19 See Charles H. Kraft, *Christianity in Culture* (Maryknoll, NY: Orbis, 1979); Charles H. Kraft, *Communicating the Gospel God's Way* (Pasadena, CA: William Carey Library, 1983); Sherwood G. Lingenfelter and Marvin K. Mayers, *Ministering Cross-Culturally: An Incarnational Model for Personal Relationships* (Grand Rapids, MI: Baker, 1986).

20 See Paul G. Hiebert, *Anthropological Insights for Missionaries* (Grand Rapids, MI: Baker, 1985).

21 E. Thomas Brewster and Elizabeth S. Brewster, "Language Learning Is Communication—Is Ministry!," *International Bulletin of Mission Research* 6, no. 4 (1982): 160–64.

22 E. Thomas Brewster and Elizabeth S. Brewster, "Language Learning Is Communication—Is Ministry!," *International Bulletin of Mission Research* 6, no. 4 (1982): 160.

23 Lingenfelter and Mayers, *Ministering Cross-Culturally*, 22.

24 Bruce J. Malina, *Christian Origins and Cultural Anthropology: Practical Models for Biblical Interpretation* (1935; repr., Atlanta, GA: Westminster John Knox, 1986), 70.

25 Moon, "Toward True Globalism."

26 Rob Brynjolfson, "Effective Equipping of the Cross-Cultural Worker," *Connections: The Journal of the WEA Missions Commission* 3, no. 1 (February 2004): 75–77.

27 World Evangelical Alliance, *ReMAP II: Worldwide Missionary Retention Study and Best Practices* (New York: WEA Resources, 2010), http://www.worldevangelicals.org/resources/rfiles/res3_96_link _1292358945.pdf.

28 Jim Van Meter, "US Report of Findings on Missionary Retention," World Evangelical Alliance Resources, December 2003, 4, http://www.worldevangelicals.org/resources/view.htm?id=95.

29 Paul Sungro Lee, "Missionary Paternalism: Ultimate Peril of Mission," Evangelical Alliance for Preacher Training/Commission, May 25, 2012, https://www.academia.edu/27787385/Missionary_Paternalism _Ultimate_Peril_of_Mission.

30 Paul Borthwick, *Western Christians in Global Mission: What's the Role of the North American Church?* (Downers Grove, IL: InterVarsity, 2012), 152–53.

Bibliography

Borthwick, Paul. *Western Christians in Global Mission: What's the Role of the North American Church?* Downers Grove, IL: InterVarsity, 2012.

Brewster, E. Thomas, and Elizabeth S. Brewster. "Language Learning Is Communication—Is Ministry!" *International Bulletin of Mission Research* 6, no. 4 (1982): 160–164.

Brynjolfson, Rob. "Effective Equipping of the Cross-Cultural Worker." *Connections: The Journal of the WEA Missions Commission* 3, no. 1 (February 2004): 72–79.

Carpenter, Joel A. *Christian Higher Education: A Global Reconnaissance.* Grand Rapids, MI: Eerdmans, 2014.

Dowsett, Rose. *The Cape Town Commitment: A Confession of Faith and a Call to Action.* Peabody, MA: Hendrickson, 2012.

Ferris, Robert W., ed. *Establishing Ministry Training: A Manual for Programme Developers.* Pasadena, CA: William Carey Library, 1995. https://weamc.global/archive/Ferris_Ministry-Training.pdf.

Glover, Robert Hall. *The Bible Basis of Missions.* Chicago, IL: Moody, 1946.

Hiebert, Paul G. *Anthropological Insights for Missionaries.* Grand Rapids, MI: Baker, 1985.

———. *Transforming Worldviews: An Anthropological Understanding of How People Change.* Grand Rapids, MI: Baker Academic, 2008.

Hull, Bill. *The Disciple-Making Church.* Old Tappan, NJ: F. H. Revell, 1990.

Kim, Myung Ho. "The Dialogical Approach and Spiritual Growth: Discipleship Training in Korea." PhD diss., Trinity Evangelical Divinity School, 2006.

Kim, Sangkeun. "Sheer Numbers Do Not Tell the Entire Story." *Ecumenical Review* 57, no. 4 (2005): 463–472.

Kraft, Charles H. *Anthropology for Christian Witness.* Maryknoll, NY: Orbis, 1996.

———. *Christianity in Culture.* Maryknoll, NY: Orbis, 1979.

———. *Communicating the Gospel God's Way.* Pasadena, CA: William Carey Library, 1983.

Lane, Denis. *Tuning God's New Instruments*. Singapore: World
    Evangelical Fellowship, 1990.

Lee, Paul Sungro. "The Impact of Missionary Training on Intercultural
    Readiness in Seoul, Korea." PhD diss., Oxford Graduate School,
    2014.

———. *Missionary Candidate Training*. Merrifield, VA: Evangelical
    Alliance for Preacher Training Commission, 2008.

———. "Missionary Paternalism: Ultimate Peril of Mission."
    Evangelical Alliance for Preacher Training/Commission,
    May 25, 2012. https://www.academia.edu/27787385/Missionary
    _Paternalism_Ultimate_Peril_of_Mission.

Lingenfelter, Sherwood G., and Marvin K. Mayers. *Ministering Cross-
    Culturally: An Incarnational Model for Personal Relationships.*
    Grand Rapids, MI: Baker, 1986.

Malina, Bruce J. *Christian Origins and Cultural Anthropology: Practical
    Models for Biblical Interpretation.* 1986. Reprint, Atlanta, GA:
    Westminster John Knox, 1935.

Moon, Jay. "Toward True Globalism in World Missions." *Lausanne
    Global Analysis* 8, no. 1 (January 2019). https://www.lausanne
    .org/content/lga/2019-01/toward-true-globalism-in-world
    -missions?fbclid=IwAR3QlIgHGeirOuiPvrMhUel1Y45A
    -2n7ibIix98cq4fLfAMObR2d7g8HcBQ.

Morris, Thomas V. "The Coherence of the Incarnation." In *Christian
    Apologetics: An Anthology of Primary Sources*, edited by Khaldoun
    A. Sweis and Chad V. Meiste, 260–270. Grand Rapids, MI:
    Zondervan, 2012.

Noebel, David A. *Understanding the Times: The Religious Worldviews
    of Our Day and the Search for Truth*. Eugene, OR: Harvest
    House, 1997.

Pate, Larry D. "The Changing Balance in Global Mission."
    International Bulletin of Mission Research 15, no. 2 (1991): 56–61.

———. *From Every People: A Handbook of Two-Thirds World Missions with Directory, Histories, Analysis.* Monrovia, CA: MARC, 1989.

Reisacher, Evelyne Annick. "The Processes of Attachment between the Algerians and French within the Christian Community in France." PhD diss., Fuller Theological Seminary, 2001.

Van Meter, Jim. "US Report of Findings on Missionary Retention." World Evangelical Alliance Resources, December 2003. http://www.worldevangelicals.org/resources/view.htm?id=95.

World Evangelical Alliance. *ReMAP II: Worldwide Missionary Retention Study and Best Practices.* New York: WEA Resources, 2010. http://www.worldevangelicals.org/resources/rfiles/res3_96_link_1292358945.pdf.

10

Migrating Discipleship

A Dream for Discipling the Asian Diasporas

David Mark Ball

Discipling the Diasporas

While many politicians and policy makers see global migration as a threat to the sovereignty of nations, the unprecedented movement of people almost certainly offers the greatest opportunity for mission in the history of the world. Since the publishing of *The Cape Town Commitment* in 2010, thinking about and the practice of the Christian mission "to, through and beyond" people on the move in the twenty-first century have begun to take their rightful places in the church and mission thinking.[1] The response to the gospel among migrants worldwide is creating new momentum, and the gospel is naturally flowing across cultural lines in diverse locations through diaspora communities. However, the opportunities and challenges of the global diaspora are about sharing the good news not only of the love of God in Jesus Christ but also of making disciples who can in turn make disciples of others.

In April 2015, the members of the Increase Association began to explore the possibilities for discipleship in the context of the dispersed peoples of the world.[2] Building on the missiological thinking that emerged from the Lausanne Movement's Diaspora Issue Group, the Increase Association recognized how God uses global migration for mission in the following four ways:[3]

1. **Mission to the diaspora:** When immigrants arrive and settle in their new countries, local churches, organizations, and individuals in the host countries reach out to the diaspora communities with the love of Christ. Often people show greater openness to the gospel in foreign lands and do not have religious and sociocultural restraints as in their countries of origin.

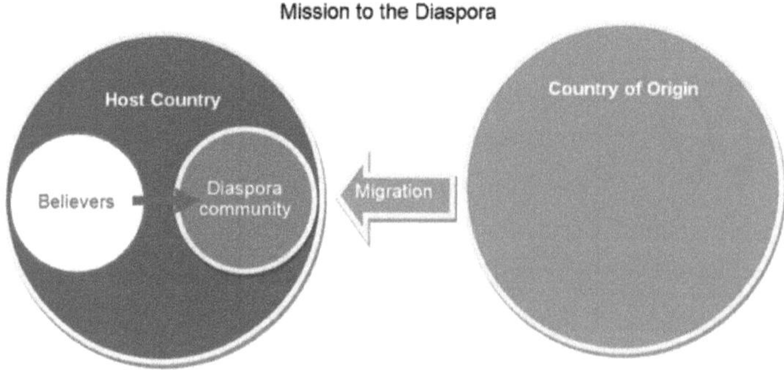

2. **Mission in the diaspora:** Immigrant Christians share the love of Christ with the members of their communities in their adopted destination countries on account of their renewed spiritual passion and cultural proximity to their people in a foreign country. They exhibit a greater burden and boldness to share the gospel than in their countries of origin.

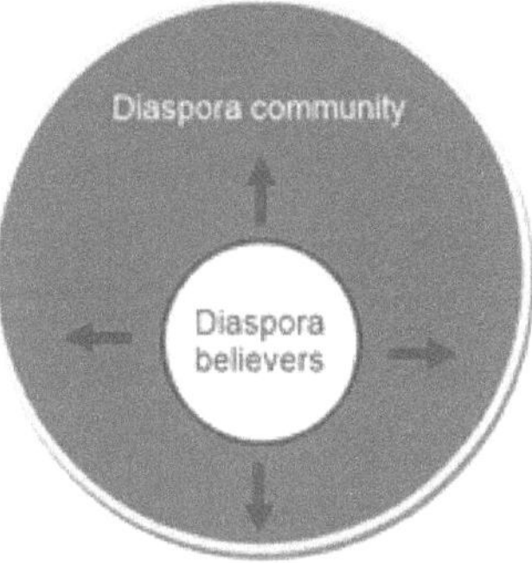

3. **Mission by the diaspora:** When believers return to or interact with their families and friends in their ancestral homelands, they can share the love of Christ in a way that foreign missionaries could never do. Often those who have come to know the Lord Jesus in their host countries are motivated to share their newfound faith with those in their countries of origin. They also give and support mission work in their countries of origin and get involved in different forms of ministries.

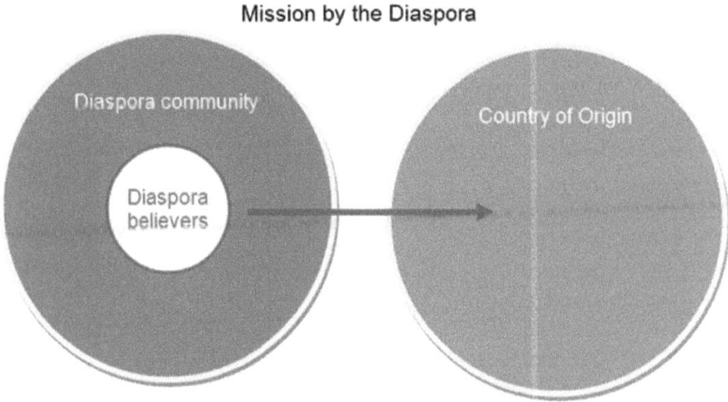

4. **Mission beyond the diaspora:** In this category, mission is done by migrants Christians and those who have become Christian after coming to new countries. The migrants turn into missionaries just as missionaries were migrants in the past. They evangelize and minister to people in their host countries and other ethnic groups in their host societal contexts. They revive Christianity in their host countries where it is mostly declining and bring fresh impetus for missions everywhere.

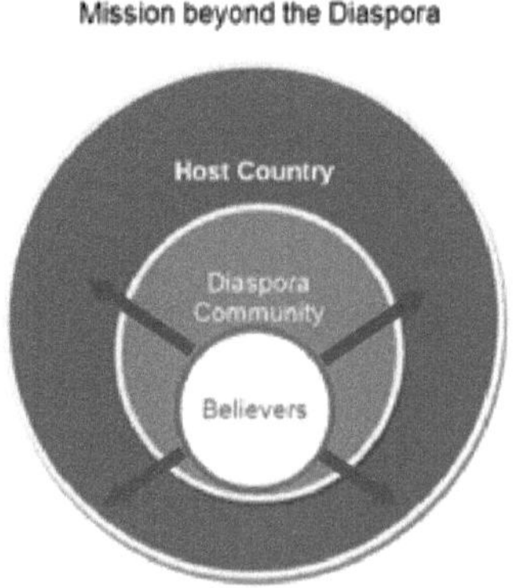

These different examples of diaspora missions show both the new realities and the new possibilities in the context of global migration. Once we recognize the nature of the church itself as a "diaspora" community, as foreigners and exiles, as migrants and refugees, every Christian believer and every church necessarily becomes part of this global phenomenon, not just as outsiders, showing pity to others, but as insiders, people who as a result of our new identity in Christ can and must identify with those who are scattered in this world. The Great Commission of Jesus is to be accomplished not (and never has been) only by sending missionaries to foreign countries but also by living as God's scattered people in this world.[4]

But what about the question of discipleship? If global migration at the start of the twenty-first century offers the greatest opportunity for mission in the history of the world, what sort of dream do we have for discipleship in the context of the global diasporas? Can we dare to dream, with the apostle Peter, of a church that takes the theology of the priesthood of all believers seriously (1 Pet 2:9) and, with the apostle Paul, of one that strives to present all believers mature in Christ (Col 1:28, 29)? Can we dare to dream that each congregation will have the resources to disciple its members to maturity? Can we dare to dream that one day the church will rise and live out the true meaning of its creed that all believers are equally called to mission and ministry? Can we even dream of a situation where all around the world, believers from the majority ethnic language and culture will be able to sit down together with believers from the minority ethnic languages and cultures to study God's word as brothers and sisters in Christ, learning what it is to follow Jesus in our diverse world?

Is this a dream that can inspire us to rise to the challenge of equipping disciples to engage in mission to, in, by, and beyond the diaspora? This was the focus of the members of the Increase Association at their conference in Chiang Mai, Thailand, in November 2017, and they adopted a diaspora statement. The conference participants committed to partnering with like-minded churches, organizations, and networks in Asia and beyond to enable discipleship, ministry, and mission training to take place among and through diaspora believers. Let us further explore the role of theological education by extension (TEE) as a tool to equip and empower local congregations for discipleship and then consider some real examples of how diaspora believers are being discipled in Asia and among Asian diasporas.

TEE as a Tool to Equip and Empower

TEE began in Central America in the 1960s as a "tool to equip and empower" believers located in contexts where access to seminaries and Bible schools was limited to well-educated urban Christians. The rural believers who were able to attend Bible colleges often never returned to the churches and congregations that so desperately needed indigenous leaders. As some leaders recognized the inadequacy of residential theological education for people in rural indigenous communities, courses began to be developed to meet the needs of ordinary believers with little or no formal education. For example, SEAN International developed courses for indigenous leaders and believers in Paraguay, Chile, and northern Argentina using the following foundational principles:[5]

1. **Simple:** Traditional theological education was aimed at those with formal education and those at the higher levels of the educational ladder. But this alternative educational model was aimed at those who had little or no formal education and spoke Spanish as their second language.
2. **Biblical:** Every effort was made to give a clear biblical exegesis, providing different interpretations and leaving controversial points open ended for each denomination to explain its position.

3. **Practical:** The Sea of Galilee receives and gives out
    water, and hence it is alive. Contrarily, the Dead
    Sea receives but does not give out water, and so it is
    dead. Likewise, this training model expected people
    to apply what they had learned in their discipleship
    and the ministry of their churches. It is only when
    we pass on what we have learned that it becomes
    effective.[6]

The application of learning extended beyond the formal
ministry of the people's churches and affected their families,
communities, marketplaces, and societies at large. The learning found greater acceptance, as the insights came from their
own people and in a very contextualized fashion. Since the
words and examples used were drawn from their commonly
used language and not complicated foreign theological or
philosophical ideas, it found greater penetration. The biblical truths were not only made transferrable easily, but they
multiplied quickly as the recipients became confident enough
to share them with others.

SEAN's basic discipleship course Abundant Life and its
two-year ministry-training course the Life of Christ proved
so popular that requests for the course were received from all
over the world. As a result, these materials have now been
adapted and translated into more than eighty languages and
are used in more than one hundred countries worldwide.
In the meantime, the TEE method had been adopted in
many Asian countries, including India and Pakistan, where
courses were being written for various local contexts.[7] Some
of these courses were developed in Asia, including popular
ones like Big Picture (Abundant Light), which has been
translated and adapted for use globally.

Simple, biblical, and contextually relevant course materials are vital for effective discipleship. However, these are not sufficient on their own. The enduring strength of TEE around the world has been that it takes place in a group meeting in the context of a local church where students can think through the application of their learning to daily life issues. By combining the three elements of personal study, group learning, and practical application, TEE recaptures William Tyndale's vision of enabling even common and illiterate people to understand the Scriptures. These strands are not exceptional on their own, but when woven together, they make a stronger chord. When repeated week after week, this learning cycle becomes a habit integrated into the routine of the learners. As Jerry Yer Soung notes, "The method of studying alone and then discussing what you learn in small groups adds to the implementation of new knowledge: meeting in our small groups brings us closer together. As a group, we discover different areas in our lives that need to be developed or worked on. Alone, we may never realize these in ourselves but meeting as a group we are able to help each other in these areas and see people's lives being changed."[8]

Across Asia, the lives of ordinary believers are being changed as they study the Scriptures with carefully designed workbooks and as they meet together to discern how to apply their learning in their own lives and in the lives of their churches and communities. At least one hundred thousand Asian Christians are in regular TEE groups, and a large proportion are believers of non-Christian backgrounds who are keen to grow in their new faith and share it with others. Most of the group members and their leaders are laypeople with ordinary jobs. These everyday Christians in their everyday lives are uniquely placed to reach their neighbors of other faiths. They do not have cultural or language hurdles to cross and do not require visas to minister to others. It is primarily through them that the gospel is advancing in Asia today. The millions who know Christ can reach the billions who do not.

What if this same tool that is being used across Asia to disciple and train Asian Christians to grow in their knowledge of the Scriptures and to apply them to their daily lives was available to do the same in the diaspora? How can the same and other tools be employed to nurture new believers in their newfound faith and develop them into leaders in their local contexts? How can these study materials be used by people when they or others in their families or communities migrate to nearby cities or across the world for employment? In the next section, we will see some examples of what is happening and the implications of the Christian discipleship of Asian diaspora communities.

Discipling the Diaspora in Asia and Beyond: Some Case Studies

The challenges and opportunities of discipling the peoples of the Asian diaspora within Asia and beyond have never been greater. A record number of Asians in different countries are moving out of their villages to cities within their countries (domestic or internal migration) and to nearby as well as faraway lands (international migration). Since courses have been translated into so many Asian languages and are widely used across Asia, they can provide a significant breakthrough in this task. The church-based TEE courses are already available in more than seventy languages. For example, migrants from Myanmar, Nepal, Pakistan, Cambodia, Indonesia, and other countries have started discipleship courses right away in their mother tongue in different migrant destination countries. As the group facilitators are from the same cultural backgrounds, informal groups spring up like mushrooms wherever the believers of a particular language group gather. They disciple one another themselves without much support or needing help from professionals.

The materials are flexible enough to spin off new study groups according to the convenience of the students. They are not highly structured and controlled by hierarchies. Many find this format to be suitable for their erratic lives and the work of the diaspora peoples. The proximity and trustworthiness of the group leaders are other factors that are important for the effectiveness of discipling diaspora peoples. People can study together with others of different ethnicities and nationalities as well. Everyone can study and do their homework in their own languages, while group discussions take place in a common language. The materials offer opportunities for discipleship. After accepting Jesus, there is a real need to learn how to follow him and to understand the Bible. When believers of different ethnic backgrounds can sit down together at the table of brotherhood, there is a foretaste of the biblical vision of the nations coming to worship the Lord together (Ps 86:9; Rev 7:9, 10) and the Pentecostal reality of diaspora peoples all hearing and understanding God's word in their own mother tongue (Acts 2:8–11). Here are different models of diaspora mission as reflected in the way TEE is being used in Asia and beyond:

1. **Discipling to the diaspora:** In several places in the world, host churches have discovered how TEE can be used to disciple diaspora believers in their midst.

This phenomenon is especially growing in Europe, where many churches are using "Come Follow Me" among Muslim-background believers. This discipleship course was written specifically for new believers in Jesus from Muslim backgrounds. It is relevant to the issues they face and is based on inductive Bible study methods. A British Christian using the course in the United Kingdom acknowledges, "I'm doing a 'Come Follow Me' course with a small group of Iranians using the Farsi edition. It is working fabulously. I don't think I've ever worked with a more enthusiastic group; they are really enjoying it and growing very fast. I think there are a couple of leaders developing among the group. And they are encouraging me."[9]

Elsewhere in Europe, another Christian who used the course among Afghani refugees admits, "I do think the course has helped these men to become real believers. Some of them say that they had told lies in their interviews in [other countries], and now they want to have a 'new start' and tell the truth, even though it means that they will not get asylum in [this country]. They say it is better to have a clean conscience with God than stay [here] because of lies!"[10]

Another example of discipleship to the diaspora is in Malaysia, where churches are ministering among diaspora communities. Nearly one million Nepalis are working as security guards, as factory workers, or in other low-paid jobs in Malaysia. The local Christian ministries involved in outreach to these workers have partnered with the national TEE program in Nepal. As a result, 380 students led by forty-two group leaders have been able to study God's word in their mother tongue at times that are convenient to them. A TEE student found that "these courses have helped him to understand God's Word and hope to pass it on to others. When his contract finishes in Malaysia, he wants to return to Nepal and plans to start discipleship groups in his village."[11]

In Malaysia, churches are using TEE courses among Burmese and Urdu speakers to strengthen the faith of migrant believers who speak those languages. One of the most exciting areas of growth through the use of TEE has been across the former Soviet countries in Central Asia, where despite various levels of persecution, churches have found that they are able to train and equip new believers to grow in their faith. In eastern Russia, one couple working among the Central Asian migrant communities use TEE materials to serve the migrants because the courses are so easy to understand, and they found it to be a helpful discipleship tool. Many of the migrants they encounter have very basic or no education at all. There are examples of people who have learned to read and write through TEE courses!

2. **Discipling in the diaspora:** In the United Kingdom, Nepali churches are discipling about one hundred Nepali believers using courses published by ITEEN. In the Gulf countries, there are groups of Indians, Nepalis, and Pakistanis who meet together to study God's word in their ethnic churches. More than a quarter of a century ago, the Vietnamese District of the Christian and Missionary Alliance started using SEAN's the Life of Christ course in

Vietnamese to train and equip ministers among their diaspora communities in the United States. Similarly, the Christian and Missionary Alliance churches in the United States began to use courses in the Hmong and Khmer languages to equip leaders in their churches. These churches continue to use TEE materials to train second- and third-generation migrants in the United States. The later generations often use English-language courses.

3. **Discipling by the diaspora:** As believers are equipped in the diaspora, they also begin to turn their attention to equipping the believers back in Asia. For example, the materials that had been used by the Vietnamese believers in the United States were taken to Vietnam. In 1992, a Vietnamese pastor in California bought six course books of the Life of Christ and knew such training would work back in his village. From a diaspora network of churches in the United States, the Vietnamese courses not only have become a significant way of training believers in Vietnam itself but are also used among diaspora believers in Christian and Missionary Alliance churches in Australia.

    Migrants from Central Asia not only have spread across the former Soviet Union but are also present in large numbers in Korea. After the collapse of the Soviet Union, many Russian speakers, mainly from Uzbekistan, migrated to Korea, so there are now about fifty thousand Russian-speaking ethnic Koreans and over twenty thousand Russian speakers of other nationalities in Korea. In 2017, Pastor Dmitrii Hen from Suniy Church invited leaders from the Russian and Uzbek TEE organizations to Korea to introduce TEE course materials to the Russian-speaking churches in Korea. As a result of this training seminar, fifty-seven believers, including forty pastors, are now equipped to lead TEE groups in Russian-speaking Korean churches. In one church alone, over two hundred believers have now become TEE students, and more groups have started in other churches.

4. **Discipling beyond the diaspora:** Across Asia and the wider world, the mainland Chinese have migrated in large numbers over long periods and assimilated within different nations. For example, the majority of Malaysian believers are from the Chinese community. Moved by the love of God in Christ, many of these believers have been involved in missions among the Indigenous Malaysian communities. Into this situation, the leaders of the largest Chinese TEE movement came to Malaysia and started training Chinese believers in local churches. Those who have been trained using these materials have now been inspired to translate the materials into Bahasa Malaysia to enable the Indigenous believers to grow in their faith amid growing persecution and pressure from the majority community. A new Malaysian TEE movement has been formed as churches have sought to minister to diaspora communities. In turn, this has led to these communities translating discipleship materials for the Indigenous Malaysian churches.

So we have seen that discipleship using TEE can take place to, in, by, and beyond the diaspora peoples of Asian backgrounds. To these few examples could be added ones of Russian-speaking migrants studying in Turkey; Spanish speakers in Tokyo; Filipinos,

Pakistanis, Indians, and Nepalis in the Gulf; Farsi and Arabic speakers in Europe; Hmong speakers throughout the world; Chinese speakers in Burma, the United States, and Europe; and so the list goes on. The situation among migrant workers is often difficult, as they usually form the lowest-paid groups in their places of settlement. Their time for study is limited, and they often have little energy left after working long hours. They often are not connected with churches back home or aware of appropriate resources that could be used. They find that the Christians and churches of their host nations are unable to minister to them effectively on account of language and cultural barriers. Yet amid this, God is doing something remarkable in equipping his people for mission and ministry in the most difficult of workplaces and enabling them to live out his calling in their day-to-day lives.

The Increase Association Commitment: A Call to Participate

So we return to the commitment that was made at the Increase Association conference in Chiang Mai, Thailand, in November 2017. A total of 168 participants, comprising leaders from church-based training programs across Asia and mission organizations, met together to reflect on what God is doing across Asia with the theme of "Empowering Churches, Equipping Disciples." The focus of the conference was on discipling diaspora believers. Arising out of this conference was the commitment of its participants to take diaspora discipleship seriously and to make available course materials in different languages to Asian migrants worldwide.

The conference statement on the diaspora marks a sea change in the TEE movement, which has traditionally focused on discipling believers within national and geographic boundaries. With this commitment, the members of the Increase Association have committed themselves to enabling discipleship and leadership training to take place wherever diaspora communities may exist. This is a task that these organizations cannot accomplish on their own. In order to fulfill their vision, they have committed themselves to working alongside Christian churches and organizations that share this same vision. The materials developed and translated to Asian languages and contexts could now be used around the globe and called for the next level of partnership with churches and ministries in different countries to leverage impact among Asian diasporas.

As people engage with the Scriptures in their local church contexts using simple and flexible courses available at a price they can afford, we are seeing the emancipation of people across Asia from biblical illiteracy. We are seeing a fulfillment of Tyndale's vision to train all people to know the Scriptures. As the truth of God's word is made clear in the languages of ordinary people, they are being transformed into the likeness of his Son. In Isaiah's words, we are seeing valleys exalted and hills and mountains made low (40:4). We are seeing the glory of the Lord revealed as the church of many nations is discipled.

Together, those who are called to diaspora mission can work with those who are part of the vibrant Asian TEE movement. We could provide tools to equip and empower all Christian believers to grow in Christ and serve him actively in their local churches and communities. Collectively, we can see the church rise up and live out as all believers are equipped for the mission of God in the world, wherever that may be. This greatly reduces our dependence on professional mission workers and current funding mechanisms for global missionary tasks. This model of discipleship and leadership training creates a greater momentum at the grassroots level in every church, and Asian diaspora Christians become an unparalleled global missionary force for taking the gospel to all people and ends of the earth, as Asians are the largest and the most widely dispersed diaspora community in the world.

Notes

1 See Rose Dowsett, *The Cape Town Commitment: A Confession of Faith and a Call to Action* (Peabody, MA: Hendrickson, 2012), sec. II C, https://www.lausanne.org/content/ctc/ctcommitment#p2-1.

2 The Increase Association connects and strengthens theological education by extension (TEE) and other church-based training movements across Asia and beyond. See "About the Increase Association," Increase Association, accessed April 15, 2022, https://www.increaseassociation.org.

3 Lausanne Movement and Global Diaspora Network, *Scattered to Gather: Embracing the Global Trend of Diaspora*, rev. ed. (Vernon Hills, IL: Parivar, 2017), 23–25. See D. M. Ball, "Reflecting on the Nature of the Church as a Diaspora Community and Some Implications for Mission and Discipleship," Increase Association, November 2016, https://www.increaseassociation.org/resources/diaspora/95-foreigners-and-exiles.

4 See Sadiri Joy Tira and Tetsunao Yamamori, eds., *Scattered and Gathered: A Global Compendium of Diaspora Missiology*, rev. ed. (Cumbria, UK: Langham, 2020).

5 *SEAN* was originally an acronym for Seminario por Extensión Anglicano. It was based on 2 Tim 2:2 NIV: "[to] be qualified to teach others." *SEAN* now stands for Study by Extension for All Nations. See https://www.seaninternational.org.

6 Tim Green and David Mark Ball, "The Worldwide Spread of TEE," in *TEE in Asia: Empowering Churches, Equipping Disciples*, ed. H. R. Wingerden, T. Green, and G. Aylett (Cumbria, UK: Langham, 2021), 32.

7 The Open Theological Seminary (originally known as PAKTEE) in Pakistan and the Association for Theological Education by Extension both started in 1971 and developed courses for their contexts before adapting courses from elsewhere as appropriate. SEAN was also formed in 1971.

8 Quoted in H. R. Wingerden, "Thailand: Growing Together in Christ," in Wingerden, Green, and Aylett, *TEE in Asia*, 53.

9 See "What They Say," Come Follow Me, accessed January 11, 2019, https://come-follow-me.org/about/what-they-say.

10 "What They Say" (brackets in the original).

11 Green and Ball, *TEE in Asia*, chap. 16.

Bibliography

Ball, D. M. "Reflecting on the Nature of the Church as a Diaspora Community and Some Implications for Mission and Discipleship." Increase Association, November 2016. https://www.increaseassociation.org/resources/diaspora/95-foreigners-and-exiles.

Dowsett, Rose. *The Cape Town Commitment: A Confession of Faith and a Call to Action.* Peabody, MA: Hendrickson, 2012.

Green, Tim, and David Mark Ball. "The Worldwide Spread of TEE." In Wingerden, Green, and Aylett, *TEE in Asia*, chap. 5.

Increase Association. "About the Increase Association." Accessed April 15, 2022. https://www.increaseassociation.org.

Lausanne Movement and Global Diaspora Network. *Scattered to Gather: Embracing the Global Trend of Diaspora.* Rev. ed. Vernon Hills, IL: Parivar, 2017.

Tira, Sadiri Joy, and Tetsunao Yamamori, eds. *Scattered and Gathered: A Global Compendium of Diaspora Missiology.* Rev. ed. Cumbria, UK: Langham, 2020.

Wingerden, H. R. "Thailand: Growing Together in Christ." In Wingerden, Green, and Aylett, *TEE in Asia*, chap. 16.

Wingerden, H. R., T. Green, and G. Aylett, eds. *TEE in Asia: Empowering Churches, Equipping Disciples.* Cumbria, UK: Langham, 2021.

11

International Student Diasporas of Asia

Phil Jones

Introduction

"Would you please explain Christianity to me?" Fifteen years ago, who could have imagined a Muslim student from Sudan asking this of an Indonesian Christian student in China? An African student learning about the gospel of Jesus Christ from another international student in Asia. In tandem with the rapid economic development of Asian nations, the international student population in, out of, and within Asia has surged significantly over the last decade or so. These people on the move are not ethnically homogeneous and constitute a modern diaspora group that seeks educational advancement in places far away from home.

This movement of enthusiastic and open-minded high achievers represents a hugely strategic missional opportunity for the Asian and the global church but comes with many challenges.[1] God is moving students and scholars to countries around the world where they can more easily hear and respond to the gospel. This chapter explores the Asian student diaspora both within Asia and outside of Asia. While this chapter addresses the whole of Asia, from the Middle East to East Asia, the author focuses on China, which is currently the largest Asian sender and receiver of international students. The framework of diaspora missiology is anchored on biblical texts like those saying that God has "marked out their appointed times in history and the boundaries of their lands" (Acts 17:26 NIV) and beckons them to come "from every nation, tribe, people and language" (Rev 7:9 NIV).[2] When the people of the kingdom of God undertake ministry by faith, God produces bountiful fruits by his power (2 Thess 1:11).

The transnational movement of learners and scholars is truly a global and growing phenomenon. International student ministry (ISM) has a rich history, at least in the West, dating back to John R. Mott and the Edinburgh mission conference in 1910.[3] Very few students ever went abroad for studies in the nineteenth century, and the number of international students increased significantly after the Second World War and postcolonial era.[4] Over the last five decades or so, ISMs have been developed and successfully implemented in many college ministries and churches in the West. They have seen remarkable results through their impact on the future leaders of nations with the gospel when they were students in local colleges in foreign countries. The local churches and ministries in every nation can take advantage of the strategic opportunity that God is bringing to their doorsteps to impact the world for Christ without having to send missionaries overseas. They, in turn, have a great impact on their nations when they return upon the completion of their studies.

However, this trend of international students is a relatively new phenomenon in Asia, and focused ministries for them are yet to be fully realized by churches, college ministries, and mission organizations in Asia.[5] ISM in Asia will require an Asia-specific contextualized missiology, and the challenge is not only to "de-Westernize" mission for Asia but to develop forms appropriate to its diverse cultural and sociopolitical contexts.

International Students and Asia

Asian nations are both senders and receivers of international students both inside and outside the region. In recent years, record levels of students have been sent from and received in Asia. The *Asian international student diaspora* could refer to (1) students who are coming to Asia from non-Asian countries, (2) those going out of Asia to non-Asian countries for studies, and (3) those moving from one Asian country to another. These international students could range from schooling (few), college, graduate, doctoral, and postdoctoral research students. They seek admission to foreign schools and enter foreign countries with the appropriate visa rules for international students in those countries. We may consider four categories of international students of Asia as per table 11.1, each with its own specific issues and opportunities.

Table 11.1: Four categories of
international students of Asia

	Receiving	Sending
Asia	**RA:** receiving students from within Asia	**SA:** sending Asian students within Asia
Outside Asia	**RO:** receiving students from non-Asian countries	**SO:** sending Asian students to non-Asian countries

Historically, Asian students have pursued higher education in specialized and professional fields abroad in Western nations because of the perceived economic advantage it offers. Besides seeking a superior quality of education, they also avail much-required exposure and connections for better prospects in the future. They acquire foreign languages and cultural fluencies and act as brokers between nations. Some students pursue foreign education in order to migrate overseas or take up careers in advanced workplaces.

Recently, a variety of factors have driven the development of Asia as an educational center: Asian universities have become attractive due to their steady rise in world rankings; the cost of living remains relatively low; cultural, religious, and physical proximity reduces stress; and scholarships have been liberally offered to select nations in the pursuit of "soft power." Asian students are increasingly studying abroad, and Asia is becoming a sizeable receiver of foreign students. In 2017, China was the world's largest receiver of Anglophone African students studying abroad,[6] and new policies in some countries are attracting international students to them, such as India, Singapore, Malaysia, Hong Kong, the Philippines,

and the United Arab Emirates.[7] Many universities in Asia
have steadily risen in the ratings of educational institutions
worldwide and attract many to explore advanced studies in
Asia's top-ranked universities.[8]

Table 11.2: The multidirectional flow of students

Country	International students[*]	Year
China	492,185	2019
Russia	334,497	2019
Japan	188,384	2018
Turkey	148,868	2018
South Korea	123,850	2017
United Arab Emirates	77,469	2017
Malaysia	60,244	2017
India	45,424	2017
Philippines	12,278	2018

* Details for China, Russia, Japan, the United Arab Emirates, Malaysia, India, and the Philippines are from "Project Atlas," Institute of International Education, accessed December 4, 2019, https://www.iie.org/Research-and Insights/Project-Atlas/Explore-Data/China. Details for Turkey are from "Higher Education in Numbers," Study in Turkey, accessed December 4, 2019, http://www.studyinturkey.gov.tr/StudyinTurkey/_PartStatistic. Details for South Korea are from Kerrie Kennedy, "South Korea Sees Record International Student Numbers in 2017," PIE News, February 13, 2018, https://thepienews.com/data/south-korea-record-high-growth-in-intl-student-numbers/.

1. SO Students: Sending Asians outside of Asia

Asian students leaving Asia have traditionally gone to North America, Western Europe, and Australia. As a result of the influx of Asian and other foreign students, these regions have developed national ISMs, such as InterVarsity USA.[9] Many valuable lessons can be learned from them about approaches to and responses of the international students. They have recognized their joyful duty of welcoming strangers among them and ways to share Christ with those coming from countries closed to the gospel. Recently, some have called for a paradigm shift in missions to move ISM from a peripheral effort to the core of the kingdom mission strategy.[10]

In addition, several regional, even global, networks have been established to encourage and support various ISMs. Two notable examples are the ISM Issue Group of the Lausanne Movement and the International Fellowship of Evangelical Students Europe's collaboration with national ISMs.[11] The West need no longer view SO student ministry as a ministry *to* a diaspora. There are Christian students from the majority world who are coming to the West, where the church is on the decline, and they have much to offer to the host nations, from cultural enrichment to discipleship. The Western church can co-labor in ministry *with* and *alongside* the Christian Asian students in the West.

2. SA Students: Sending Asian Students within Asia

This is perhaps the fastest-growing group of students: those who move across borders within Asia to gain a *glocal* (global but local) education. From a missional perspective, Christian students being sent in this category have a wide-open door for ministry to fellow Asian students. Churches would do well to prepare such students to be mission minded as they step into a new university with potentially open-minded fellow international students from other parts of Asia. It is very strategic to send Christian Asian students who are motivated, equipped, and available for ministry to other countries, especially those that are closed to the gospel. One significant challenge for this group is the natural tendency to stick together in tight ethnolinguistic cliques, which militates against both the embracing of anyone different and "going outside the circle" to engage with others.

3. RA Students: Receiving Fellow Asian Students

From the receivers' perspective, this group of Asian international students presents a different but equally strategic opportunity for gospel proclamation. The largest block of students coming to China, for example, is fellow Asians (60 percent).[12] The open door here is for the host churches to see them as a vulnerable group of foreigners in their midst who desperately need to know the good news of Christ. So many of these arriving students come from nations where they are unlikely to hear the name of Jesus. Reaching them should not be looked down on or considered a substandard mission. The churches in the receiving nations must prioritize ministry to international students in their cities with a welcoming posture.

4. RO Students: Receiving Students from outside of Asia

These non-Asians arriving in Asia to study are perhaps the most complex to consider. They are culturally very different and face many linguistic and cultural barriers. The first category is Western international students, who tend to come for shorter periods on an exchange or for intensive language courses. Though they are there for a short duration, they are more outgoing, friendly, and open to new experiences.

The second and perhaps the fastest-growing category is African and South Pacific Islander international students who enroll for complete undergraduate and postgraduate degrees. They may be in Asia between two and seven years if they pursue multiple degrees and if they have to do a year of language learning. The students from Africa make up the second-largest block of international students in China by continent (17 percent), after students from Asia. Many of them are shocked by the extreme weather conditions and struggle with the differences in food, culture, and leisure activities. African students in China, India, and Singapore have faced racial prejudice and deal with continual discrimination in their host nations. These RO students are often isolated from locals. But if this can be overcome, whether Christian or not, they can be huge blessings to the churches of their host countries through enriching cross-cultural exposure and seeing a global view of God's mission in the world.

Challenges

We shall now focus on the challenges of and opportunities for ministry from the perspective of the receiving Asian church—RA and RO students. The missional activity of the Asian church toward these students is perhaps the most undeveloped and unrealized at present, the challenges are not insignificant, and the gospel-strategic opportunities are truly incredible.

Monoculturalism. Some Asian societies that enjoy a multicultural heritage are not so surprised by foreign students on university campuses. Others have been historically closed and are mostly monocultural. This makes the cultural chasm between locals and foreigners frighteningly vast. The university policies in China segregate foreign students in separate dorms, classes, and even campuses in order to maintain a nonintegrationist view toward foreigners. Isolating internationals hinders local churches from reaching them. Racism toward dark-skinned students may be minimized among mature local disciples, but it inevitably works against genuine and open love toward foreigners.

Inferiority. The reverse of racism is xenophilia, where some international students are elevated, resulting in a similar distancing effect. The presence of culturally agile foreigners moving with ease in a heterogeneous international student world can starkly contrast the at-home Asian, nervous and fearful about engaging across the cultural divide. This inferiority is compounded by the desire to "get it right" and to shy away from risky exchanges. The presence of international churches in these contexts is both a plus and a minus, effectively embracing international students but alleviating the necessity of local churches to do so.

Political constraints. More and more Asian countries are actively attracting international students for long-term economic gains and their own geopolitical influence. The political and religious constraints on the ground can be huge challenges for ISM. Though they are liberal compared to other Islamic countries, Indonesia and Malaysia have strict laws regarding conversion, halal food, and even headdress for women. Christians may experience pressure and limitation when engaging with foreign students. In recent years, more intense, politically motivated religious policy in communist China has only increased the segregation of foreign students away from local Christians. Non-Asian foreign students posed a security risk for unregistered congregations in China. The recent incidents in Liaoning and Hubei show that the Three-Self churches can be off-limits to internationals.[13] When local churches are under such pressure, how should they respond to this influx of open-minded international students? Is it a form of outreach they are "allowed" not to do, to be left at the feet of foreign believers?

Not a real mission. A campus worker in China expressed how hard it is to raise support from her Chinese church for ISM "because they don't see it as a real mission." The same view was expressed by an Asian leader of a global mission organization who was a grateful recipient of earlier ISM in the West. Some, if not most, Asian Christians view ISM as not "the real thing," since it doesn't involve any suffering. Going to Saudi Arabia would cross the threshold to be a "real mission," but staying at home in Jakarta and daily making friends at the next-door university is not counted as mission. This view of ISM is not unique to Asia, but in the West, there have been a few more years of reflection and more voices to challenge this unbiblical perspective. For Asia to embrace ISM widely, Asian churches and mission leaders must champion the legitimacy of this ministry.

Scope and growth. Not only are the numbers of international students in Asia staggering, but this increase stands in paradox with the limitations of the context. The United States has approximately 1,200 ISM workers to 1.2 million international students, a ratio of 1:1,000. Over a dozen organizations are doing ISM at a national level, with many churches and ministries focused locally. Any international student can easily find a church or campus ministry where they can investigate Christ and will most likely be welcomed.

In China, the ratio of ISM workers to students is closer to 1:25,000. Apart from the thirty to forty international churches, an international student in China has virtually no access to organized Christian witness. International student numbers in Asia are very likely to keep growing strongly because of underlying factors and the small percentage they represent in the total education arena, meaning the academic system has the potential to absorb and serve many more.

Language myth. Another challenge to overcome is the unfounded belief that ISM is done in English. In China, English is neither used nor needed by many international students. Central and Southeast Asians and Arabic- and Spanish-speaking students routinely spend a year learning Chinese, followed by a bachelor's or master's degree in Chinese. Asian churches must recognize that if students learn and operate in their local host languages, then they can offer a natural sought-after commodity that international students want: conversations with native speakers. This opens the door not only for English corners but also Chinese, Vietnamese, and Thai corners.

Complexity. International students are a complex diaspora, ethnically and culturally diverse. There has been an increased awareness and embracing of diaspora missions, as is evident by the theme of the 2019 conference of the Asia Missions Association—"Migration and Mission."[14] The main focus has been on *homogeneous diasporas*, such as Filipino maids in the Middle East. By contrast, international students are *heterogeneous*, composed of multiple ethnicities. Some cultures maintain a simplistic view of an us-versus-them distinction between locals and foreigners, and foreign students are considered "not us." The recent growth of international student numbers and this complexity mean that organizations and churches may struggle to see how they fit in an overall mission strategy. As a result, international students are simply not on the radar of Christians as they ought to be.

Mission confusion. In line with near-cultural or proximate missions, Chinese churches are sending Chinese pastors to Africa to reach the Chinese diaspora there. Should Thai churches send Thai pastors to reach the Thai students in China? The advantages seem obvious: there would be no culture or language gap, and less training would be required. But does it mean local churches should not be doing cross-cultural ministry in their own backyards and abandon cross-cultural ministry in other nondomestic contexts? This is not the direction that churches historically have taken, nor is it biblically justifiable. There is a real danger of abdicating the gospel responsibility of reaching out to the people close to you regardless of their ethnicity and cultural distance. Moreover, it's impractical to send culture- or language-specific workers to reach every individual group of students. The responsibility to love internationals with the gospel must fall on local churches, wherever they are, as has been done in the West.

Opportunities

Global impact. International students in any context are by nature not representative of their original societies; they are the top layer. They are the very best, up-and-coming leaders, handpicked scholarship recipients, and the future CEOs, policy makers, and political leaders of their respective homelands. Therefore, ISM has a disproportionately heavy impact, as it influences future influencers. Moreover, students from countries that are not represented much in the West are more likely to be studying in Asia. To reach international students in Asia is to reach the world.

Returnees. Simply having studied outside one's own culture makes one less afraid of the "other" and more linguistically and culturally agile. Such an Asian student may return from the West with models of ministry experiences in church- or campus-based ISMs. This makes Asian Christian returnees potential catalysts for ISM in their own countries if they survive reentry and (re)integrate into healthy local churches. Western ISMs are catching on to how strategic these returnees may be for their homeland churches and are now casting a vision of ministry far beyond reentry for these globally experienced students. As they pick up the ISM challenge, Asian churches can impart this greater gospel vision to "returning diasporas" sent back from Asia to their own contexts.

Benefits to local churches. Churches the world over suffer from ministry myopia, an inability to see outside of their own contexts. Engaging with ISM brings God's sovereign movement of people and his global kingdom purposes right up close and makes Asian churches aware of this bigger picture. This will only enlarge whatever vision for mission a church or ministry may hold. ISM also allows involvement in global missions by every member regardless of their age or training because it happens right where they are.

Legitimate mission. The gospel-strategic value of reaching international students must in the long run legitimize this area of ministry. Many opportunities exist for churches, mission agencies, and Bible and theological training institutions to formally recognize ISM as a ministry area that requires

its own specialized training and expertise. This will increase
interest and the number of qualified personnel to carry out
this ministry. More reflections and well-researched resources
on ISM from different contexts must be produced and dis-
tributed widely to improve the credibility of such ministries.

Networking. Asian missiologists and mission practitioners
need to network regarding ISM and its contextualization.
ISM will look different in Japan, China, Singapore, Malaysia,
India, and the Middle East. Clearly, one cannot blindly adopt
strategies developed in the West, though there are lessons to
be shared. How was this ISM vision developed and imparted
to local churches? How were ministry structures birthed and
grown to embrace what God was doing? What can international church networks do for international students?

Strategic contexts. Numerous opportunities exist to research
specific Asian contexts where international students are con-
centrated. Are there certain student categories that are strategic yet underreached, such as Pakistani medical students
in China or Christians from India studying in American
schools in the Middle East? Are there international students
in cities without any international churches? What local organizations are ready to take up this challenge and consider
deploying ministry effort to love these foreigners among them?

In the light of mapping the growing international student diaspora in Asia and exploring the various challenges
and opportunities before ISMs in Asia (mentioned above),
I suggest following six strategies for missional engagement
with the student diaspora in Asia. First, establish trust-based
networking relationships among Christian leaders in Asia
committed to praying for and reaching the international student diaspora with the gospel of Christ.[15] Second, reflect on
the cultural issues of monoculturalism, inferiority, and the

English-language myth, and critique these against the biblical mandate to love the foreigners in our midst. Third, recognize that evangelizing and discipling international students and then sending ministry-minded returnees back across the globe have strategic impacts for the gospel. Fourth, challenge the shortsighted view that ISM is not a real mission, and work to clarify and legitimize ISM's place in churches' overall mission strategies. Fifth, recognize the challenges of political constraints, and work creatively to imagine appropriate ministry models. Finally, research cities and regions in Asia where international students are present to identify strategic locations or subgroups for Christian witness.

Conclusion

The international student diaspora of Asia concerns Asian students studying outside and within Asia as well as non-Asian students studying in Asia. Just as God has allowed the Western church to respond to the presence of international students, so now he calls the Asian church to courageously and creatively love these new arrivals on its doorstep. Leiton Edward Chinn writes, "Clearly, the vision for ISM is being embraced by the Asian missions community and is gradually being incorporated by churches and campus ministries in Greater Asia. ISM is taking root in Greater Asia, in addition to the Greater European and North American regions, after sixty years of tilling the soil, seeding, and watering."[16] The challenges are many; the opportunities are strategic and exciting. Will the international students of Asia have a strategic diasporic gospel impact on the entire globe for the glory of Jesus Christ?

Notes

1 Leiton Edward Chinn, "International Student Ministry: A Most Strategic Yet Most Inexpensive Global Mission Opportunity Arises in Asia," *Asian Missions Advance*, no. 42 (January 2014): 2–7, http://www.asiamissions.net/asian-missions-advances/.

2 See Sadiri Joy Tira and Tetsunao Yamamori, eds., *Scattered and Gathered: A Global Compendium of Diaspora Missiology*, rev. ed. (Cumbria, UK: Langham, 2020).

3 Leiton Edward Chinn, "The Global ISM Movement," in *Diaspora Missions to International Students*, ed. Enoch Wan (Portland, OR: Western Seminary Press, 2019), 119–38.

4 See Issue Group for Diasporas and International Students, "Diasporas and International Students: The New People Next Door," Lausanne Movement, Lausanne occasional paper no. 55, October 2004, 28–36, https://lausanne.org/content/lop/diasporas-and-international-students-the-new-people-next-door-lop-55.

5 See Phil Jones, "International Students in China: Who Will Reach This Vast and Strategic and Yet Invisible Group?," *Evangelical Missions Quarterly* 54, no. 2 (April 2018): 46–57.

6 See Beth Daley, "China Tops US and UK as Destination for Anglophone African Students," Conversation, June 27, 2017, http://theconversation.com/china-tops-us-and-uk-as-destination-for-anglophone-african-students-78967.

7 See "Why Southeast and East Asia Are Increasingly Popular among International Students," Study International, March 22, 2018, https://www.studyinternational.com/news/southeast-east-asia-increasingly-popular-among-international-students/. Also see Yojana Sharma, "Internationally Mobile Students Head for Asia," University World News, January 31, 2014, https://www.universityworldnews.com/post.php?story=20140131102318847.

8 For example, "China has 154 universities ranked in Top 1000, among which 66 are in Top 500, 4 are in Top 100." People's Republic of China, "Shanghai Ranking's Academic Ranking of World Universities 2019 Press Release," Shanghai Ranking, August 15, 2019, https://www.shanghairanking.com/news/arwu/2019.

9 Stacey Bieler and Lisa Espineli Chinn, "History of International Student Ministry in InterVarsity/USA," in Wan, *Diaspora Missions*, 79–117.

10 See Jack D. Burke, *Paradigm Shift: Why International Students Are So Strategic to Global Missions* (Bloomington, IN: WestBow, 2019).

11 Chinn, "Global ISM Movement," 119–38.

12 See "Statistical Report on International Students in China for 2018," Ministry of Education of the People's Republic of China, April 17, 2019, http://en.moe.gov.cn/documents/reports/201904/t20190418_378692.html.

13 Gu Xi, "African Christian Students Can't Practice Their Faith in China," *Bitter Winter*, October 15, 2019, https://bitterwinter.org/african-christian-students-cant-practice-their-faith-in-china/.

14 See a recent publication from this conference: Steve K. Eom, *Migration and Mission* (Seoul: AMA, 2021).

15 Leiton Edward Chinn and Lisa Espineli Chinn, "Agents of Diaspora Missions in and from the Academic World," in Tira and Yamamori, *Scattered and Gathered*, 263–80.

16 Leiton Edward Chinn, "Foreign Student Mission Vision Is No Longer a Blind-Spot and Asia Is Embracing the Vision" (paper presentation, Asia Missions Association's 13th Triennial Convention, November 2019). The convention's theme was "migration and mission," with "foreign students and mission" being a subtheme.

Bibliography

Bieler, Stacey, and Lisa Espineli Chinn. "History of International Student Ministry in InterVarsity/USA." In Wan, *Diaspora Missions*, 79–117.

Burke, Jack D. *Paradigm Shift: Why International Students Are So Strategic to Global Missions*. Bloomington, IN: WestBow, 2019.

Chinn, Leiton Edward. "Foreign Student Mission Vision Is No Longer a Blind-Spot and Asia Is Embracing the Vision." Paper presented at the Asia Missions Association's 13th Triennial Convention, November 2019.

———. "The Global ISM Movement." In Wan, *Diaspora Missions to International Students*, 119–38.

———. "International Student Ministry: A Most Strategic Yet Most Inexpensive Global Mission Opportunity Arises in Asia." *Asian Missions Advance*, no. 42 (January 2014): 2–7. http://www.asiamissions.net/asian-missions-advances/.

Chinn, Leiton Edward, and Lisa Espineli Chinn. "Agents of Diaspora Missions in and from the Academic World." In Tira and Yamamori, *Scattered and Gathered*, 263–280.

Daley, Beth. "China Tops US and UK as Destination for Anglophone African Students." Conversation, June 27, 2017. http://theconversation.com/china-tops-us-and-uk-as-destination-for-anglophone-african-students-78967.

Eom, Steve K. *Migration and Mission*. Seoul: AMA, 2021.

Institute of International Education. "Project Atlas." Accessed December 4, 2019. https://www.iie.org/Research-and-Insights/Project-Atlas/Explore-Data/China.

Issue Group for Diasporas and International Students. "Diasporas and International Students: The New People Next Door." Lausanne Movement, Lausanne occasional paper no. 55,

October 2004. https://lausanne.org/content/lop/diasporas-and
-international-students-the-new-people-next-door-lop-55.

Jones, Phil. "International Students in China: Who Will Reach This Vast and Strategic and Yet Invisible Group?" *Evangelical Missions Quarterly* 54, no. 2 (April 2018): 46–57.

Kennedy, Kerrie. "South Korea Sees Record International Student Numbers in 2017." PIE News, February 13, 2018. https://thepienews.com/data/south-korea-record-high-growth-in-intl-student-numbers/.

Ministry of Education of the People's Republic of China. "Statistical Report on International Students in China for 2018." April 17, 2019. http://en.moe.gov.cn/documents/reports/201904/t20190418_378692.html.

People's Republic of China. "Shanghai Ranking's Academic Ranking of World Universities 2019 Press Release." Shanghai Ranking, August 15, 2019. https://www.shanghairanking.com/news/arwu/2019.

Sharma, Yojana. "Internationally Mobile Students Head for Asia." University World News, January 31, 2014. https://www.universityworldnews.com/post.php?story=20140131102318847.

Study International. "Why Southeast and East Asia Are Increasingly Popular among International Students." March 22, 2018. https://www.studyinternational.com/news/southeast-east-asia-increasingly-popular-among-international-students/.

Study in Turkey. "Higher Education in Numbers." Accessed December 4, 2019. http://www.studyinturkey.gov.tr/StudyinTurkey/_PartStatistic.

Tira, Sadiri Joy, and Tetsunao Yamamori, eds. *Scattered and Gathered: A Global Compendium of Diaspora Missiology*. Rev. ed. Cumbria, UK: Langham, 2020.

Wan, Enoch, ed. *Diaspora Missions to International Students*. Portland, OR: Western Seminary Press, 2019.

Xi, Gu. "African Christian Students Can't Practice Their Faith in China." *Bitter Winter*, October 15, 2019. https://bitterwinter.org/african-christian-students-cant-practice-their-faith-in-china/.

12

The Contextualized Worship of the South Asian Punjabi Christian Diaspora

Yousaf Sadiq

The Contextualized Psalms (the Punjabi Zaburs)

The Punjabi psalms are a model of contextualization where scriptural truths are presented to ordinary people within their own language, culture, and context.[1] The local melodies and language bring to them the message of God with spontaneity and ease. When Christians in Punjab were given the liberty to use natural ways to praise God, they developed innovative and indigenous forms of Christianity.[2] *Zabur* is an Arabic word that is used to refer to the psalms in the Old Testament. The same word occurs in the Qur'an in reference to the Psalms of David.[3] The psalms translated into the Punjabi language in versified form can unequivocally be regarded as the most accustomed, read, sung, recited, and memorized part of the Bible by Christians in Pakistan.[4]

The first work of the committee for the Punjabi Psalter was published in 1892. It was a collection of fifty-five psalms with musical notations and titled *Zabur Punjabi Nazm Men Tarjuma Kiya Gaya* (Psalms translated in Punjabi verse). Two thousand copies of the 1908 edition of the Psalter were printed at the Medical Hall Press in Benares with the title *Punjabi Zabur: Desi Ragan Vich* (Punjabi psalms: In local melodies). This selection of psalms was published in Roman script, and the preface indicates that there were plans for its publication in Persian script. The committee for the Punjabi psalms consisted of Rev. Dr. David Smith Lytle, Miss Mary Jane Campbell, Rev. Dr. Thomas Fulton Cummings, Rev. Dr. Imam-ud-Din Shahbaz, and the lady musicians, including Miss Mary Henrietta Cowden, Mrs. William McKelvey, Miss Mary Rachel Martin, and Miss Emma Josephine Martin.[5]

After Shahbaz prepared the poetry, the next step was to evaluate the translation of the psalms using the original text of the Psalter. The third and final phase involved the musical arrangements of the Punjabi metrical psalms. The missionaries with musical skills worked tirelessly to collect data. Frederick Stock mentions that in order to collect data and listen to the various commonly used tunes, the missionaries spent a considerable amount of time at ordinary shopping and eating places.[6] Young acknowledges the help received from a group of nomadic singers. A gifted missionary in music, Mary Rachel Martin, with the help of Henrietta Cowden, Josephine Martin, and Mrs. William McKelvey, wrote down the musical tunes in Western notations so that the Western missionaries could sing and play them.[7]

It was the pioneering work of Andrew Gordon and Samuel Martin on the Urdu metrical psalms that paved the way for the poetic psalms in Punjabi. The success of the 1892 trial version led to the availability of the entire book of Psalms in versified form in 1908. The beautiful melodies of these psalms were modeled after the bhajan style, and the cultural fondness was given special preference in gathering musical data for them. The United Presbyterian missionaries of North America prepared the musical notations, the Muslim-convert Shahbaz put them in versified form, and the Hindu singer Radha Kishan and the wandering minstrels assisted with the tunes of the psalms in Punjabi.

The Punjabi Psalter and the Indian Subcontinent

"I wonder sometimes if the songs of David ever sounded sweeter in Hebrew tongue sung in the hills of Judea and the great temple in Jerusalem than they do in the plains and hills and humble mud churches in the villages of Punjab on the day of worship."[8] These words of Emma Anderson compliment the Punjabi Psalter. It is noteworthy that no other language in the Indian subcontinent (it may well be the only one in Asia) has the honor of having the entire book of Psalms in a versified form that has been used for Christian worship. Punjabi is unique in that sense, and therefore, the luminous and "remarkable" work of Shahbaz can truly be regarded as a precious gift to the Punjabi Christian community in the Indian subcontinent.[9] James Massey asserts that the contributions of Shahbaz are in fact for the whole of the Indian church.[10]

It is fascinating to find that the Punjabi Psalms are used among the Punjabi congregations in India with immense enthusiasm. "The best example is the translation of the Psalms into Punjabi by the Rev. Imam-uddin Shahbaz, which are still in use in most of the northern parts in India as far as Delhi and Uttar Pradesh. In some parts of Northwest India, the worship service does not start unless the Zaboors (Psalms) are sung. Since they are composed in the popular forms of classic ragas, they can be used in the whole of the northern region."[11]

The picture of a rural service in the Indian Punjab portrayed by Ernest Campbell looks so identical to a rural service in the Pakistani Punjab that it is impossible to differentiate between them: "The opening song is a Zabur or psalm, to a fine old Punjab tune. 'I was glad when they said, come let us go to the House of the Lord.' The traditional final hymn is sung, *Rahega nan sada thikar* (The name of Christ will remain forever! It will remain as long as the sun remains . . . and all men will receive grace from His name)."[12] Likewise, the use of similar instruments for worship and the singing of the Punjabi psalms at the beginning and the end show that it is no different from a Christian service in the rural areas of Punjab in Pakistan. The Punjabi psalms were published in the Gurumukhi script in 1930.

These versified psalms have played a central role in the theological development of the Punjabi church in India and Pakistan. Punjabi Christians, especially the older generation, know several of the Punjabi psalms by heart. Most of them have no formal schooling, and the memorization of God's word in the form of the Punjabi psalms helps them learn God's truth. Michael Nazir-Ali, the former bishop of Rochester and Raiwind, regards these psalms as "the basis of the spirituality of the Pakistani church" and remarks that "one thing that has really influenced me in thinking about God is the Psalms in Punjabi."[13] Arthur Victor finds that "these

Zaburs have touched the deep chord in the hearts of the Punjabi Christians."[14]

The content of the psalms attracted the oppressed and depressed people of lower castes, who enthusiastically embraced the message of hope, deliverance, protection, and justice in them. It was the cooperation of the various Western mission agencies working in the Punjab region that made it possible for the Punjabi Christians to have the Psalter and to enjoy the beautiful book of Psalms in poetic form.

Whether it is an occasion of celebration or sorrow, the Punjabi psalms can be heard widely. The Punjabi Christian community in the Indian subcontinent uses them in their religious and social gatherings. Regardless of denominational affiliations, the Punjabi psalms are used by all Christian churches in Punjab. They have helped create unity and harmony among Christians across denominational and doctrinal lines. They equally belong to the Presbyterians, Anglicans, Methodists, Baptists, Brethren, Pentecostals, Charismatics, Roman Catholics, and anyone else who uses them to worship God. When they get together for communal worship, they have one thing in common to sing, and that is the metrical Punjabi psalms by which they can praise God. Thus, Punjabi psalms have broken down denominational boundaries, and it is fascinating to observe the variety of ways in which the psalms are being used in liturgical and cultural settings.

The Communal Worship of the South Asian Punjabi Diaspora

The Punjabi psalms are extensively used among Punjabi-speaking churches worldwide. The corporate worship in

Punjabi diaspora churches is considered incomplete without Punjabi psalms. Hence they can be viewed as the heart of Christian worship among the global Punjabi church. They have made an unfathomable impact on the Punjabi Christian spirituality and have given it "an unrivaled familiarity" with the lovely book of Psalms.[15]

The Punjabi psalms also play a vital role in the church liturgy. It would not be unjust to count the second part of Psalm 24 (vv. 7–10) as the most familiar Punjabi psalm used in diaspora churches and as an opening song at church services. Another reason for its rising popularity has to do with its use of excessive repetitions, which make it easier to remember. The members of an Indian-Pakistani church in Phoenix (Arizona) can be seen in a video carrying palm branches as they enter the church in a lively procession while singing Psalm 24; it shows the practice followed by diaspora and home churches alike. In this video, a man rides on a symbolic plush donkey, signifying Jesus's triumphant entry into Jerusalem.[16]

The people of the South Asian Punjabi Christian diaspora living in the Western world continue to make use of the Punjabi Zabur in their communal worship. St. Andrew's Church in Ilford (London), Calvary Chapel Norbury (London), Punjabi Masihi Church (Surrey, BC), Cornerstone Asian Church (Mississauga, ON), Asian Christian Church (Edmonton, AB), Bethlehem Punjabi Church (New York City), and Trinity International Christian Church (Philadelphia, PA) are some examples of the diaspora churches that sing the Punjabi Zabur with great enthusiasm.

As the psalms were put to local melodies, they are best suited to be played on traditional Indian musical instruments. A tabla (a pair of twin hand drums) and a harmonium (a hand-pumped organ) are the two most used instruments among the diaspora Punjabi churches.[17] Other commonly used musical instruments for Christian worship are a *dholak* (a double-headed cylindrical drum) and the tambourine. As a general practice, the diasporic South Asians of all religious backgrounds enter barefoot and sit on the floor at places of worship, and Punjabi Christians follow the same practice primarily when making their way to the pulpit to pray, read Scripture, or deliver a sermon.

The Punjabi metrical psalms are a classic example of native Christian music that was composed by and is used to this day with enthusiasm by the Punjabi Christian diaspora. Jeffrey Cox claims, "It is in Punjabi hymnody, rather than in bureaucratic creations of the missions, that one finds the fullest expression of indigenous Punjabi Christianity."[18] The work of Shahbaz exhorts the Punjabi Christian diaspora to perceive these psalms as a precious heritage.

The older generation of Punjabi Christians living outside of India and Pakistan primarily use the Punjabi language, or in some cases Urdu, or the combination of both Urdu and Punjabi. However, children born abroad, especially in the Western world, are most familiar with and fluent only in English. The mother tongue is confined to usage in the home and with parents. Since parents love to sing the Punjabi psalms, children hear the Zaburs either at home or in church settings. However, one of the major challenges for the new generation of the Punjabi Christian diaspora to learn the Punjabi psalms is the lack of resources. Many of them struggle to speak their mother tongue, and unlike their parents, almost all of them are unable to read the Persian/Urdu script.

The most common way to handle the challenge of the unfamiliar script is to transliterate the content using the Roman script or to employ biscriptal use.[19] The Punjabi Christian diaspora has primarily adopted the Roman script and used dual-scripted songbooks to introduce Zaburs to the next generations. Here it is worth mentioning that the book *Upper Room Praise* was published by Metropolitan New Revival Church in Brooklyn, New York, in 2019, which includes hymns in Urdu and all of the Zaburs transliterated in Roman script. Gabreal Mehboob, born in the United States and only thirteen years of age, has been instrumental in its preparation. He learned to read and write Urdu at home and compiled the aforementioned book. This is an encouraging trend among South Asian Christians globally.

Celebrating the Heritage of Punjabi Zaburs

The largest Pakistani Christian community in the United States lives around northeast Philadelphia. It is estimated that there are approximately eight hundred families, and their numbers continue to grow. There are twenty-five Pakistani churches of various denominations in the area. An event called "Celebration of the Heritage of Punjabi Zaburs" was hosted by Trinity International Christian Church in Philadelphia on August 7, 2021. Earlier, in 2013, the church had organized a similar event to mark the heritage of Punjabi Zaburs, and Calvary Chapel Norbury in the United Kingdom had organized a Sham-e-Mazamir (psalm night) event in 2012. This author had the honor to speak at both events.

The special worship night was led by the Trinity Choir, and the environment was serene, beautiful, and awe-inspiring. Psalm 136 was the opening Zabur, which was followed by Psalms 24 and 4, while Zabur 72 was the closing song. This author cannot express his delight in words to participate and speak at this event, a video of which is available on the social media page of the church.[20] It is worth noting that those of the fourth generation of the American missionaries and Indian Christian workers who contributed to the making of the Punjabi Psalter in the late nineteenth century in colonial India were present at the event in Philadelphia. They were celebrating the work that their forefathers did together over 150 years ago. Janette Gordon Weldon and Rachel Sharp (the great- and great-great-granddaughters of Andrew Gordon), Promeet Singh and Pranav Singh (the great-great-grandsons of Imam-ud-Din Shahbaz), and Tariq Waris (the principal designate of the Full Gospel Assemblies Theological Seminary in Lahore, Pakistan) were among the esteemed guests at the event.

The audience deeply appreciated the event and learned about their distinctive Christian heritage as well as their identity and roots. The event presented challenges faced in sharing the gospel by those who went from Philadelphia to Punjab in the late nineteenth century, and now in the early twenty-first century, many from Punjab live in Philadelphia. It informed them about the sacrifices made for the gospel to get to their forefathers and the value of worshipping in the mother tongue and cultural context. Some young folks who were either born in Philadelphia or came here when they were very young made the commitment to play their role in bringing the gospel to insiders and outsiders both in Philadelphia and in Punjab. Several committed that they will start singing and teaching the Zaburs to their young kids. In his feedback about the event, Pastor Azhar Alam affirms, "Celebration of Punjabi Zaburs was truly an informative and soul-stirring event. Despite being one of the first events organized after the pandemic, we reached nearly two-hundred people in person and over a thousand online on social media platforms who were in attendance for this event."[21]

In conclusion, Punjabi psalms are an excellent example of a contextualized form of Christian worship.[22] The versified translation of the psalms in the Punjabi language plays a vital role in the personal and communal worship of South Asian Punjabi Christians in the diaspora globally. It has helped establish unity and harmony among Christians of different churches and denominations. When they get together for communal worship, they have one thing in common to sing and praise God—the metrical Punjabi psalms. The Punjabi psalms have broken down the walls of denominational boundaries. It is very encouraging that South Asian diaspora churches have started to organize events to celebrate the unique heritage of the Punjabi psalms.

Notes

1 For more on this, see Yousaf Sadiq, *The Contextualized Psalms (Punjabi Zabur): A Precious Heritage of the Global Punjabi Christian Community* (Eugene, OR: Wipf & Stock, 2020).

2 Jeffrey Cox, "George Alfred Lefroy, 1854–1919, a Bishop in Search of a Church," in *After the Victorians: Private Conscience and Public Duty in Modern Britain*, ed. Peter Mandler and Susan Pedersen (London: Routledge, 1994), 67.

3 Thomas Hughes, *A Dictionary of Islam* (London: Allen, 1895), 698.

4 Yousaf Sadiq, "A Precious Gift: The Punjabi Psalms and the Legacy of Imam-ud-Din Shahbaz," *International Bulletin of Mission Research* 38, no. 1 (January 2014): 36.

5 Sadiq, *Contextualized Psalms*, 21.

6 Frederick Stock, *People Movements in the Punjab: With Special Reference to the United Presbyterian Church* (Pasadena, CA: Carey, 1975), 120.

7 William Young, *Sialkot Convention Hymn Book: Notes on Writers and Translators* (Daska, Pakistan: s.n., 1965), 4.

8 Emma Anderson and May J. Campbell, *In the Shadow of the Himalayas: A Historical Narrative of the Missions of the United Presbyterian Church of North America as Conducted in the Punjab, India, 1855–1940* (Pittsburgh, PA: UPBFM, 1942), 114–15.

9 Banarsi Das Jain, "Panjabi," in *Encyclopedia of Literature*, ed. Joseph Shipley (New York: Philosophical, 1946), 554.

10 James Massey, "Punjabi Christian Writer's Response to the Gospel," in *Oxford Encyclopaedia of South Asian Christianity*, ed. Roger Hedlund (New Delhi: Oxford University Press, 2012), 574.

11 Vidyasagar Dogar, *Rural Christian Community in Northwest India* (Delhi: ISPCK, 2001), 22.

12 Ernest Campbell, "The Church in the Punjab: Some Aspects of Its Life and Growth," in *The Church as Christian Community: Three Studies of North Indian Churches*, ed. Hayward Victor (London: Lutterworth, 1966), 165.

13 Michael Nazir-Ali, "The Good Fight," interview by Huw Spanner, Third Way, accessed August 2021, https://thirdway.hymnsam.co.uk/editions/nov-2011-/high-profile/the-good-fight.aspx.

14 Arthur Victor, "Impact of Punjabi Culture on Punjabi Christian Literature," *Religion and Society* 38, no. 2 (June 1991): 39.

15 John O'Brien, *The Construction of Pakistani Christian Identity* (Lahore, Pakistan: Research Society, 2006), 567.

16 See Promila Wilson, "Palm Sunday 2018 Church Service," Facebook, March 25, 2018, 1:14:20, https://www.facebook.com/promila.wilson/videos/2138298879530439.

17 Gerry Farrell, "Harmonium (India)," in *Continuum Encyclopedia of Popular Music of the World*, ed. John Shepherd (New York: Continuum, 2003), 307.

18 Jeffrey Cox, *Imperial Fault Lines: Christianity and Colonial Power in India, 1880–1940* (Stanford, CA: Stanford University Press, 2002), 148.

19 Hye Pae, *Script Effects as the Hidden Drive of the Mind, Cognition, and Culture* (New York: Springer, 2020), 216.

20 Trinity International Christian Church, "Trinity International Christian Church," YouTube, August 7, 2021, 2:32:24, https://www.youtube.com/watch?v=yqcZ1OMhrAQ.

21 Azhar Alam, letter to author, August 9, 2021.

22 Michael Nazir-Ali, *Frontiers in Muslim-Christian Encounter* (Oxford: Regnum, 1987), 81.

Bibliography

Anderson, Emma, and May J. Campbell. *In the Shadow of the Himalayas: A Historical Narrative of the Missions of the United Presbyterian Church of North America as Conducted in the Punjab, India, 1855–1940.* Pittsburgh, PA: UPBFM, 1942.

Campbell, Ernest. "The Church in the Punjab: Some Aspects of Its Life and Growth." In *The Church as Christian Community: Three Studies of North Indian Churches*, edited by Hayward Victor, 137–220. London: Lutterworth, 1966.

Cox, Jeffrey. "George Alfred Lefroy, 1854–1919, a Bishop in Search of a Church." In *After the Victorians: Private Conscience and Public Duty in Modern Britain*, edited by Peter Mandler and Susan Pedersen, 55–76. London: Routledge, 1994.

———. *Imperial Fault Lines: Christianity and Colonial Power in India, 1880–1940.* Stanford, CA: Stanford University Press, 2002.

Das Jain, Banarsi. "Panjabi." In *Encyclopedia of Literature*, edited by Joseph Shipley, 552–556. New York: Philosophical, 1946.

Dogar, Vidyasagar. *Rural Christian Community in Northwest India.* Delhi: ISPCK, 2001.

Farrell, Gerry. "Harmonium (India)." In *Continuum Encyclopedia of Popular Music of the World*, edited by John Shepherd, 307–308. New York: Continuum, 2003.

Hughes, Thomas. *A Dictionary of Islam*. London: Allen, 1895.

Massey, James. "Punjabi Christian Writer's Response to the Gospel." In *Oxford Encyclopaedia of South Asian Christianity*, edited by Roger Hedlund, 574–575. New Delhi: Oxford University Press, 2012.

Nazir-Ali, Michael. *Frontiers in Muslim-Christian Encounter*. Oxford: Regnum, 1987.

———. "The Good Fight." Interview by Huw Spanner. Third Way. Accessed August 2021. https://thirdway.hymnsam.co.uk/editions/nov-2011-/high-profile/the-good-fight.aspx.

O'Brien, John. *The Construction of Pakistani Christian Identity*. Lahore, Pakistan: Research Society, 2006.

Pae, Hye. *Script Effects as the Hidden Drive of the Mind, Cognition, and Culture*. New York: Springer, 2020.

Sadiq, Yousaf. *The Contextualized Psalms (Punjabi Zabur): A Precious Heritage of the Global Punjabi Christian Community*. Eugene, OR: Wipf & Stock, 2020.

———. "A Precious Gift: The Punjabi Psalms and the Legacy of Imam-ud-Din Shahbaz." *International Bulletin of Mission Research* 38, no. 1 (January 2014): 36–39.

Stock, Frederick. *People Movements in the Punjab: With Special Reference to the United Presbyterian Church*. Pasadena, CA: Carey, 1975.

Victor, Arthur. "Impact of Punjabi Culture on Punjabi Christian Literature." *Religion and Society* 38, no. 2 (June 1991): 37–46.

Young, William. *Sialkot Convention Hymn Book: Notes on Writers and Translators*. Daska, Pakistan: s.n., 1965.

Index

About the Authors

SAM GEORGE, PHD, serves as a catalyst for diasporas of the Lausanne Movement and the director of the Global Diaspora Institute at the Wheaton College Billy Graham Centre (United States). After a bachelor's in mechanical engineering and master's in management, he worked in engineering and technology firms for ten years. Later he studied practical theology and missiology in the United States and the United Kingdom. He lives with his wife and their two boys in the suburbs of Chicago (United States). His recent publications include *Refugee Diaspora* (William Carey), *Diaspora Christianities* (Fortress), and *Desi Diaspora* (SAIACS Press). He teaches migration, diaspora mission, and world Christianity at five seminaries across Asia, Africa, and the Americas.

MIYON CHUNG, PHD, is a Korean American who is a faculty member at Morling College, Sydney, Australia. Earlier she taught at Torch Trinity Graduate University, Seoul, South Korea. She completed her PhD in theology at Southwestern Baptist Theological Seminary. She has also served as the vice president of the Baptist World Alliance and the chair of theological education for the Asian Pacific Baptist Federation.

Prince Kumar Tamilarasan recently completed his PhD from Mysore University and is a faculty member in the Old Testament department of the South Asia Institute of Advanced Christian Studies in Bangalore, India. Earlier he served as a discipleship pastor of the  First Assembly of God Church in Bangalore. He holds a bachelor's degree in mathematics and several master's degrees in English, philosophy, divinity, and theology.

Tereso C. Casiño, ThD, PhD, joined the School of Divinity at Gardner-Webb University in South Carolina, United States, as a professor of mission and evangelism in 2010 and served earlier as a professor of systematic theology and intercultural studies/missions at Torch Trinity Graduate School of Theology in  Seoul, South Korea, for eight years. He has authored numerous journal articles and is the editor of the *Asia-Pacific Journal of Intercultural Studies*. He is a native of the Philippines and married to Dr. Cecilia J. Casiño, who taught pastoral care in Seoul, and they have two adult children.

Daniel D. Lee, PhD, serves as the assistant provost for the Center for Asian American Theology and Ministry and the assistant professor of theology and Asian American ministry at Fuller Theological Seminary. He developed  the center and Fuller's Asian American program. His research areas focus on the Reformed tradition and theological contextuality, and he brings broad ministry experience to his work. He is the author of the book *Double Particularity: Karl Barth, Contextuality, and Asian American Theology* (Fortress) as well as several articles and book chapters.

NARRY F. SANTOS, PhD, is the assistant professor of practical ministry and intercultural leadership at Tyndale Seminary in Toronto and the vice president of the Evangelical Missiological Society Canada. He completed his first doctorate in New Testament from Dallas Theological Seminary and another PhD in Philippine studies (including anthropology and psychology) from the University of the Philippines. He also serves as a part-time senior pastor of Greenhills Christian Fellowship (GCF) Peel and York. Earlier he was the pastor of Saddleback South Manila, and he ministered at GCF in different pastoral roles for twenty years, including planting six churches in Canada and four in the Philippines.

CHANDLER H. IM, PhD, was born in South Korea and immigrated to the United States in 1980; currently serves as a teaching missionary in Tokyo, Japan, an adjunct professor of mission at Faith Seminary (Tacoma, WA), and the Korean World Mission Council's director of global relations; previously served as the director of the Ethnic America Network and the Billy Graham

Centre at Wheaton College (2008–16); and coedited, with Amos Yong of Fuller Seminary, *Global Diasporas and Mission* (Regnum).

ANDREW Y. LEE, PhD, is the associate director of the Global Diaspora Institute at Wheaton College. He has previously taught at several seminaries, including the Southern Baptist Theological Seminary and Gordon-Conwell Theological Seminary. His pastoral experience includes serving at the largest Chinese churches in New York City and in the Midwest. He holds a PhD in religion from Baylor University.

PAUL SUNGRO LEE, PhD, has served as the international director of the Evangelical Alliance for Preacher Training/ Commission since 1996. He facilitates schools of mission in Africa and Asia in cooperation with the Christian and Missionary Alliance in Korea, raising up the next generation of missionaries. He teaches at a number of seminaries in the Philippines, including the International Graduate School of Leadership. He authored *Missionary Candidate Training: Raising Up Third World Missionaries*, which is used as a missionary-training manual around the world.

DAVID MARK BALL, PhD, was born in Kenya, where his parents were missionaries. His doctoral research was in New Testament studies from Sheffield University. He and his wife spent fifteen years in India working with  the Association for Theological Education by Extension. He is currently the director of the GOLD Project (www .goldproject.org) and a part-time consultant for SEAN International. He is also the chair of the Increase Task Group on the Diaspora as well as an increase equipper. In his spare time, he is an active member of the Christian Motorcyclists Association.

PHIL JONES (pseudonym) has been working among international students, previously in his home country in the West and currently in China. He is becoming aware of the opportunities to reach the nations who have come to Asia. He is a mentor, trainer, mobilizer, and networker for the benefit of international students in Asia.

YOUSAF SADIQ, PhD, is an assistant  professor of anthropology at Wheaton College in Illinois, United States. He is originally from Pakistan and earned his doctorate from the London School of Theology, United Kingdom. His research draws attention to the contextualization of the psalms in the Punjabi language and sociolinguistic issues facing the Punjabi Christians in Pakistan. He has an ongoing interest in how language affects society's attitude and how the contextualized psalms may build bridges with people of other faiths in the South Asian context.